# Design on the Edge

# Design on the Edge
## The Making of a High-Performance Building

David W. Orr

The MIT Press
Cambridge, Massachusetts
London, England

First MIT Press paperback edition, 2008
© 2006 Massachusetts Institute of Technology

MIT Press books may be purchased at special quantity discounts for business or sales promotional use. For information, please e-mail <special_sales@mitpress .mit.edu> or write to Special Sales Department, The MIT Press, 55 Hayward Street, Cambridge, MA 02142.

This book was set in Sabon by Graphic Composition, Inc.
Printed on recycled paper and bound in the United States of America.

Library of Congress Cataloging-in-Publication Data

Orr, David W., 1944–
Design on the edge: the making of a high-performance building / David W. Orr.
    p.    cm.
Includes bibliographical references and index.
ISBN 978-0-262-15117-7 (hc : alk. paper)—978-0-262-65112-7 (pb : alk. paper)
1. Adam Joseph Lewis Center (Oberlin, Ohio). 2. Oberlin College—Buildings.
3. Buildings—Ohio—Oberlin—History. I. Title.
LD4170.A32O77   2006
727'.3077123—dc22

                                                                2006044259

10  9  8  7  6  5  4  3  2

For Adam

# Contents

# IV  Pedagogy

# Acknowledgments

The Lewis Center is a collective accomplishment, and in naming those deserving credit I will undoubtedly omit some—a frailty of memory, not of gratitude. Success of the project owes much to my colleagues past and present at Oberlin: David Benzing, Beverly Burgess, Norman Care, Leo Evans, Karen Florini, Dierdre Holmes, David Love, Al MacKay, Brad Masi, Gene Matthews, John Petersen, Bob Scheren, Harlan Wilson, Cheryl Wolfe-Cragin, and President Nancy Dye who allowed it to proceed.

Among those whose generosity made it possible, I owe a special acknowledgment to Adam and Peter Lewis, Peter and Mimi Buckley, the George Gund Foundation, Dick and Mim Hallock, the Heinz Foundation, Randall Jones, Pete Lavigne, Carl McDaniel, John Powers, Michael Stranahan, and the Educational Foundation of America.

The building described below reflects the vision, design skill, and stamina of the lead architects William McDonough + Partners, particularly Kevin Burke for his patience, dedication, and talent; Bill McDonough for his incandescence; and Russell Perry, who defines coolness under fire. The building also reflects the extraordinary skills of the members of the design group assembled around the project: John Lyle, who gave us heart and guidance, but did not live to see the results; Bill Browning, Carol and Colin Franklin, Amory Lovins, Ron Perkins, Shanti Pless, Michael Shaw, Steven Strong, John Todd, Paul Torcellini, Adrian Tuluca, Jeff Wartelle, and the engineers at Lev Zetlin.

The actual building reflects the practical talents, labor, and dedication of its builders and those who made it work, including David Benzing, Leo Evans, Stan Peters, John Petersen, Marty Plato, Chad Porter, and Don Van Dyke.

I appreciate the time, skill, and good judgment of those who read the early drafts of the book, and whose comments, criticisms, and suggestions made it a better book than it otherwise would have been: David Benzing, Bob Longsworth, Wilson Orr, and one anonymous reader who knows a lot about the theory and practice of punctuation. To Clay Morgan at The MIT Press, I owe special thanks for his interest in the book. I appreciate the editorial skill of Deborah Cantor-Adams and Cindy Milstein, who improved the manuscript. But each is absolved of any remaining flaws herein. And to Elaine, a lover of children, music, and greenness, heartfelt gratitude for enduring the time that went into both the building and this book.

# Introduction

This is the story of a small building in Ohio that was one of the first, if not the first, substantially green or high-performance buildings on a college campus. It spans the decade between 1995 and 2005. In that time, Americans impeached a president, balanced the federal budget and then unbalanced it again, witnessed the largest corporate bankruptcy ever, opted out of the Kyoto treaty, suffered a major terrorist attack, fought wars in the Balkans, Afghanistan, and Iraq, evacuated a major city, and became acutely aware of our vulnerability to malice, the forces of nature, and incompetence and malfeasance in high places. Ostensibly the story is about the art and science of ecological design, a specific building, a particular college, and education of the higher sort. But it is also a thread in the larger narrative of our time and the uncertain struggle to calibrate global civilization with the realities and limits of the biosphere. We are not faring particularly well in that effort and the stakes are rising. For Americans, with our SUVs, sprawling suburbs, and peculiar blend of manifest destiny, religiosity, militarism, and consumerism, larger connections are sometimes hard to see. Yet see them we must. We might have had an easier path to walk had we had the good sense to pay serious attention to the problems of energy, the environment, and security put before the public by the Carter administration in *The Global 2000 Report* (1980). Instead, we did the national equivalent of a quarter-century Australian walkabout, mostly ignoring energy efficiency, solar energy, the preservation of natural systems, and the national remodeling implied by the necessities of sustainability and resilience. Ronald Reagan's "morning in America" is ending in the twilight of terrorism, war, debt, inequity, ecological decline, greater oil dependency, and national division some twenty-five years later. And we still have no adequate national strategy to move the nation toward energy efficiency and solar energy, preserve farmland and forests, restore our lakes and rivers, eliminate waste and pollution, and build a society secure by design, and hence little capacity to truly honor our children and their future. The story told here, however, is not so much about politics but about a college building and its wider implications.

This is the first of two books on the Adam Joseph Lewis Center at Oberlin College. The second book, written by the designers, architects, and engineers who worked on the project, will provide more of the technical details about the building having to do with process, performance, outcomes, and a design revolution now well underway that is changing architecture, community design, materials, energy systems, and much more. My intention here is to tell the story of the project, placing it into its larger educational, design, and institutional context. For me, it is a personal tale and I tell it as such—equal parts memoir, reflection, analysis, and exposition. But it is also a story of institutional behavior in a global context we are only beginning to fathom. Against the backdrop of global change, the question is whether institutions that purport to advance learning can themselves learn, measured not just by their success in the competition for available students and funding but in response to human-driven changes in the biogeochemical cycles of Earth (Steffen et al. 2004). We have good reason to believe that those changes will alter the human prospect to our disadvantage, perhaps sooner than later. That alone gives us cause, both individually and collectively, to adjust our priorities and behavior; hence, the attempt to make the substance and process of education accord with the ecological realities while equipping the young for a world different from any humankind has ever known.

Beyond the particulars of the building, its larger importance, I think, lies in the fact that most of us live out our lives in organizations and institutions of all kinds. In our frontier past, for better or worse, people were more self-reliant. But those days are long gone. The present reality is that we live in a world of large organizations and institutions that educate, nurture, house, govern, adjudicate, imprison, execute, license, tax, provision, employ, loan, give, entertain, heal, protect, inform, and more. When they do these things with competence, compassion, honesty, transparency, fairness, imagination, and foresight, we are all the better for it. When they perform otherwise, we all suffer. For example, the failure of the U.S. auto industry in the face of Japanese competition and declining oil supplies is a matter of no small import. Instead of leading advances in quality, automotive engineering, and fuel efficiency, U.S. automakers coasted on their past laurels, to our national disadvantage and eventually their own, selling oversized fuel-guzzling behemoths with lots of cup holders. One could similarly lament other organizational and institutional failures in churches, corporations, philanthropies, government agencies, city governments, planning boards, and institutions of higher education. The truth is that innovation within most organizations is often difficult, slow, and painful. The typical response to new ideas is often to oppose them and defend established routines and vested interests or ignore them because of lethargy, lack of imagination, perverse incentives, obsolete rules, and the fear of change. But organizations sometimes learn, improve, innovate, and plan with foresight. The difference between organizational learning and the failure to learn is increasingly important to our prospects in the twenty-first century.

This case concerns the behavior of one small college within that group of organizations that is sometimes described as the "industry" of higher education—a telling word. The significance of this case lies only in the light it might shed on the realities of organizational innovation and learning in educational institutions and perhaps in organizations more generally. Nevertheless I offer no theory of organizational change or any grandiloquent summation of the human condition. I intend only to tell the story of a building, place it in a larger context, and say what I think it meant to the design professions, educational institutions, and the students of one college. My target audience includes all of those who have ever tried to change an organization for the better; architects who need to know how to sell important design innovations to wary clients; college and university administrators and trustees who will spend billions of dollars on new buildings over the next few years; teachers of all kinds whose deepest professions may be undermined by the buildings and campuses where they work; and all of those who wish to preserve a habitable planet.

The first section below places the building into a larger historical and design context. There are, more or less, seven sources of design beginning with vernacular traditions rooted in the particularities of place and tradition. Beyond vernacular building styles and everyday needs for reliable shelter, humans early on virtually everywhere began to develop monumental ceremonial structures of which Stonehenge is the most famous. The purposes of these structures are unknown, but they were designed to mirror the cycles of nature as well as the regularities of the sun, the moon, and the stars. For their part, the Greeks contributed the ideas of proportionality and perspective to the design arts along with the possibility of human rationality. The makers of Gothic cathedrals ushered in another stage of design by joining engineering advances such as the flying buttress to theology and the notion that humans might create mnemonic spaces of light and majesty that invited the actual presence of divinity. The industrial stage of design reflects no cosmic patterns, substantive rationality, or any understanding of theology beyond that associated with the pursuit of pecuniary advantage. It is, rather, a reflection of the assumptions embedded in the resource- and energy-intensive market economies that flourished in the nineteenth and twentieth centuries. Art, style, and varying aesthetic standards are yet another source of design—what might be called form making, evident prominently in the artistry of Frank Gehry. Finally, the green building movement is based on ecological patterns and the design wisdom of 3.8 billion years of evolution. In some ways it reflects the intent of the earliest designers to mirror a larger reality, but it is now grounded in the modern scientific study of natural systems and processes of nature transposed to the built environment.

The various stages of design, however many there may be, are a kind of lamination of purposes, philosophies, and possibilities by which we make the human presence on Earth. We still design and build with some sense, more or less explicit, of larger realities. Some still do so in the hope of fostering a higher level of rationality. Others continue to design and build to invite mystery and majesty into the built form. And all of us make our way in a practical world of supply and demand. The ecological design revolution is a culmination of sorts that acknowledges that we will have to accommodate the realities of entropy and ecology, especially in a full world of 6.5 billion humans that grows by another 75 million each year. But ecological design need not be a grudging recognition of reality. To the contrary, it ought to be the basis for yet another advance in the human condition—one powered by sunshine and buildings, neighborhoods, and cities that reflect "elegant solutions predicated on the uniqueness of place," as my friend John Todd puts it. Further, ecological design is a finer calibration of our buildings and communities with our own senses and evolutionary past (Kellert 2005).

The second section of this book is about the particulars of the making of the Lewis Center. The Center began as an attempt merely to solve a space problem for a growing academic program, but it grew into a mission to build the first substantially green building in higher education. My involvement in the project was more than incidental since I had helped to start it, was eventually charged with raising funds for it from "sources not otherwise likely to give to the college," and had to keep it on track when it was derailed for one reason or another. The actual history of the project is as much about institutional politics and strategies of change as it is about architecture and engineering. In the telling, I've divided the story into component parts on origins, landscape, the actual building, fundraising, building performance, and something called "political economy." I've included a great deal in this section that is personal, but I think it is useful in shedding light on how the project actually developed. All in all, it is a partial success story. The building was completed, much as intended, and has flourished in ways we could not have foreseen. It is widely remarked, awarded, emulated, and studied. But the process that Peter Senge (2000) calls institutional learning was not entirely successful and the reasons are, I think, instructive for what they say about innovation in colleges and universities as well as other organizations.

The third section begins with an account of my own learning process and is necessarily told as a personal story. In the late 1970s I had ventured out of the safety of academic employment into the wilds of the Arkansas Ozarks with my family and my brother and his to start an environmental organization on fifteen hundred acres located in the fifth-poorest county in the forty-ninth-wealthiest state. After my eleven years at the rural periphery, I never saw the world the same again and certainly not what passes for education. I came to believe that education is more problematic and uncertain than commonly thought, and only sometimes under unpredictable circumstances leads to real learning, which is a lifelong and mostly mysterious process. This, too, would be irrelevant except for the fact that it led me to very different ideas about education, which in turn led to the Lewis Center and are embedded in its design. Chapter 12 is about education, curriculum, and the green campus movement, of which high-performance buildings are a significant part. I end this first book on the Lewis Center with what Paul Harvey would call "the rest of the story": some of the projects that grew from the project—none of which could have been foreseen at the beginning. Buildings, however grand and noble, are best regarded as a means to some larger end. In the case of academic buildings and the Lewis Center in particular, the ends have to do with the students whose lives, purposes, and intellectual and moral capacities have become the rest of the story.

*Earth, Air, Fire, Water, and Spirit*

We are made of earth and to earth we all return
We are deep-air mammals living at the bottom of an ocean of air
We live by the slow fire of oxidation
In landscapes shaped by fire, air, and water
We are creatures more water than solid; eddies in one watershed or another
All part of one great watershed
We are spirits made matter, but we are spirit and that matters
We are sojourners in a mystery called time

# I

## Context

# 1

## A Meditation on Building

Architecture is the art that most tries, in its rhythm, to reproduce the order of the universe, which the ancients called *Kosmos*.
—Umberto Eco

My grandfather, a preacher who reportedly did not know which end of a hammer was which, caused one house to be built in Charlotte, North Carolina, and one church, which is still a downtown landmark even though it is no longer used as a church. My father, a Presbyterian minister and college president who certainly did know which end of a hammer was which, built four houses, one church, and seventeen college buildings in his eighty-nine years. My brother, a farmer at heart but a jack-of-all-trades as well as the best mechanic and coolest backhoe operator I've ever seen, has built several dozen buildings of various kinds—all more or less still standing. Somewhere between my father and grandfather's skill level, I have been involved in a half-dozen construction projects, including the one described here. This is the story of a building: its place, its institutional setting, its meaning, and the people around it—the originators, facilitators, designers, builders, philanthropists, and critics. But most important, this is the story of an experiment at the intersection of ecological design and education. The *New York Times* (March 9, 1999) once described the Lewis Center as "perhaps the most remarkable" of a new generation of college buildings. Whatever else it is, it took much of my life for the ten years required to raise the money, design, build, and fine-tune. It was a source of joy and exasperation, often in the same day.

Aside from language, our desire to build is perhaps the most distinctive thing about humans. Building for us, clever apes, is not just a nesting instinct but the way by which we manifest our ideas and values. The act of building is a form of language that puts us on public display. Inevitably, our fears, obsessions, fantasies, loves, hatreds, ambitions, limitations, needs, and social rank are spoken in the tangible forms of the Great Pyramids, cityscapes, suburbs, big-box stores, and sprawling developments. Buildings do not just reflect our values; they later become causes in their own right. Winston Churchill's famous observation in 1943 that "we shape our buildings, and afterwards our buildings shape us" captures the essence of the matter. Frank Lloyd Wright is reported to have once said that he could design a house that would cause a newly married couple, madly in love, to divorce in a matter of months. Aggregations of buildings can have comparable effects on a larger scale, causing whole societies to become less sociable and less engaged with nature. Shopping malls, freeways, and suburbs tend to isolate, segregate, and increase social pathologies, however well housed and affluent some may be. To build, in other words, is to reveal and to cause. But what is revealed depends on the capacity not merely to see but to observe, and we seldom know in advance what we set in motion, whatever it was that we intended to do.

The idea of building permeates our ways of speaking, suggesting a deep resonance between our facility for language and our activities as Homo faber. We construct arguments. We lay foundations. We build companies. We hammer out solutions. We forge ahead. We structure deals. Some fabricate stories. And a few are busy deconstructing this or that. We think metaphorically, and the most common metaphors are those originating either in what nature makes or what we've made of nature. We are also visual creatures, strongly influenced by what we see or think that we see. Size and scale become powerful symbols of our collective power and importance. Official buildings reflect politicians' need for recognition and maybe that of the public for belonging to some larger enterprise. Aware of our mortality, we think about transcendence. The easy way to become immortal is to build something that will presumably last a while. But what are intended as thousand-year Reichs often have short life spans, and who now remembers the names of the pharaohs who caused the Great Pyramids to be built? And who cares?

To what extent such deeper motives really move us cannot be known. In a commercial culture greed and display are probably more significant factors. In the United States and many parts of the world those with enough money can build whatever they choose. Zoning laws and various land-use restrictions are more often than not paper barriers permeable by those with enough cash, which buys connections. So deals are cut and casinos spring up in places like mangrove wetlands along the Mississippi coast—gambling with nature that owns the house so to speak. Highways crash through prime woodlands. Suburban housing tracts with bucolic names sprawl over rich farmland from sea to shining sea. The Front Range of the Rockies is becoming one long string of weary housing tracts stitched together by pavement and strip development. Close up we call this progress, but from a sufficient perspective it is a terrible blight spreading across the face of the planet. What we build, too, reflects the larger appetites of consumers who have forgotten how to be citizens. The average house has nearly doubled in size in the last half century. Trophy palaces in places like Aspen are measured in tens of thousands of square feet. In midwestern fields, starter mansions grow instead of corn. What will all of this building frenzy look like to those living a century hence? What have we set in motion? Wendell Berry once noted that we do not know what we have done because we do not know what we have undone. So, how much has been undone to build the American way of life, and how much more will be undone in the attempt to maintain it all?

Americans, not famous for restraint or subtlety, set the standards for the last half of the twentieth century. We emerged as the preeminent nation after World War II with enough ecological slack (or access to it) to fuel another boom, and we did as opportunity and our expansionist disposition beckoned. To a world recovering from war and needing development, our example of hypermaterialism organized around the automobile set the standard. On reflection, I've concluded that no one should be permitted to build anything larger than a woodshed without first having sat for a time in the midst of some ancient ruin—the Roman Forum would do—and written one term paper on the ephemerality of all human endeavors using only the book of Ecclesiastes as a reference. The experience, properly digested, might cure much of the grandiosity that afflicts our skylines and the emptiness of our souls. The second assignment would be to visit some place—say Devon, England—where the human presence and the landscape have been braided together with great intelligence at a human scale over several millennia. That term paper should cite only Jacquetta Hawkes's classic *A Land*—arguably a cure for the disease afflicting the minds of those building strip malls, industrial "parks," and suburban "developments." A third assignment would be to observe an Amish barn raising to see how a community supports its own using local resources to build useful things; no term paper required.

It is easy to get caught up in the excitement of building. I vividly recall the "house raising" my dad organized when I was eight years old, to build a vacation cottage on an old stone foundation in a hemlock grove one mile from the Allegheny River in western Pennsylvania. The site was once the home of the Mays family, who operated a small farm and mill powered by water from Mays Run. The house had burned decades before, leaving only a barn that had been converted into a house and a garage, remnants of a mill run filled then with skunk cabbage and grass, and an overgrown orchard. To restore the place, Dad invited two dozen men to the event, including one contractor to keep things square. At day's end, after lots of sawing, nail pounding, and camaraderie, the frame and roof of a house stood where there once had been an abandoned foundation. It was the cheap way to do the job, but that's not why he did it that way. He knew the difference between means and ends. Properly led under the right circumstances, people can do wonderful and important things.

At the other end of the scale is the instructive example of Albert Speer, who served as Adolf Hitler's young genius architect for a decade. Subsequently he had lots of time to reflect on architecture, the Third Reich, and other things at public expense. There is little in the way of a contemporary record about those designing and building the big-box stores that now blight our landscapes. By one estimate we will attempt to build more buildings in the next fifty years than humans did in the past five thousand. Most of this will use a lot more energy and materials than necessary and a great deal more than we can safely use. The total numbers are sobering. It is estimated that the construction, maintenance, and operation of buildings in the United States consumes about 40 percent of the country's raw materials and energy and is responsible for about 40 percent of our $SO_2$ and $NO_2$ pollution, 33 percent of our $CO_2$ emissions, 25 percent of our wood use, and 16 percent of our water use (Wilson and Yost 2001). In 1990, 70 percent of the 2.5 million metric tons of nonfuel materials that moved through the economy were used in construction (Geiser 2001, 55). In other words, we will often solve immediate problems of space and ego at the expense of spirit, coherence, and longevity. Most of this development will be driven by individuals operating in a market system that does not account for losses of farmland, forests, wetlands, or biological diversity, or for the human need for community. Much of it will be done on the assumption that fossil energy will be cheap and abundant forever, even as the end of the fossil fuel era looms dead ahead. Much of it, too, will be done in the fervent belief that affluence and comfort will cure what ails us. It is destined, in large part, to disappoint.

Buildings mean different things at different times. To the instigator, a structure is aimed to solve one problem or another, including that of social status. To those that follow, however, buildings have a different purpose. Time, water, sunlight, insects, freezing and thawing, and wear and tear do their work. Paint peels, wood rots, metal rusts, stones shift, grass grows between cracks, surfaces abrade, and people become inattentive. In time, things come undone and few buildings age gracefully. Those that do, do so because they receive special attention and maintenance effort; the rest are destined to become ruins. Property values decline, crime becomes more common, and investors look elsewhere—a syndrome common to U.S. inner cities. What were once trophy mansions for the robber barons along Euclid Avenue in Cleveland are gone or are faded and derelict properties with only a hint of their former glory—places subject to "urban renewal," and the cycle begins again: prospect to problem to ruin, and sometimes to rebirth.

I once asked a class whether there is such a thing as "soul" in buildings. The students seized on the question avidly, but failed to identify the quality of soul. Perhaps this is a mark of youth and the number-saturated mentality of our time, yet more likely it reflects the elusive qualities of great buildings that cannot be captured easily by words. If some buildings do have the quality of soul, whatever that means, it surely differs greatly from one building to another. To some, the Parthenon has soul, or maybe it offers grandeur hitched to a lot of history. But in the right light and the right circumstances, you can feel the presence of the past in that place as if time were an illusion.

On a hot, humid July day in the low country of South Carolina I strolled around Hampton, the ancestral home of the Rutledge family, with a descendant of the slaves who once worked the plantation. We walked down the long, circular drive, once traveled by the likes of George Washington and Marquis de Lafayette, lined by giant water oaks decked out in Spanish moss, past the remnants of slave quarters and the graveyard heaped in a mound, around the mansion with its paint peeling, through the Rutledge family graveyard with large stones full of portentous epitaphs, and down the pathway to the Santee River, once the exit route for Francis Marion, the "swamp fox" of Revolutionary War fame. Soul? I don't know. Memory, mystery, distant echoes of pain, glory, sin, and maybe redemption, certainly. Before that there were others, the Creek and Catawba peoples who once hunted those forests and fished the low country rivers. The archaeology of human habitation; maybe with enough layers soul happens. Twenty years earlier, I had visited Hampton with my parents and met Archibald Rutledge, then the poet laureate of South Carolina. His son, the last of the direct line, reportedly shell-shocked in the Korean War, was living in the old plantation cookhouse. The old caretaker of the place, a man I'd met as a boy, told me that the last of the Rutledge line, had been buried in the slave graveyard by his own request. Circles in time. Maybe the working out of sin and redemption is what gives a place soul. If so, places like Auschwitz have a long way to go.

The purposes for which buildings are built and the structures themselves are temporary marriages at best. Most buildings begin their useful life serving one purpose and over time serve many others. If successful, I suppose, the ultimate distinction is for a building to become a tourist attraction or sacred site thereafter maintained at public expense. Whatever we intend for our buildings, they take on their own purposes. Churchill had it right—buildings influence our moods and psychology, our conversations and silences, our sense of place and history. They isolate or join and connect or disconnect us to time and history, seasons and nature. They celebrate the natural world of sunlight, wood, stone, and water, or they desecrate. By their ongoing requirements for energy and materials, they can create wider circles of damage. With better design and more care, could they lead to regeneration? As clusters, towns, cities, and finally, metropolitan regions, buildings affect our sociability, energy use, affinity for nature, and larger prospects in ways we seldom stop to consider. Above all they educate, but mostly in ways we fail to notice.

As a boy of fifteen, I attended a new consolidated high school in my hometown in Pennsylvania. The building had the rough shape of a T, with its intersection of two long corridors. Everything about the building, the curriculum taught in it, and the people worked at right angles. It was square, solid, forthright, and no-nonsense, as were my teachers. The geometry of the place reflected commonly held values and probably affected students' perceptions as well. The United States was the center of things, with heaven somewhere above, hell below, men in charge, and women subordinate; children were to be seen and not heard; Presbyterian certainty through and through. It was not an unpleasant school, as schools go, nor were the people mean-spirited. To the contrary, they were giving and caring. But the place taught more, and less, than anyone intended. I do not believe that architecture causes things in any straight-line way, yet it certainly influences what we pay attention to and what we can pay attention to.

The power of architecture and what is called "the built environment" is that few see it for what it is: a form of education. But the buildings, freeways, shopping malls, and sprawling suburbs of our society are a powerful and pervasive kind of instruction. Much of the message of contemporary design is that of human dominance, speed, power, individualism, the importance of the new over the old, and above all the centrality of consumption. The unavoidable lesson is that we need take no thought for the morrow; Devil-take-the-hindmost, not "in God we trust." Toss in television and the Internet, and the possibility for anything like real education—drawing forth—is considerably diminished. Even so, what's drawn forth often reflects only what's been implanted by thousands of hours of advertising, staged violence, and the deep silliness of commercial society. We are becoming people of surfaces instructed by the places we've made.

We are also becoming people accustomed to ugliness. Biochemist Rene Dubos (1972) once said that the worst thing we could do to our children would be to convince them that ugliness is normal. Much of what we've built in the post–World War II boom has been award-winning ugly, or has caused ugliness somewhere else or at some later time. A full recounting of our sins in this regard could take on the flavor of a hellfire and brimstone sermon, which I am by family background prepared to deliver. But the only useful questions have to do with how and how long it will take to transform ugliness into something lovely and to improve our skill in dwelling.

I regard it as axiomatic that we are predisposed to what biologist Edward O. Wilson (1984) calls "biophilia," or "the innate affinity for life and lifelike processes." By the same logic, most people most of the time have strong feelings about beauty, order, and harmony, and at some level are wounded by their absence. A sense of beauty is not, in other words, simply in the eye of the beholder; it comes with our hard wiring. Most people have dramatically different responses to a traffic jam and a walk along a forest path, loud street noises and whip-poor-wills of a quiet evening, a junk-strewn commercial strip and unpaved rural lane. These are not just matters of opinion unless one counts the opinions of our tissues and genes—a democracy of the whole organism. On the surface, there are wide disparities about what's beautiful and what's not, but there is a deeper level of consensus. We heal faster in the presence of natural beauty. We have an affinity for trees, water, animals, broad vistas, sky, and mountains, and I think, an inborn sense of harmony that is part of our evolutionary equipment. After millions of years, it would be surprising were it otherwise.

The architectural expression of this evolutionary tug is all around us: gardens, landscaping, mown grass, white painted tires in front of modest homes in the hills. Most of us lavish affection, if not skill and ecological competence, on the real estate under our direct control. Moreover, few of us vacation in places associated with urban violence and decay, like Newark or South Central Los Angeles, and few live in such places solely by choice. The expression of beauty changes in different places and times, and although the possibilities for creating it are not equal, our built-in sense of beauty and place is expressed in many different ways. That sense of place, however, breaks down as the scale increases. And driven by population growth, industrialization, and mechanization, the scale of human civilization has increased with astonishing speed in the past two centuries. Villages became cities; cities became metropolitan areas and then formless, sprawling, megalopolitan regions. The word sprawl doesn't quite describe what is more like an eruption of humankind fueled by easy access to ancient sunlight, and the draw down of the ecological capital of soils, forests, and biological diversity—that is, ecological disease. Sprawl brings a range of human health problems. Suburbanites living in isolation from each other and dependent on the car for transportation are more obese, suffer more often from heart disease, are more prone to asthma, and are victims of other diseases rare in more concentrated communities (Frumkin, Lawrence, and Jackson 2004).

Our collective behavior is comparable, as someone once put it, to yeast cells in a wine vat, destined to grow until overcome by our own waste products. The result is equivalent to a binge—yeast cells feeding on sugars; humans feeding on fossil fuels. If there is a better analogy, I have not heard it. The difference is that, unlike yeast cells, we supposedly have the possibility of foreknowledge that the morning after looms ahead and presumably the intelligence to do something smarter.

The important questions for us have to do with the nature of the transition to a society that can be sustained and, hopefully, will be spiritually sustaining as well. This transition will change much that we now take for granted, all having to do with our ingrained belief in the efficacy of brute force over nature. We live in the age of paradox. Our buildings are taller, but our purposes are shorter. We have more laborsaving devices, but less time for neighbors and friends. We have more money but less fairness; more weapons but less security; more power over nature, but a less-stable nature than ever before. We have more science, research, and intellectual capability than ever, but less common sense and good judgment in our public affairs. The old Enlightenment belief that with enough rationality and science we could make cause and effect transparent, has come undone in a tsunami of complexity and unintended consequences. I do not think that it is too much to say that we are midway through the hinge point of human history—a time in which we make a midcourse correction or risk losing it all.

The problem is not that we, Homo sapiens, have failed but that we've succeeded too well. We have conquered, dominated, surmounted, advanced, progressed, multiplied, and grown prosperous, and now, paradox of paradoxes, at the pinnacle of our success we can see the end of it all—with a whimper or a bang, or perhaps some of both. That awareness can immobilize us like the famous deer caught in the advancing headlights. And there is now a global debate about how we might make things "sustainable," but no one knows what that will require of us, and few except misanthropes ask why a precocious yet terribly destructive and immature biped deserves to be sustained at all—a harder question. That aside, to start we will need instructive models of sustainability, small enough to get our minds around, but big enough to give us leverage at a larger scale. In the decades and century immediately ahead, the sum total must be a remaking of the human presence on Earth that stabilizes the climate; preserves soils, forests, habitats, and other species; reduces the human population; builds habitable cities; improves our collective ability to make wise decisions; and does all of this while creating greater equity within and between generations. The journey ahead will be gut-wrenching or an adventure—the choice is ours—but if we intend to stay awhile, there is no other agenda.

## Sources of Design

The act of building begins with the needs for durable shelter, but architecture, it is said, represents a higher urge. Since humans do not live by bread alone, the drive toward novelty and artistic expression is evident from early architectural structures of antiquity to the present. But design is a blend of the practical with the transcendent—points along a continuum. The recent movement to design buildings fitted to the ecology of their places in our time is not dissimilar to the efforts of the makers of megalithic monuments to fit into larger patterns of cosmic harmony as perceived in their day (see table 1.1). Considerations of style and practicality, too, are everywhere present in all stages of design. The great change in our time is the imperative that design must now be a careful calibration of human intentions and the things that we make with the ecological realities of place and planet.

### Vernacular
Rounding a curve on a narrow winding road in the southern Appalachians, one sees the hollow open to a wider valley with a cluster of mostly

**Table 1.1**
Sources of Design

| | Vernacular | Cosmos | Rationality | Religion | Market | Art | Ecological |
|---|---|---|---|---|---|---|---|
| Example | All cultures | Stonehenge | Parthenon | Gothic cathedral | Modern city | Style | Twenty-first century? |
| Model | Place | Cosmos | Rationality | Heaven | Machine | Fashion | Ecosystems |
| Human as: | Limited | Conjurers | Striving for excellence | Within chain of being | Masters of nature | Form maker | Partner with nature |
| Metaphor | Nature | Unknown | Myth | Clock | Machine/computer | Man as creator | Biotic community |
| Language | Vernacular | Unknown | Philosophy | Theology | Economics | Aesthetic | Ecology/systems |
| Assumptions | Preserve tradition | Unknown | Possibility of rationality | Heaven and hell | Cheap energy | Art mirrors/shapes life | Interrelatedness |
| Scope | Local | Isolated | City-state | Europe | Global | Temporal | Local/global networks |
| Purpose | Practical | Appease/worship | Arête-excellence | Salvation | Maximize wealth | Originality | Sustainability |

dilapidated farm buildings dating to the early years of the nineteenth century. Of these, one barn in particular stands out. Made of chestnut timbers still showing the marks of saw and adze, the two-story "crib barn" still rests firm on a carefully laid stone foundation. On the lower level, the barn timbers are notched at the corners with a timber-framed upper floor cantilevered out at one end. The insults of time, insect, and weather have been borne with an unusual degree of grace. The builders, perhaps buried in the graveyard of the old church nearby, knew something about building barns that is now mostly forgotten. It is safe to say that no architect drew the plans and no engineer certified the drawings. Rather, the building skills were those of mostly unschooled people taught by the farming culture of northern Europe and disciplined by the realities of the southern Appalachians. The chestnut forests that provided some of the finest wood ever grown have long since disappeared, but the skills of barn building and those necessary to organize barn raisings still flourish among the Amish communities of Pennsylvania, Ohio, and Indiana.

Vernacular architecture arises from the particularities of place, culture, and tradition, and the need to provide shelter against the weather, predators, and enemies. The impulse is thoroughly practical, but the results are often elegant solutions to common problems. A Bedouin tent made of woven materials that block the sun yet permit the air to pass, as Bill McDonough points out, provides an appropriate, cheap, and elegant shelter for desert environments. The hallmarks of vernacular design are practicality, durability, simplicity, repairability, and reliance on local resources. And for cultures without professional engineers and architects, or the money to pay them, the skills necessary to building were widely known and often practiced communally.

Vernacular design is not, however, a thing of the past or characteristic only of less-developed societies. The necessity to build simply and make do with locally available materials, or the deeper need to build in ways that reflect and honor place, will never disappear. Indeed, words like sustainable, green, and high performance, often conceal more than they reveal about human intentions and design choices as well as their results. If buildings are measured by what happens in them, the shack where Aldo Leopold ([1949] 1987) once wrote *A Sand County Almanac,* for example, is a high-performance building. The structure was a converted chicken coop—little more than boards, nails, tar paper, a smoky fireplace, and salvaged windows assembled as a ramshackle weekend family getaway infused with lots of eloquent wisdom and heart. But the words written there that began the rational discussion about the proper role of humans in the land are priceless.

All buildings result from choices having to do with design intent, size, materials and their sources, energy intensity, convenience, ecological impacts, cultural information, and how well they fit particular places. Building performance, at its best, is a means to improve the depth and quality of human experience—for which there is no one formula. In our time, architecture has become highly professionalized, but the results are not necessarily more beautiful or soul serving. Designing ecologically is not synonymous with vernacular design, yet perhaps it is close, and a rough comparison is useful (see table 1.2).

## Cosmos

Driving west from central London, we pass miles of buildings that reluctantly give way to open space and verdant countryside. The British have

**Table 1.2**
Modern and Vernacular Design Compared

|  | Current Practice | Vernacular |
| --- | --- | --- |
| Scale | Large | Small, localized, fitted to place |
| Material intensity availability | High | Dependent on local |
| Energy requirements | High | Low; locally sourced |
| Convenience | High; design for automobile | Adapted to function |
| Comfort | High | Moderate to high |
| Controls/technology | High; 72°F year-round | Low |
| Ecological impacts | Global | Local |
| Cultural information | Low | High; mostly local skills |
| Design strategies | Professional standards | Public, participatory, educational |

been more successful than North Americans at containing urban sprawl and preserving open space; even so, a landscape once full of charm, villages, and small farms is clearly under assault by industrial agriculture and what is called, with no sense of irony, development. For those with eyes to see, this is a war zone. Small farms have been removed in a process of consolidation that began in the eighteenth century and reached an apogee of sorts with the industrial farming that now dominates the landscape. By U.S. standards, however, the farms are still small and the countryside is still magical, now often more cosmetic than real. Rural landownership was traditionally controlled by the Crown and its designated lords. That system persists, supplemented by a small number of large corporate owners. Access to "roam" freely across the land on a system of trails and back roads is a major issue in Britain, as is the recent contention about the old aristocratic tradition of foxhunting with hounds—a mixture of pageantry, sport, and sadistic pleasure.

Driving farther west, the flatness of Sussex rises gradually onto the historic Salisbury Plain, one of the most ancient inhabited landscapes in Britain. Turning off the M-3 onto a smaller road, A303, the traveler has to look diligently for the few signs to Stonehenge. Were it located in the United States, we would have been passing giant billboards announcing Stonehenge and one commercial opportunity or another just ahead. Motels, hotels, and the paraphernalia of tourism and commerce would have blighted the landscape, all but obliterating the main attraction. Disciplined by a culture three or four millennia old, the Brits know better. Over a slight rise, the ancient megalithic structure appears on a hill straight ahead. Somber lichen-covered stones were placed in an arc between 2550 and 1900 BC by a people whose intentions have long since receded into the mists of time. The best guesses about their purposes are just that: guesses. What we know is that with great effort and considerable skill these people moved giant stones from as far away as the Preseli Mountains in Wales, a distance of 135 miles, into a formation consisting of two outer circles and two horseshoe-shaped formations inside, open to the East. The place appears to have once served as a device to mark the seasons and chart the night skies as part of ceremonial functions the nature of which no one now knows. After several centuries of debate about its uses as a celestial observatory, a calendar, or a primitive astronomical computer, one archaeologist concludes sensibly that Stonehenge is best regarded as an "ancient sacred place" depicting the cosmology of its builders (Chippindale 2004, 236–237). Whatever its builders' intention, the measurements of the sun and the moon were remarkably accurate for a people who we think of as primitive. But what moved them to calculate, sweat, build, and celebrate, and what gods or demons they hoped to appease or mollify by doing so we cannot fathom. Whatever they intended, the site is moving in its silent grandeur and indifference to time and tourist alike. We are safe to presume that it also moved those who once went there to worship, appease, or just be in ways perhaps no longer accessible to us.

The landscape around Stonehenge features burial mounds called barrows, ceremonial avenues (cursus) extending for miles, and even more ancient monuments like that at nearby Avebury. At about the same time that Stonehenge was being built, other cultures throughout much of the inhabited world were building similar kinds of monuments in Ireland, the Orkney Islands, Crete, Egypt, and the lowlands of Central America an ocean distant. Not knowing why or even how they were built, we see such places as museums, interesting for a time but unrelated to our own buildings or lives. Nor do we see the cosmology of such places as anything more than curious astronomical puzzles. What we miss, I think, is a fundamental need buried deep in the human psyche for meaning and connection to something that transcends ourselves. Stonehenge and similar places are dramatic evidence of a desire to connect to a larger reality and model a larger cosmology. They were also intended, in some unknown way, to explain, console, or simply acknowledge the reality of death. But it is said that the average visitor spends ninety-three minutes at the site, and unaware of the irony or possibly afraid of being caught in some mysterious vortex of time, hurries on to some other, and maybe safer, destination. Conforming to modern notions of time, we spend the requisite ninety minutes and head on to Devon, our next stop.

### Rationality

Several thousand miles and two millennia distant, the Greeks built the Parthenon on top of a rock outcropping called the Acropolis. Prominent above a natural harbor, the site was ideal as a fortified center for the city of Athens, and later for civic and ceremonial functions. Today, it is the most famous ruin in the world as well as a symbol of the Greek contribution to the development of rational thought, science, art, and democracy. But our knowledge of its origins, the intentions of its instigator, Pericles, and its architect, Iktinos, and the circumstances of its construction are remarkably sketchy. Other than one by Plutarch, the only reference to the Parthenon in the ancient world is from one Pausanias, who wrote a paragraph about it in a *Guidebook to Greece* six hundred years after its construction (Beard 2003, 23). Yet we do know that the building of the Parthenon coincided with the apogee and decline of the Greek empire between AD 447 and 404 as its most eloquent physical expression. The Parthenon, the first temple built entirely from marble, represented the height of the refinement of temple design. Iktinos's art lay in his use of deception so that almost no line in the structure is entirely straight. In appreciation, Paul Valery once wrote:

Standing before a building in which mass was so sensitively lightened, a building that seemed so simple, no one was aware that the sense of happiness he felt was caused by curves and bends that were almost imperceptible yet immensely powerful. The beholder was unaware that he was responding to a combination of regularity and irregularity the architect had hidden in his work, a combination as strong as it is impossible to describe. (quoted in Meier 2000, 350)

From a sufficient distance the Parthenon looks absolutely square; the eye is deceived by the practice of making the columns swell slightly toward the middle (entasis), and bending them slightly inward while they rest on a slightly convex platform (Hurwit 2004, 118). The Parthenon is deceptive in other ways that are neither so artistic nor admirable. It was funded by the profits of the Greek empire and built from marble mined by slaves at the onset of the wars that ended Athenian democracy. In the words of Loren Samons, it "is not a testament to Athenian democracy, humanism, or liberalism . . . [but] first and foremost a monument to Athenian power, glory, and victory over both barbarians and . . . other Greeks" (quoted in Hurwit 2004, 55).

Still, from the site of the forum or agora below, it is possible to hear the distant echoes of conversations that occurred in that brief moment in time about life, meaning, purpose, and the possibility that humans could rise above sophistry and irrationality. If Stonehenge had to do with cosmology, the Parthenon symbolizes the possibility that humans may one day emerge from the shadows of the cave into the full sunlight of rational thought and action—a hope that seems oddly distant after the world wars, gulags, genocide, and terrorism of the past hundred years. To this endeavor the Greeks gave architectural expression, raising the arts of proportion, harmony, and building science to a level some think has never been surpassed.

## Theology

Fifteen hundred years later, the great era of Gothic cathedral building began with the construction of the Abbey Church of St. Denis, seven miles north of Paris. The style of the cathedral was quickly emulated throughout much of Europe and Scandinavia. From start to finish the era lasted about four hundred years. The first example of Gothic design in Britain occurred between 1175 and 1184 with the rebuilding of part of the great cathedral at Canterbury destroyed by fire. Westminster Abbey, built by Edward the Confessor between 1042 and 1066, was done over in elaborate Gothic style by Henry III between 1246 and 1272 at what is estimated to be 5 percent of his available wealth (Jenkyns 2004). Much of that work has survived to the present. Britain alone, a country smaller than the state of Alabama with a population of six million, built twenty-seven Gothic cathedrals, hundreds of abbeys and monasteries, and thousands of parish churches, in a time of recurring famines, wars, and plagues. The average construction time for the larger cathedrals and abbey churches was nearly three centuries at costs we would most certainly regard as prohibitive (Scott 2003, 42–43).

Gothic cathedrals exhibited an abundance of ornamentation, elaboration, and symbolism that is difficult for us to comprehend—the religious zeal that motivated the builders and worshippers alike has been long since assigned to other, more secular tasks. Cathedrals were, in Robert Scott's words (2003, 120), "a space where people could get a taste of heaven . . . a literal representation of the thing itself." Drawing from Saint Augustine, the elaborate geometry of cathedrals was assumed to be a kind of applied theology imitating the work of God. At the heart of cathedral building were new construction techniques including the use of ribbed vaults and flying buttresses that allowed for greater building height and penetration of light. Above all, cathedrals were intended to be places showing God's nature as divine light—"akin to a great lens created to gather the diffuse ambient light of the divine spirit and focus it to a particular geographical location, where it becomes available for human worship and supplication" (153–154). The vast scale of cathedrals was further intended to be large enough to "attract the sacred and induce it to settle and stay . . . and substantial enough not only to contain and confine the sacred, but also to ensure that it will remain strong, vibrant, and alive—keeping its powers from dissipating" (152). Cathedrals were also designed to be mnemonic devices to instruct and remind worshippers of heaven, earthly temptations, and the torments of hell. Icons, carvings, gargoyles, and statuary filled cathedral spaces to remind mostly illiterate parishioners of the story of Christianity, honor the dead, preserve the relics of the faith, and provide an abode for deceased saints. For people living in the highly uncertain, chaotic, and often violent world of the Middle Ages, cathedrals and the church liturgy were intended also to assure worshippers of the existence of a higher order, cosmic regularity, coherence, and structure missing in ordinary life. No less important, the great cathedrals and abbey churches provided a focal point for the surrounding community as economic drivers and places of pageantry and public charity.

The Christian cosmology that fueled ambitions, fears, and devotion has faded with the centuries, and the feudal system that paid for it is long gone. Only 2 percent of British people regularly attend church services of any kind. The cathedrals are now filled mostly by tourists marveling at the bones, and only dimly aware of the life that caused people to build them and worship in them. Our cathedrals and enthusiasms are different, but perhaps no less intense.

**The Market**
On a typical day, the intersection of Tottenham Court Road and Oxford Street in central London is filled with hurried and harried people. Overhead, facing out on the intersection on this particular March day, is a two-story billboard filled with the image of a teenage boy wearing nothing but his Calvin Klein underwear and a callow, suggestive expression. Whatever his particular abilities, it is said that he is enjoying his fifteen minutes of fame, although his expression gives no hint of enjoyment or even of much awareness. That billboard is one of many at this intersection, all showing

off the fine arts of commercial seduction in its many guises and disguises. We are exposed to several thousand such advertisements each day from billboards, television, and radio, the largest effort ever conceived to deflect human psychology and behavior, all in the service of making us dependable and dependent consumers and sedated citizens. Rats on treadmills may have greater independence and deeper thoughts.

The devotion of whole societies to the god of consumption is rooted in the theology of the market laid down by the first economist, Adam Smith, in 1776, and his neoclassic and increasingly mathematically rigorous disciples. The central principle of the market-as-theology is simply that rational individuals maximize their gains and minimize their losses as measured in pecuniary terms. Among economists and their followers that doctrine is presumed to be both an adequate description of how people actually behave and a prescription for how they should behave, a curious blend of scientific presumption and theological instruction. The theology of the market, too, has its particular architectural forms oriented unsurprisingly to utility, production, efficiency, speed, and for the wealthy, conspicuous display. No one could confuse the resulting architecture of factories, roadways, and sprawling cities with beauty; yet its purpose is not beauty but merely pecuniary gain—a different kind of aesthetic. The working out of market theology remorselessly stripped away all values that could not be rendered into profit, changing the face of the land, cities, cultures, and human psychology. Land, forests, wildlife, the waters of Earth, and even persons have all been rendered into an abstraction called resources. No theology was ever as total or demanded such total fealty.

From the air, the result is apparent in vast malls that function as cathedrals of consumption, endless highways to permit access to the many opportunities for consumption, suburbs stretching to the far horizon, and the blanket of brown haze that envelops it all. More distant and hidden from view are the clear-cut forests, mines, agribusinesses, refineries, chemical factories, and fuel storage depots—the extractive apparatus supplying the market economy. On the fringes one finds the growing blight of abandoned factories, malls, and mines—the unlovely detritus of the extractive economy. Caught in between are the slums, trailer parks, bars, and tawdriness of those unfortunate enough to be sacrificed to the market.

Their numbers are growing, if not their consciousness, as Karl Marx once predicted.

I arrived at my office just before nine on the morning of September 11 to find the departmental secretary in tears. The first plane had just hit the North Tower; a second plane heading for the South Tower was only minutes away from impact. Two stark, soaring square towers that dominated the New York skyline and symbolized U.S. dominance in the global economy collapsed within the hour. The World Trade Center was not beautiful architecture, nor was that its purpose. Its function was strictly utilitarian. It is now famous as the intersection of hatred and structure, and a turning point in history. The twentieth century was born in a spirit of optimism that was transmuted by two world wars, insane ideologies, gulags, holocausts, killing fields, and terrorism into escapism and a kind of controlled despair. The twenty-first century began with another mind-set born of the growing disparity between rich and poor, and between our technological prowess and ecological decline. The fate of the Twin Towers is a symbol of that starting point—history deflected along a path the end of which we cannot foresee. September 11, 2001, may some day be seen as the beginning of the end of the design experiment that formed around the ideas of industrialization, economic growth, and our total mastery of nature. The commercial economy with its iconic architecture of giant towers, commercial malls, and urban sprawl is failing, and we are uncertain where to turn.

Whatever its specific purposes may have been, Stonehenge was designed to mirror what its builders knew of the cosmos. Again, we cannot know with any certainty what they intended, but we may reasonably infer that its building was driven by a desire to transcend earthly existence. Standing on the Acropolis, the Parthenon is the western epitome of proportion, perspective, and reason—a symbol of the belief that life ought to mirror larger harmonies as an orderly endeavor lived to standards of excellence that the ancient Greeks called arête. The Parthenon and the agora were the stage for the brief Athenian experiment with the idea that we might become reasonable and self-governing people. The designers of Westminster Abbey and the great cathedrals of Europe attempted to mirror Christian theology in light, form, symbolism, and majesty. In time each of these design revolutions came undone, the result of changing circumstances and history. But each in its own way represented the human endeavor to establish order and meaning in ways characteristic of its particular age. Design established on the proposition that human affairs and the physical world could be built around the abstraction of the market is in the process of disintegration as well.

We no longer have a cosmology that orients us to space and time or ties us to each other. We know too much, or too little, to say with certainty where we are or why we exist. The carnage and excesses of the twentieth century exacted a heavy toll on our faith about the possibilities of rational thought and a rational ordering of human affairs. And caught between fundamentalisms and secularism, organized religion is no longer the source of stability, consolation, and certainty that it once may have been. Our architecture shows the strain. We build lavishly, grandly, and ostentatiously, but no longer in a way that binds, challenges, explains, and orients. Some build "cost-effectively," but we pay for that economy too, because of the damage done to Earth and our spirits. Architect Christopher Alexander describes it in these words (2001–2004, 1:6): "In the 20th century we have passed through a unique period, one in which architecture as a discipline has been in a state that is almost unimaginably bad. Sometimes I think of it as a mass psychosis of unprecedented dimension, in which the people of earth—in large numbers and in almost all contemporary societies—have created a form of architecture which is against life, insane, image-ridden, hollow." In large measure, the cause is that the great determinant of contemporary architecture is finance capital. But imagine the creators of Stonehenge, the Parthenon, or Westminster aiming to be merely cost-effective. They built nobly because they suspected a higher order of things beyond their apprehension that they wanted to placate, mirror, exploit, or worship—or perhaps they were just hedging their bets. We build less grandly and worship lesser deities. But our starting point is the same as once described by Vitruvius: "the need to shelter human activity (commodity), to durably challenge gravity and the elements (firmness), and to be an object of beauty (delight)" (Rybczynski 2001, 4).

# 2

## Origins of Ecological Design

Ask the animals, and they will teach you; the birds of the air, and they will tell you; ask the plants of the earth, and they will teach you; and the fish of the sea will declare to you.
—Job 12:7–9

Imagine living in a chaotic, random world without order, in which no rules applied and effects followed no discernible pattern of cause. Such a world would be alien to intelligence, morality, and foresight, governed instead by caprice, chance, and whimsy, which is to say that it would be a kind of hell. Design presumes, on the contrary, the possibility of order and begins in the faith that matter is ordered and that order matters. But to the questions of exactly what is ordered and how there is no one answer. The more we know, the more mysterious the world appears to be. Beyond the regularities of changing seasons, birth, and death, the world that we experience is often chaotic, violent, and capricious, governed as much by fate as by foresight. Still, even that awareness fuels the effort to discover larger patterns, the mastery of which will permit us to establish a safe haven or, for some, heaven on Earth. For the builders of megalithic monuments like Stonehenge, the clues to order lay in the observed regularities of the night sky and the movements of the sun, the moon, and the stars relative to Earth. The Greeks, believers in the possibility of reason, discovered geometric proportions and mathematical harmony in the world. Some thought that the cultivation of reason might lead to entire societies in which reasonable people might collaborate reasonably to manage public affairs in a state of democracy, yet another level of harmony. For the ancient Jews, the basis of order was otherworldly—a moral order evident in the laws God first gave to Moses. For the builders of the great cathedrals, that belief was extended into architectural form blending Greek geometry with Judeo-Christian theology in service to the idea that inspired humans could design so artfully as to create sacred spaces that were a portion of heaven on Earth.

The designers of Gothic cathedrals presumed a more remote God who had once created a clockwork universe and had the good sense thereafter not to meddle with it, leaving it to run on remote control. Isaac Newton deciphered the scientific laws God had once purportedly used, and rendered these into science and the metaphor of a machine. Adam Smith took that metaphor to describe our tendency to truck and barter as the working out of an invisible hand administering the laws of supply and demand in a mechanistic world. Smith's economy is a kind of machine that sifts order from the chaos of individual self-interest. We continue to live in that faith, now extended to a further abstraction called the global economy.

Each of the design stages persists in some degree in subsequent stages like the layers of successive geologic eras. Unlike the more discrete scientific revolutions described by Thomas Kuhn—in which one paradigm overthrows another less adequate one—our sense of order is a kind of lamination in which earlier thinking persists whether in science, social structures, language, or even commonplace superstitions. Each transformation in our understanding of how to make the human presence on Earth surrendered in due course to time, human frailty, and its own inherent shortcomings; but those earlier ways of understanding did not altogether disappear. The megalithic belief in a larger order evident in the rising and setting of the sun, lunar cycles, and movements of the stars survives in the belief that patterns of ecology represent a larger ordering applicable to human systems. The belief that human reason might yet bring order from unreason and caprice also survives. The Greek experiment in rationality flourished in the Christian era as part of what Arthur O. Lovejoy ([1936] 1974) once described as "the great chain of being." If humans had the capacity of reason, might they not also discern the very mind of God? The Neoplatonism of the medieval world, in Lovejoy's words, "rested at bottom upon a faith . . . that the universe is a rational order . . . a coherent, luminous, intellectually secure and dependable world, in which the mind of man could go about its business of seeking an understanding of things in full confidence" (327–328). Faith in a rational order and the powers of rationality survives into our time, magnified by the Enlightenment of the eighteenth century into the creed of inevitable progress. The faith of the medieval clergy survives not just in the millenarian assumptions of nearly every ideological movement but in the belief that what we make on Earth ought to reflect higher obligations than those of self-interest. That, too, is an echo of the ancient belief in a divine order that would lead to the final triumph of right.

The increasingly homogeneous industrial civilization that now stretches around the world is the signature accomplishment of the capitalist revolution, but its future is troubled for reasons that any moderately well-informed high school student could recite in detail. Its prospects are clouded, first, because it is inflicting a rising level of ecological damage evident as impaired ecological functions, the loss of biological diversity, mutilated ecological systems, spreading blight, pollution, and climate change. For the scientists who study Earth processes and ecology the facts are well-known. Due to the loss of habitat and pollution, the number of species on Earth will decline by one-quarter to one-third in this century. The carbon content of the atmosphere has increased by more than a third from its preindustrial level of 280 parts per million and is rising at a rate now over 2 parts per million each year, a harbinger of worse to come. The human population has increased sixfold in the last two centuries and will grow to eight or nine billion before it will presumably level off. The number of large predatory fish in the oceans has decreased by 90 percent. Worldwide soil loss is estimated to be twenty to twenty-five billion tons per year. Forests are disappearing at the rate of 9.4 million hectares per year, an area roughly the size of Portugal. Within a few years, maybe a decade or two, we will reach the peak of the era of cheap oil, and start down the backside of the curve where supply and demand diverge, which may well trigger bitter geopolitical conflicts. Harvard biologist Edward O. Wilson (2002) refers to the decades ahead as a "bottleneck," an uncertain passage through constraints caused by the loss of species, climatic change, and population growth. The scientific evidence documenting the decline of the vital signs of Earth is overwhelming, and so too is the burden of pondering such complicated and dire things, which may help to explain the growing popularity of escapism, religious zealotry, overconsumption, and other modes of denial.

The industrial experiment is also failing because of growing inequities and violence. After a century of economic growth, a majority of people experience life close to the bone. Over one billion people live in absolute poverty at the edge of starvation. Their daily reality is hunger, insecurity, and hopelessness. At the other end of the spectrum, another billion live in affluence and suffer the consequences of having too much. Powered by cheap fossil energy, their world is one of traffic jams, suburban malls, satiation, fashion, fad diets, addiction, boredom, and commercial entertainment. In spite of high rates of economic growth, the trend toward greater and greater inequity is leading to a world dominated by a handful of corporations and a few thousand super wealthy. These two worlds appear to be diverging, but in fact their destinies are colliding. Security, once a function of distance and military might, has been radically changed by terrorism and the diffusion of heinous weaponry. National borders no longer provide safety. The powerful and wealthy are vulnerable now precisely because their power and wealth makes them targets for terrorists and malcontents. And ethics, once a matter of individual behavior, now includes the conduct of whole societies and entire generations whose choices often cast long shadows across the planet and into the far future.

The inability to solve ecological and social problems points to deeper flaws. Like the proverbial fish unaware of the water in which it swims, we too have difficulty perceiving fatal flaws in our ideas, paradigms, and behavior that we take for granted until it is too late. In Jared Diamond's words (2005, 438), "human societies and smaller groups may make disastrous decisions for a whole sequence of reasons: failure to anticipate a problem, failure to perceive it once it has arisen, failure to attempt to solve it after it has been perceived, and failure to succeed in attempts to solve it." In our time, the inability to perceive and solve problems is often related to our faith in technology that leads some to believe that we are masters of nature and smart enough to manage it in perpetuity. That presumption, in turn, rests on an improbably rosy view of human capabilities and the faith, as Robert Sinsheimer (1978) once put it, that nature sets no traps for unwary species. Our optimism is, I think, a product of a particular era in human history shaped by the one-time drawdown of cheap fossil fuels—the "age of exuberance," in William Catton's words (1980, 6). Our politics, economics, education, as well as personal expectations were shaped by the assumption that we had at last solved the age-old problem of energy. Ancient sunlight fueled rapid economic growth, vastly increased mobility and agricultural productivity, and a level of affluence that our ancestors could not imagine. But it also weakened social cohesion, encouraged overconsumption, polluted our air and water, and contaminated our politics, while creating a fragile and temporary energetic basis for a complicated civilization vulnerable to breakdown for many reasons. Anthropologist Joseph Tainter summarizes this by saying (1988, 195) that "as stresses necessarily arise, new organizational and economic solutions must be developed, typically at increasing costs and declining marginal return. The marginal return on investment in complexity accordingly deteriorates, at first gradually, then with accelerated force. At this point, a complex society reaches the phase where it becomes increasingly vulnerable to collapse." In other words, foresight fails to anticipate problems that outrun solutions, thereby aggregating into crises and then into a systemwide crisis of crises. The sense of care, always a limited resource, falters; human ingenuity, however considerable, fails; and things come tumbling down (Homer-Dixon 2000). The story is an old one—a lack of foresight, the intoxication of power, tragedy, arrogance, stupidity, and angry gods.

The fox, Isaiah Berlin (1953) once noted, knows many things, but the hedgehog knows one big thing. Ecological designers, like the hedgehog, know one big thing: that everything is hitched to everything else as systems within larger systems and patterns that connect across species, space, and time. Ecological design begins with the recognition that the whole is more than the sum of its parts, that unpredictable properties emerge at different scales, and that as a result we live in a world of surprise and mystery. Those who design with nature work in the recognition that the world is one and indivisible, that what goes around comes around, that life is more paradoxical than we can ever know, and that health, healing, wholeness, and holy too are inseparable. Ecological design is the careful meshing of human purposes with the patterns and flows of the natural world as well as the study of those patterns to inform human intentions, leaving wide margins for error, malfeasance, and the unknown. Ecological design requires an efficiency revolution in the use of energy and materials, a transition to renewable energy, changes in land use and community design, a transition to economies that preserve natural capital, and a recalibration of political and legal systems with ecological realities. Most important, it requires a change in how we think about our place in the natural world.

The origins of ecological design can be traced back into our prehistoric ancestors' interest in the natural regularities of the seasons, the sun, the moon, and the stars, as well as in the Greek conviction that humans, by the application of reason, could discern the laws of nature. Ecological design also rests on the theological conviction that we are obliged, not merely constrained, to respect larger harmonies and patterns. The Latin root for the word religion—bind together—and the Greek root for ecology—household management—suggest a deeper compatibility and connection to order. Further, ecological design builds on the science and technology of the industrial age, but for the purpose of establishing a partnership with nature, not domination. The first models of ecological design can be found throughout the world in the vernacular architecture and the practical arts that are as old as recorded history. It is, accordingly, as much a recovery of old and established knowledge and practices as it is a discovery of anything new. The arts of building, agriculture, forestry, health care, and economy were sometimes practiced sustainably in cultures that we otherwise might dismiss as primitive. The art of applied wholeness was implicit in social customs such as the observance of the Sabbath and holy days, the Jubilee year, or the practice of potlatch, in which debts were forgiven and wealth was recirculated. It is evident still in all of those various ways by which communities and societies gracefully cultivate the arts of generosity, kindness, prudence, love, humility, compassion, gentleness, forgiveness, gratitude, and ecological intelligence.

In its specifically modern form, ecological design has roots in the Romantic rebellion against the more extreme forms of modernism, particularly the belief that humans armed with science and a bit of technology were lords and masters of creation. Francis Bacon, perhaps the most influential of the architects of modern science, proposed the kind of science that would reveal knowledge by putting nature on the rack and torturing her secrets from her—a view still congenial to some who have learned to say it more correctly. The science that grew from Bacon, Galileo, and René Descartes overthrew older forms of knowing based on the view that we are participants in the forming of knowledge and that nature is not dead (Merchant 1982). The result was a science based on the assumptions that we stand apart from nature, that knowledge is to be judged by its usefulness in extending human mastery over nature, and that nature is best understood by reducing it into its components. "The natural world," in the words of E. A. Burtt (1954, 104), "was portrayed as a vast, self-contained mathematical machine, consisting of motions of matter in space and time, and man with his purposes, feelings, and secondary qualities was shoved apart as an unimportant spectator." Our minds are so completely stamped by that particular kind of science that it is difficult to imagine another way to know in which comparably valid knowledge might be derived from different assumptions along with something akin to sympathy and a "feeling for the organism" (Keller 1983).

Among the dissidents of modern science, Johann Wolfgang von Goethe, best known as the author of *Faust,* stands out as one of the first theorists and practitioners of the science of wholeness. In contrast to a purely intellectual empiricism, what physicist and philosopher Henri Bortoft (1996) calls the "onlooker consciousness," Goethe stressed the importance of observation grounded in intuition so that objects under investigation could communicate to the observer. Descartes, in contrast, reportedly began his days in bed by withdrawing his attention from the contaminating influence of his own body and the cares of the world, to engage in deep thinking. He thereby aimed to establish the methodology for a science of quantity established by pure logic. Goethe, on the other hand, practiced an applied science of wholeness in which "the organizing idea in cognition comes from the phenomenon itself, instead of from the self-assertive thinking of the investigating scientist," explains Bortoft (240). Rather than the intellectual inquisition proposed by Bacon and practiced subsequently, Goethe suggested something like a dialogue with nature by which scientists "offer their thinking to nature so that nature can think in them and the phenomenon disclose itself as idea" (242). The facilitation of that dialogue required "training new cognitive capacities" so that Goethean scientists, "far from being onlookers, detached from the phenomenon, or at most manipulating it externally . . . are engaged with it in a way which entails their own development" (244). As Bortoft also observes (242), "The Goethean scientist does not project their thoughts onto nature, but offers their thinking to nature so that nature can think in them and the phenomenon disclose itself as idea," which requires overcoming a deeply ingrained habit of seeing things as only isolated parts, not in their wholeness. The mental leap, notes Bortoft, is similar to that made by Helen Keller, who blind and deaf, was nonetheless able to wake to what she called the "light of the world" without any preconceptions or prior metaphoric structure whatsoever. Goethe proposed not to dispense with conventional science but rather to find another, and complementary, doorway to the realm of knowledge in the belief that truth is not to be had through any single method, nor by any one age or culture.

Implicit in Goethe's mode of science is the old view, still current among some native peoples, that Earth and its creatures are kin and in some fashion sentient, and can this communicate to us; that life comes to us as a gift; and that a spirit of trust, not fear, is essential to knowing anything worth knowing. That message, in Calvin Martin's words (1999, 107, 113), "is riveting . . . offering a civilization strangled by fear, measuring everything in fear, the chance to love everything" and to rise above "the armored chauvinism" inherent in a kind of insane quantification. It is, I think, what Albert Einstein meant in saying (Calaprice 2005, 206):

A human being is part of a whole, called by us the universe, a part limited in time and space. He experiences himself, his thoughts and feelings, as something separated from the rest—a kind of optical delusion of his consciousness. This delusion is a kind of prison for us, restricting us to our personal desires and to affection for a few persons nearest us. Our task must be to free ourselves from this prison by widening our circles of compassion to embrace all living creatures and the whole of nature in its beauty.

Goethe proposed a kind of jailbreak from the prison of Cartesian anthropocentrism, and from beliefs that animals and natural systems were fit objects to be manipulated at will. His intellectual heirs include all of those who believe that the whole is more than the sum of its parts, including systems thinkers as diverse as mathematician and philosopher Alfred North Whitehead, politician and philosopher Jan Smuts, biologist Ludwig von Bertalanffy, economist Kenneth Boulding, and ecologist Eugene Odum. Goethe's approach continues in the study of nonlinear systems in places like the Santa Fe Institute. Biologist Brian Goodwin (1994, 198), for one, calls for a "science of qualities" that complements and extends existing science. In Goodwin's view, conventional science is incapable of describing "the rhythms and spatial patterns that emerge during the development of an organism and result in the morphology and behavior that identify it as a member of a particular species . . . or the emergent qualities that are expressed in biological form are directly linked to the nature of organisms as integrated wholes" (198–199). Goodwin, like Goethe, advocates a "new biology . . . with a new vision of our relationships with organisms and with nature in general . . . [one] that emphasizes the wholeness, health, and quality of life that emerge from a deep respect for other beings and their rights to full expression of their natures" (232). Goodwin, Goethe, and other systems scientists aim for a more scientific science, commensurate with the fullness of life.

While Goethe's scientific work focused on the morphology of plants and the physics of light, D'Arcy Thompson, one of the most unusual polymaths of the twentieth century and one who "stands as the most influential biologist ever left on the fringes of legitimate science" (Gleick 1987, 199), approached design by studying how and why certain forms appeared in nature. Of Thompson's *magnum opus On Growth and Form* (1917), Sir Peter Medawar said that it was "beyond comparison the finest work of literature in all the annals of science that have been recorded in the English tongue" (quoted in Gleick 1987, 200). Thompson seems to have measured everything he encountered, most notably natural forms as well as the structural features of plants and animals. In so doing, he discovered the patterns by which form arises from physical forces, not just by evolutionary tinkering, as proposed by Charles Darwin. Why, for example, does the honeycomb of the bee consist of hexagonal chambers similar to soap bubbles compressed between two glass plates? The answer, Thompson discovered, was found in the response of materials to physical forces, applicable as well to "the cornea of the human eye, dry lake beds, and polygons of tundra and ice" (Willis 1995, 72). By showing the physical and mechanical forces behind life-forms at all levels, Thompson challenged the Darwinian idea that heredity determined everything. His notions inspired subsequent work in biomechanics, evolutionary biology, architecture, and biomimicry, including that by Paul Grillo, Karl von Frisch, and Steven Vogel.

Von Frisch, for example, explored the ingenuity of architecture evolved by birds, mammals, fish, and insects. He found that African termite mounds a dozen feet high maintain a constant temperature of ~78°F in tropical climates (von Frisch 1974, 138–149). Nests are ventilated variously by permeable walls that exchange gases, and by ventilation shafts opened and closed manually as needed with no other instructions than those given by instinct. Interior ducts move air and gases automatically by convection. The system is so ingeniously designed that chambers deep underground are fed a constant stream of cool, fresh air that rises as it warms before being ventilated to the outside. The nests are constructed of materials cemented together with the termites' own excretions, eliminating the problem of waste disposal. Desert termites, with no engineering degrees as far as we know, bore holes forty meters below their nests to find water. Beavers construct dams one thousand feet or more in length; their houses are insulated to remain warm in subzero temperatures. Other animals, less studied, build with comparable skill (Tsui 1999, 86–131). Considerable as it is, human ingenuity pales before that of the many other animals who design and build remarkably strong, adaptable, and resilient structures without toxic chemicals, machinery, hands with opposable thumbs, fossil fuels, and professional engineers.

The idea that nature is shaped by physical forces as much as by evolution is also evident in the work of Theodor Schwenk, who explored the role of water as a shaper of Earth's surfaces and biological systems. As Schwenk wrote (1989, 24):

In the chemical realm, water lies exactly at the neutral point between acid and alkaline, and is therefore able to serve as the mediator of change in either direction. In fact, water is the instrument of chemical change wherever it occurs in life and nature. . . . In the light-realm, too, water occupies the middle ground between light and darkness. The rainbow, that primal phenomenon of color, makes its shining appearance in and through the agency of water. . . . In the realm of gravity, water counters heaviness with levity; thus, objects immersed in water take on buoyancy. . . . In the heat-realm water takes a middle position between radiation and conduction. It is the greatest heat conveyer in the earth's organism, transporting inconceivable amounts of warmth from hot regions to cooler ones by means of the process known as heat-convection. . . . In the morphological realm, water favors the spherical; we see this in the drop form. Pitting the round against the radial, it calls forth that primal form of life, the spiral. . . . In every area, water assumes the role of mediator. Encompassing both life and death, it constantly wrests the former from the latter.

Moving water shapes landscapes. As ice it molds entire continents. At a microscale, its movement shapes organs and the tiniest organisms. But at any scale it flows, dissolves, purifies, condenses, floats, washes, and conducts, and some believe that it even remembers. Our language is brimful of water metaphors; we have streams of thought or dry spells. The brain literally floats on a water cushion. Water in its various metaphors is the heart of our language, religion, and philosophy. We are much given to the poetry of water as mists, rain, flows, springs, light reflected, waterfalls, tides, waves, and storms. Some of us have been baptized in it. But all of us stand ignorant before the mystery that D. H. Lawrence called "the third thing," by which two atoms of hydrogen and one of oxygen become water, and no one knows what it is (Lawrence 1971, 515).

"Form patterns," Schwenk wrote (1996, 34), "such as those appearing in waves with new water constantly flowing through them, picture on the one hand the creation of form and on the other the constant exchange of material in the organic world." Water is a shaper, but the physics of its movement is also the elementary pattern of larger systems "depicting in miniature the great starry universe" (45). Water is the medium by and through which life is lived. Turbulence in air and water have the same forms and mechanics as vortices whether in the ocean, the atmosphere, or space. Sound waves and waves in water operate similarly. In short, Schwenk's great contribution to ecological design was to introduce water as a geologic, biological, somatic, and spiritual force, a reminder that we are creatures of water, all of us eddies in one great watershed.

The profession of design as an ecological art probably begins with the great British and European landscapers such as Capability Brown (1716–1783), famous for developing pastoral vistas for the rich and famous of his day. Looking out from the massive ostentation of Blenheim Palace across the surrounding lakes, trees, and grazing sheep you are witness not to the natural landscape but to Brown's version of the pastoral—an orderliness of considerable comfort to the creators of the British empire. In U.S. history, the early beginnings of design as ecology are apparent in the work of the great landscape architect and creator of Central Park in New York, Frederick Law Olmsted, and later, in that of Jens Jensen, who pioneered the use of native plants in designed landscapes of the Midwest. Ian McHarg (1969, 27), a brilliant revolutionary, merged the science of ecology with landscape architecture, aiming to create human settlements in which "man and nature are indivisible, and that survival and health are contingent upon an understanding of nature and her processes." His students, including Frederick Steiner, Pliny Fisk, Carol Franklin, and Ann Whiston Spirn, continued that vision armed with the sophisticated methodological tools of geographic information systems and ecological modeling applicable to the broader problems of human ecology.

While the degree of influence varied, many early efforts toward ecological design were inspired by the arts and crafts movement in Britain, particularly the work of William Morris and John Ruskin. In U.S. architecture, for example, Frank Lloyd Wright's attempt to define an "organic architecture" has clear resonance with the work of Morris and Ruskin as well as the transcendentalism of Ralph Waldo Emerson. Speaking before the Royal Institute of British Architects in 1939, Wright (1993, 302, 306) described organic architecture as "architecture of nature, for nature . . . something more integral and consistent with the laws of nature." In words Morris and Ruskin would have applauded, Wright argued that a building "should love the ground on which it stands" (307), reflecting the topography, materials, and life of the place. Organic architecture is "human scale in all proportions," but is a blending of nature with human-created space so that it would be difficult to "say where the garden ends and where the house begins . . . for we are by nature ground-loving animals, and insofar as we court the ground, know the ground, and sympathize with what it has to give us" (309). Wright's vision extended beyond architecture to the larger settlement patterns that he called "Broadacre City," asserting that organic architecture had to be more than an island in a society with other values. Wright, with his attempts to harmonize building and ecology as well as his pioneering efforts to use natural materials and solar energy, is a precursor to those involved in green building movement. And in his often random musings about an "organic society," he foreshadowed the present dialogue about ecological design and the sustainability of modern society.

Ecological design, however, is not just about calibrating human activities with natural systems. It is also an inward search to find patterns and order of nature written in our senses, flesh, and human proclivities. There is no line dividing nature outside from inside; we are permeable creatures inseparable from nature and the natural processes in which we live, move, and have our being. We are also sensual creatures with five senses that we know and others that we only suspect. At its best, ecological design is a calibration, not just of our sense of proportion that the Greeks understood mathematically, but a finer calibration of the full range of our sensuality with the built environment, landscapes, and natural systems. Our buildings are thoughts, words, theories, and entire philosophies crystallized for a brief time into a physical form that reveals what's on our mind and what's not. When done right, they are a kind of dialogue with nature and our own deeper, sensual nature. The sights, smells, texture, and sounds of the built environment evoke memories, initiate streams of thought, engage, sooth, provoke, bind or block, and open or close possibilities. When done badly, the result is the spiritual emptiness characteristic of a great deal of modern design that reveals, in turn, a poverty of thought, perception, and feeling manifest as ugliness.

We are creatures shaped inordinately by the faculty of sight, yet seeing is anything but simple. Oliver Sacks once described a man blind since early childhood who, once his sight was restored, found it to be a terrible and confusing burden, and preferred to return to blindness and his own inner world. "When we open our eyes each morning," Sacks writes (1993, 64), "it is upon a world we have spent a lifetime *learning* to see." And we can lose not only the faculty of sight but the ability to see as well. Even with twenty-twenty vision, our perception is always selective because our eyes permit us to see only within certain ranges of the light spectrum, and because personality, prejudice, interest, and culture further filter what we are able to see. Sacks notes that individual people can choose not to see, and I suspect the same is true for cultures as well. The affinity for nature, a kind of sight, is much diminished in modern cultures.

Collective vision cannot be easily restored by more clever thinking, but as David Abram puts it (1996, 69), only "through a renewed attentiveness to this perceptual dimension that underlies all our logics, through a rejuvenation of our carnal, sensorial empathy with the living land that sustains us." Following the writings of Maurice Merleau-Ponty, Abram describes perception as interactive and participatory, in which "perceived things are encountered by the perceiving body as animate, living powers that actively draw us into relation . . . both engender[ing] and support[ing] our more conscious, linguistic reciprocity with others" (90). Further, sight as well as language and thought are experienced bodily as colors, vibrations, sensations, and empathy, not simply as mental abstractions. The ideas that viewer and viewed are in a form of dialogue, and that we experience perception bodily, runs against the dominant strain of Western philosophy. Plato (*Phaedrus* 479), by way of illustration, has Socrates say, "I'm a lover of learning, and trees and open country won't teach me anything whereas men in the town do." Plato's world of ideal forms existed only in the abstract. Similarly, the Christian heaven exists purely somewhere beyond earthly and bodily realities. Both reflected the shifting balance between the animated sacred, participatory world and the linear, abstract, intellectual one. Commenting on the rise of writing and the priority of the text, Abram says (1996, 254) that "the voices of the forest, and of the river began to fade ... language loosen[ed] its ancient association with the invisible breath, the spirit sever[ed] itself from the wind, and psyche dissociate[d] itself from the environing air." As a result, "human awareness folds in upon itself and the senses—once the crucial site of our engagement with the wild and animate earth—become mere adjuncts of an isolate and abstract mind" (267).

Through the designed object we are invited to participate in seeing something else, a larger reality. The creators of Stonehenge, I think, intended worshippers to see not just circles of artfully arranged stone but the cosmos above. The Parthenon is a temple to the goddess Athena, but also a visible testimony to an ideal existing in mathematical harmonies, proportion, and symmetry discoverable by human reason. The builders of Gothic cathedrals intended not just monumental architecture but a glimpse of heaven and a home for sacred presence. For all of the crass, utilitarian ugliness of the factories, slums, and glittering office towers, the designers and builders of the industrial world intended to reveal possibilities for abundance and human improvement in a world they otherwise deemed uncertain and violent, ruled by the laws of the jungle.

Finally, the practice of ecological design is rooted in the emerging science of ecology and the natural characteristics of specific places. The ecological design revolution is not merely a more efficient use of energy and materials, in accord with ecological realities but a deeper and more coherent vision of the human place in nature. Ecological design is, in effect, the specific terms of a declaration of coevolution with nature that begins in the science of ecology and the recognition of our dependence on "the web of life" (Capra 1996). In contrast to the belief that nature is little more than a machine and its parts merely resources, for ecological designers, nature is, as Aldo Leopold put it ([1949] 1987, 216),

a fountain of energy flowing through a circuit of soils, plants, and animals. Food chains are the living channels which conduct energy upward; death and decay return it to the soil. The circuit is not closed; some energy is dissipated in decay, some is added by absorption from the air, some is stored in soils, peats, and long-lived forests; but it is a sustained circuit, like a slowly augmented revolving fund of life. There is always a net loss by downhill wash, but this is normally small and offset by the decay of rocks.

Energy flowing through the "biotic stream" moves "in long or short circuits, rapidly or slowly, uniformly or in spurts, in declining or ascending volume," through what ecologists call food chains. For designers, the important point is that the internal processes of the biotic community—the ecological books, in effect—must balance so that the energy used or dissipated by various processes of growth is replenished (1953/1972, 162). Leopold proposed three basic ideas:

1. That land is not merely soil
2. That the native plants and animals kept the energy circuit open; others may or may not
3. That man-made changes are of a different order than evolutionary changes, and have effects more comprehensive than is intended or foreseen. (218)

Ecological design, as Leopold noted, begins with the recognition that nature is not simply dead material or a resource for the expression of human wants and needs but rather "community of soils, waters, plants, and animals, or collectively: the land" of which we are a part (Leopold 1949, 204). But Leopold did not stop at the boundary of science and ethics; he went on to draw out the larger implications. For reasons that are both necessary and right, the recognition that we are members in the community of life "changes the role of *Homo sapiens* from conqueror of the land-community to plain member and citizen of it" (204). The "upshot" is Leopold's classic statement that "a thing is right when it tends to preserve the integrity, stability, and beauty of the biotic community. It is wrong when it tends otherwise" (224–225). We will be a long time understanding the full implications of that creed, but Leopold, late in his life, was beginning to ponder the larger social, political, and economic requisites of a fully functioning land ethic.

Like Leopold's land ethic, ecological design represents a practical marriage of ecologically enlightened self-interest with the recognition of the intrinsic values of natural systems. Once consummated, however, the marriage branches out into a myriad of possibilities. Economics rooted in the realities of ecology, for example, requires the preservation of the natural capital of soils, forests, and biological diversity—that is, economies that operate within the limits of Earth's carrying capacity (Hawken, Lovins, and Lovins 1999; Daly 1996). An ecological politics requires recognizing the complexities and timescales of ecosystems in the conduct of the public business. An ecological view of health would begin with the acknowledgment that the body exists within an environment, not as a kind of isolated machine (Kaptchuk 2000). Religion grounded in the operational realities of ecology would build on the human role as steward and the obligation to care for the Creation (Tucker 2003). An ecological view of agriculture would begin with the realities of natural systems, aiming to mimic the way nature "farms" (W. Jackson 1980). An ecological view of business and industry would aim to create solar powered industrial and commercial ecologies so that every waste product cycles as an input in some other system (McDonough and Braungart 2002). And an ecological view of education would, among other things, foster the capacity to perceive systems and patterns as well as promote ecological competence (Orr 1992, 2004).

Ecology, the "subversive science," is the recognition of our practical connections to the physical world, but it does not stop there. The awareness of the many ways by which we are connected to the web of life would lead intelligent and scientifically literate people to protect nature and the conditions necessary to it for reasons of self-interest. But our knowledge, always incomplete and often dead wrong, is inadequate to the task of knowing what's in our interest—whether we wish to define that as "higher" or "lower." Science notwithstanding, frequently we do not know what we are doing or why. More subversive still are questions concerning the interests and rights of lives and life across the boundaries of species and time. Since future genetic forms of life cannot speak for themselves, their only advocates are those willing to speak on their behalf. Any number of clever arguments purport to explain why we should or should not be concerned about those whose lives and circumstances would be affected by our action or inaction. Like so many tin soldiers arrayed across the battlefield of abstract intellectual combat, they assault frontally or by flank, retreat only to regroup, and charge again, each battle giving rise to yet another. In the end, I think, such questions will be decided not by intellectual combat and argumentation, however smart, but rather more simply and profoundly by affection—all of those human emotions that we try to capture in words like compassion, sympathy, and love. In other words, love neither requires nor hinges on intellectual argument. It is a claim that we recognize as valid, yet for reasons we could never describe satisfactorily. Ultimately, it is a self-limitation on what we do and a gift we offer. Blaise Pascal's observation that the heart has reasons that reason does not know, sums up the matter. Love is a gift, but the giver expects no return on the investment, and that defies logic, reason, and even contentions about selfish genes.

After all of the intellectualization is finished and all of the clever arguments made, whether we choose to design with nature or not will come down to a profoundly simple matter of whether we love deeply enough, artfully enough, carefully enough to preserve life and the web on which all life depends. Ecological design is simply an informed love applied to the dialogue between humankind and natural systems. The origins of the practice of ecological design can be traced far back in time, but deeper origins are found in the recesses of the human heart.

# 3

## The Design Revolution: Notes for Practitioners

When you build a thing you cannot merely build that thing in isolation, but must also repair the world around it, and within it so that the larger world at that one place becomes more coherent and more whole; and the thing which you make takes its place in the web of nature as you make it.

—Christopher Alexander

Environmental design should aim at creating conditions favorable for the development of man's anatomical and physiological potentialities. It should also take into consideration the cosmic rhythms which are inextricably woven into man's biological fabric and that condition even his mental processes.

—Rene Dubos

The long-term goal of ecological design is to go "from conqueror of the land-community to plain member and citizen of it." Drawing from Sim Van der Ryn and Stuart Cowan (1996), William McDonough and Michael Braungart (2002), the basic principles of ecological design are:

- Use sunshine and wind
- Preserve diversity
- Account for all costs
- Eliminate waste
- Solve for pattern
- Protect human dignity
- Leave wide margins for error, malfeasance, and ignorance

But there is no larger theory of ecological design, nor is there a textbook formula that works for practitioners across different fields and at varying scales. And neither should we presume agreement on what it means for humankind to become a plain member and citizen of the biotic community. In other words, we have a compass but no map. Samuel Mockbee, founder of the Rural Studio, enjoined his architectural students working with the poor in Hale County, Alabama, simply to make their work "warm, dry, and noble" (Oppenheimer and Hursley 2002). Warm and dry are easier for the most part because we feel them somatically, but noble is hard because it requires us to make judgments about what we ought to do relative to some standard higher than creature comfort. Nevertheless, in the best sense of the word noble, it implies decent, worthy, generous, magnificent, proud, and resilient. And it ought to be synonymous with ecological design as well.

Having no theory to expound, what follows are notes for something like a bull session on ecological design based on a scouting expedition described further on.

## Beginnings

The human sense of order and affinity for design, forged through our long evolutionary history, goes back to our dawning sensations and experiences of life. The first safe haven we sense is our mother's womb. Our first awareness of regularity is the rhythm of our mother's heartbeat. Our first passageway is her birth canal. Our first sign of benevolence is at her breast. Our first awareness of self and other comes from sounds made and reciprocated. Our first feelings of ecstasy come from bodily release. The first window through which we see is our eye. The first tool we master is our own hand. The world is first revealed to us through the senses of touch and taste. Our first worldview is formed within small places of childhood. Our ancestors' first inkling that they were not alone was the empathetic encounter with animals. The first music they heard were sounds made by birds, animals, wind, and water. Their first source of wonder, perhaps, was the undimmed night sky. Their first models of shelter were those created by birds and animals. The first materials humans used for building were mud, grass, stone, wood, and animal skins. Their first metaphors were likely formed from their daily experiences of nature. The first models for worship were found in what early humans perceived as cosmic harmony, often replicated in the design of dwelling places.

We are creatures shaped by the interplay between our senses and the world that we experience. We have reason to believe that our senses have atrophied in the modern world. Some evidence suggests, for example, that we have a lost a rudimentary awareness of being watched. Aboriginal peoples can walk with unerring accuracy through trackless landscapes in the dark of night. But across all cultures and times, good design joins our sensuality with inspiration, creativity, place, form, and materials. Good design feels right, and is a pleasure to behold and experience for reasons that we understand at an intuitive level but have difficulty explaining (Alexander 2001–2004; Kellert 1996).

## Evolution as Model, and Nature as Standard

The starting point for ecological design is the 3.8 billion years of evolutionary history. Nature, for ecological designers, is not something just to be mastered; it is a tutor and mentor for human actions. For example, Janine Benyus (1998), author of *Biomimicry,* points out that spiders make biodegradable materials stronger than steel and tougher than Kevlar without fossil fuels or toxic chemicals. From nothing more than substances in seawater, mollusks make ceramic-like materials that are stronger and more durable than anything we presently know how to make. These and thousands of other instances are models for manufacturing, the design of technologies, farming, machines, and architecture that are orders of magnitude more efficient and elegant than our best industrial capabilities.

Ecological design, however, is not simply a mimicking of nature toward a smarter kind of industrialization but rather a deeper revolution in the place of humans in nature. In Wendell Berry's words (1987, 146), design begins with the questions "What is here? What will nature permit us to do here? What will nature help us do here?" The capacity to question presumes the humility to ask, the good sense to ask the right questions, and the wisdom to follow the answers to their logical conclusions. Ecological design is not a monologue of humans talking to nature but a dialogue that requires the capacity to listen, discern, and learn from nature. When we get it right, the results, again in John Todd's words, are "elegant solutions predicated on the uniqueness of place." The industrial standard, in contrast, is based on the idea that nature can be tortured into revealing her secrets, as Francis Bacon put it, and then by brute force and human cleverness coerced to do whatever those with power intend. One size fits all, so that industrial design looks the same and operates by the same narrow logic everywhere. But this is no great victory for humankind because the mastery of nature in truth represents the mastery of some people over others using nature as the medium, as C. S. Lewis (1946) once put it.

**All Design Is Political**

Design inevitably involves decisions about how society provides food, energy, shelter, materials, water, and waste cycling, and distributes risks, costs, and benefits. In other words, design affects who gets what, when, and how—a standard definition of politics. The environment, then, is a mirror reflecting decisions that we make about energy, forests, land, water, biological diversity, resources, and the distribution of wealth, risks, and benefits. Often cast as "conservative" or "liberal," such decisions in our time are, in fact, frequently about how the present generation orients itself to the interests of its children and grandchildren. One can arrive at a decent regard for the prospects of future generations as either a conservative or a liberal. These are not opposing positions so much as they are different sides of a single coin. But neither conservatives nor liberals have yet invested much energy, time, or thought to the design requirements of the transition to sustainability. The point is that harmonizing social and economic life with ecological realities will require choices about energy technologies, agriculture, land use, settlement patterns, materials, the handling of wastes, and water that are inescapably political, and will distribute risks and benefits in one way or another.

Further, as the Greeks understood, design entails choices that enhance or retard civic life and the prospects for citizenship. But in our time, "we are witnessing the destruction of the very idea of the inclusive city" (R. Rogers 1997, 10), and with it the arts of civility, citizenship, and civilization. By including or excluding possibilities to engage each other in convivial dialogue, the creators of urban spaces enhance or diminish civility, urbanity, and the civic prospect. It is no accident, I think, that crime, loneliness, and low participation became epidemic as spaces such as town squares, street markets, front porches, corner pubs, and parks were sacrificed to the automobile, parking lots, and urban sprawl. Better architecture and landscape architecture alone cannot cure these problems but they can help to engage people with their places as thoughtful agents in the making of the human prospect, which is the function of politics.

## Honest Accounting

In an age much devoted to the theology of the market, disciples of the conventional wisdom believe it imprudent to design ecologically if the costs are even marginally more. Based on incomplete and highly selective accounting, that view is almost always wrong because it overlooks the fact that we—or someone—sooner or later will pay the full costs of bad design, one way or another. In other words, society pays for ecological design whether it gets the benefits of it or not. Honest accounting, accordingly, requires that we keep the boundaries of consideration as wide as possible over the long term and have the wit to deduct the collateral benefits that come from doing the right things in the right way. For example, ignoring the costs of wars fought for "cheap" oil, or the costs of climate change, air pollution, and the health effects of urban sprawl, is cheap enough. But price and cost should not be confused. It is the height of folly to believe that we can eliminate forests, pollute, squander resources, erode soils, destroy biological diversity, remodel the biogeochemical cycles of Earth, and create ugliness, human and ecological, without consequence. The truth is that, sooner or later, the full costs will be paid one way or another. The problem, however, is that the costs of environmental dereliction are diffuse, and often can be deferred to some other persons and some later time. But they do not thereby disappear. The upshot is that much of our apparent prosperity is phony, and so too the intellectual and ideological justifications for it.

The standard of neoclassic economics applied to architecture in particular has been little short of disastrous. "The rich complexity of human motivation that generated architecture," in Richard Rogers's words (1997, 67), "is being stripped bare. Building is pursued almost exclusively for profit." By such logic, we cannot afford to design well and build for the distant future. The results have been evident for a long time. In the mid-nineteenth century, John Ruskin noted ([1880] 1989, 21), "Ours has the look of a lazy compliance with low conditions." But even Ruskin could not have foreseen the blight of suburban sprawl, strip development, and urban decay driven by our near-terminal love affair with the automobile and the inability to plan sensibly. The true costs, however, are passed on to others as "externalities," thereby privatizing the gains while socializing the costs. The truth is, as it has always been, that phony prosperity is no good economy at all. False economic reckoning has caused us to lay waste to our countryside, abandon our inner cities and the poor, and build auto-dependent communities that are contributing mightily to destabilizing the climate and rendering us dependent on politically volatile regions for oil.

An economy judged by the narrow industrial standards of efficiency will destroy values that it cannot comprehend. Measured as the output for a given level of input, maximizing efficiency creates disorder—that is, inefficiency at higher levels. The reasons for this are complex, but they have a great deal to do with our tendency to confuse means with ends. As a result, efficiency often becomes an end in itself while the original purposes (prosperity, security, benevolence, reputation, and so on) are forgotten. The assembly line was efficient for the manufacturing firm, but its larger effects on workers, communities, and ecologies were often destructive, and the problems for which mass production was once a solution have been compounded many times over. Neighborliness is certainly an inefficient use of time on any given day, although not when considered as a design principle for communities assessed over months and years or generations. For engineers, freeways are efficient at moving people up to a point, but they destroy communities, promote pollution, lead to congestion, change foreign policies, and eliminate better alternatives, including design that eliminates some of the need for mobility. Wal-Mart, similarly, is an efficient marketing enterprise, yet it eliminates its competitors and many things that make for good communities, including jobs that pay decent wages. Success on such terms will eventually destroy Wal-Mart and a great deal more. And of course, nuclear weapons are wonderfully efficient devices as well. Ecological design, in contrast, implies a different standard of efficiency oriented toward ends, not means, the whole, not parts, and the long term, not the short term.

## Design for Human Limitations

Ecological design, like all human affairs, has to be carried out in the full recognition of human limitations, including the discomfiting possibility that we are incurably ignorant. T. S. Eliot put it this way ([1936] 1971, 119):

Human kind
Cannot bear very much reality

In other words, we are inescapably ignorant and the reasons are many. We are ignorant because reality is infinite relative to our intellectual and perceptual capacities. We are ignorant because we individually and collectively forget things that we once knew. We are ignorant because every human action changes the very system we aim to understand. We are ignorant because of our own limited intelligence and because we cannot know in advance the unintended effects of our actions on complex systems. We are ignorant even of the proper ends to which knowledge might be put. Not the least, we are ignorant because we choose to be.

Alas, many seem to prefer it that way. From the publication of the *Global 2000* report in 1980 to the present, there is a veritable mountain of scientific evidence about human impacts on ecosystems and the biosphere, and ways to minimize or eliminate them. But our collective sleepwalk toward the edge of avoidable tragedy continues, suggesting that we are not so much rational creatures as we are adept and creative rationalizers. The reality is that we are coming to the end of a brief interlude in human history powered by ancient sunlight. Had we been a truly perceptive lot, we would have burned little of this endowment, and probably would not have industrialized in the manner or to the degree that we did. Willed or otherwise, we did both without reckoning the full costs and risks.

Similarly, designers must reckon with the uncomfortable probability that the amount of credulity in human societies remains constant. This is readily apparent by looking backward through the rearview mirror of history to see the foibles, fantasies, and follies of people in previous ages (Tuchman 1984). For all our pretensions to rationality, others at some later time will see us similarly. The fact is that humans in all ages and times are inclined to be as unskeptical and sometimes as gullible as those living in any other—only the sources of our befuddlement change. People of previous ages read chicken entrails, relied on shamanism, and consulted oracles. We, far more sophisticated but similarly limited, use computer models, believe experts, and exhibit a touching faith in technology to fix virtually everything. But who among us really understands how computers or computer models work? Who is aware of the many limits of expertise or the ironic ways in which technology "bites back"? Has gullibility declined as science has grown more powerful? No; if anything, it is growing because science and technology are increasingly esoteric and specialized, and hence removed from daily experience. Understanding less and less of either, we will believe almost anything. Gullibility feeds on mental laziness, and is enforced by the social factors of ostracism, pressures for conformity, and the pathologies of groupthink that penalize deviance.

This line of thought raises the related and equally unflattering possibility that stupidity may be randomly distributed up and down the social, economic, and educational ladder. As anecdotal evidence for the latter, I offer the observation that I have known as many brilliant people without much formal learning as those certified by PhDs. And there are likely as many thoroughgoing, fully degreed fools as there are nondegreed ones. Intelligence and intellectual clarity can be focused and sharpened a bit, but it can be neither taught nor conjured. The numerous examples of the undereducated or those who were outright failures in the academic sense include Albert Einstein, Winston Churchill, and Frank Lloyd Wright. One should conclude, however, not that formal schooling is useless but that its effectiveness, for all of the puffery that adorns college catalogs and educational magazines, is considerably less than often advertised. And there are those, as lawyer John Berry once noted, who have been "educated beyond their comprehension," people made more errant by the belief that their ignorance has been erased by the possession of facts, theories, and the adornment of weighty learnedness.

Nor does the outlook for intelligence necessarily brighten when we consider the limitations of large organizations. These too are infected with our debilities. Most of us live out our professional lives in organizations or work for them as clients, and discover to our dismay that the collective intelligence of organizations and bureaucracies is often considerably less than that of any one of its individual employees. We are baffled by the discrepancy between smart people within organizations exhibiting a collective IQ of less than, say, kitty litter. We understand human stupidity and dysfunction because we encounter it on a scale commensurate with our own. But confronted with large organizations, whether corporations, governments, or colleges and universities, we tend to equate scale, prestige, and power with perspicacity and infallibility. Nothing could be further from the truth. The intelligence of big organizations (if that is not altogether oxymoronic) is limited by the obligation to earn a profit, enlarge their domain, preserve entitlements, or maintain a suitable stockpile of prestige.

Our frailties infect even the anointed in the design professions. Buildings and bridges sometimes fall down (Levy and Salvadori 1992). Clever designs can induce an astonishing level of illness and destruction. Beyond some limit design becomes guesswork. British engineer A. R. Dykes puts it this way: "Engineering is the art of modeling materials we do not wholly understand, into shapes we cannot precisely analyze so as to withstand forces we cannot properly assess, in such a way that the public has no reason to suspect the extent of our ignorance." In various ways, the same is true in other design professions and virtually every other field of human endeavor.

The point is simply to say that human limitations will dog designers at every turn. They will infect every design, every project, and the evolution of every system, however clever. From this there are, I think, two conclusions to be drawn. The first is simply that design, whether of bridges, buildings, communities, factories, or farms and food systems, ought to maximize the capacity of a system to withstand disturbance without impairment—that is, its resilience. Ecological design does not assume the improbable: human infallibility, technologies that work without fail, or some deus ex machina that magically rescues us from folly. Rather, it does things at a manageable scale aiming for the flexibility, redundancy, and multiple checks and balances characteristic of healthy ecosystems, and in so doing avoids transgressing thresholds of the irreversible and irrevocable (Lovins and Lovins 1982, A. Lovins 2002, 177–213).

Forewarned about human limitations, we might further conclude that a principal goal of designers ought to be the improvement of our collective intelligence by promoting mindfulness, transparency, and ecological competence. The public is less aware of how it is provisioned with food, energy, water, materials, security, and shelter, and how its wastes are handled than people of any previous time. Industrial design cloaked the ecological fine print of what are often little better than Faustian bargains providing luxury and convenience now, while deferring ruin on those least able to organize or postponing it to some later time. Ecological design, on the contrary, ought to demystify the world, making us mindful of the ecological fine print by which we live, move, and have our being.

Design is always a powerful form of education. Only the terminally pedantic believe that learning happens just in schools and classrooms. The built environment in which we spend over 90 percent of our lives is at least as powerful in shaping our ideas and views of the world as anything learned in a classroom. Suburbs, shopping malls, freeways, parking lots, and derelict urban spaces have considerable impacts on how we think, what we think about, and what we can think about. The practice of design as a form of public instruction ought to free the ecological imagination from the tyranny of imposed forms and relationships characteristic of the fossil-fueled industrial age. Architecture, landscape architecture, and planning carried out as a form of pedagogy aims to instruct about energy, materials, history, rhythms of time and seasons, and the ecology of the places in which we live. Such a form would help us become mindful of ecological relationships and engage our places creatively.

**Vernacular**

Many of the best examples of ecological design have been created by people at the periphery of power, money, and influence in out-of-the-way places. The truth is that practical adaptation to the ecologies of particular places over long periods of time has often resulted in spectacularly successful models of vernacular design (Rudofsky 1964). It may well be that the ecological design revolution will be driven, at least in part, by experience accumulated from the periphery, not the center, and led by people skilled at solving the practical problems of living artfully by their wits and good sense in particular places. The success of vernacular design across all cultures and times underscores the possibility that design intelligence may be more accurately measured at the level of the community or culture, rather than at the individual level.

## The Standard

The aesthetic standard for ecological design is to work so artfully as to cause no ugliness, human or ecological, somewhere else or at some later time. In other words, the standard, requires a robust sense of aesthetics that rises above the belief that beauty is wholly synonymous with form alone. Every great designer from Vitruvius through Frank Lloyd Wright demonstrated that beauty in the large sense had to do with the effects of buildings on the human spirit and our sense of humanity. But the standards for beauty must be measured on a global scale and longer time horizon so that beauty includes the upstream effects at wells, mines, and forests where materials originate as well as the downstream effects on climate, human health, and ecological resilience. Things judged truly beautiful will in time be regarded as those that raised the human spirit without compromising human dignity or ecological functions elsewhere. Architecture and landscape architecture, in other words, are a means to higher ends, not ends in themselves.

## Education of Designers

As much art as science, the design professions are not simply technical disciplines, having to do with the intersection of form, materials, technology, and real estate. The design professions such as architecture, landscape architecture, and urban planning are first and foremost practical liberal arts with technical aspects. Writing in the first century BC, Vitruvius (1960, 5–6) proposed that architects "be educated, skilful with the pencil, instructed in geometry, know much history, have followed the philosophers with attention, understand music, have some knowledge of medicine, know the opinions of the jurists, and be acquainted with astronomy and the theory of the heavens." That is a start of a liberal and liberating education. Therefore, design education ought to be a part of a broad conversation that includes all of the liberal arts. This is, I think, what George Steiner means by saying (2001, 251–252), "Architecture takes us to the border. It has perennially busied the philosophic imagination, from Plato to Valery and Heidegger. More insistently than any other realization of form, architecture modifies the human environment, edifying alternative and counter-worlds in relationships at once concordant with and opposed to nature."

In countless ways all design, even the best, damages the natural world. The extraction and processing of materials depletes landscapes and pollutes. Building construction, operation, and demolition creates large amounts of debris. Agriculture inevitably simplifies ecosystems. Accordingly, a new breed of ecological designers must be even more intellectually agile and broader, capable of orchestrating the wide array of talents and fields of knowledge necessary to design outcomes that can be sustained within the ecological carrying capacity of particular places.

## Design as a Healing Profession

The design professions are a form of the healing arts, an ideal with roots again in Vitruvius's advice that architects ought to pay close attention to sunlight, the purity of water, air movements, and the effects of the building site on human health. The word healing has a close affinity with other words such as holy and wholeness. A larger sense of the profession of architecture, which architect Thomas Fisher (2001, 8) deems a "calling," would aim for the kind of wholeness that creates not just buildings but integral homes and communities. For example, compare the idea that "architecture applies only to buildings designed with a view to aesthetic appeal" (Pevsner 1990, 15) with architecture defined as "the art of place-making" and creation of "healing places" (Day 2002, 10, 5). In the former sense, design changes with trends in fashionable forms and materials. It is often indifferent to place, people, and time. The goal is to make monumental, novel, and photogenic buildings and landscapes that often express only the ego and power of the designer and owner. In contrast, the making of healing places signals a larger allegiance to place that means, in turn, a commitment to the health of other places. Place making is an art and science disciplined by locality, culture, and ecology, and requiring detailed knowledge of local materials, weather, topography, and the nature of particular places as well as a creative dialogue between past, present, and future possibilities. It is slow work in the same sense that caring and careful have a different clock speed than carelessness. Place making uses local resources, thereby buffering local communities from the ups and downs of the global economy, unemployment, and resource shortages (Sutton 2001, 200).

Practiced as a healing art, architecture would result in buildings and communities that do not compromise the health of people and places, drawing on the accumulated wisdom of placed cultures and vernacular skills. Architects would aim to design buildings that heal what ails us at deeper levels. At larger scales, the challenge is to extend healing to urban ecologies. Half of humankind now lives in urban areas—a percentage that will rise in the coming decades to perhaps 80 percent. Cities built in the industrial model and to accommodate the automobile are widely recognized as human, ecological, and increasingly, economic disasters. Given a choice, people leave such places in droves. But we have good examples of cities as diverse as Copenhagen, Chattanooga, and Curitiba that have taken charge of their futures to create livable, vital, and prosperous urban places—what Peter Hall and Colin Ward (1978) have called "sociable cities." In order to do that, however, designers must see their work as fitting into a larger human and ecological tapestry.

As a healing art, ecological design aims toward harmony, which is the proper relation of parts to the whole. Is there a design equivalent to the Hippocratic oath, which has informed medical ethics for two millennia? Are there things that designers should not design? What would it mean for designers to "do no harm"?

Looking ahead, the challenge to the design professions is to join ecology and design in order to create buildings, communities, cities, landscapes, farms, industries, and entire economies that accrue natural capital and are powered by current sunlight—perhaps, one day, having no net ecological footprint. The standard is that of the healthy, regenerative ecosystem. In the years ahead, we will discover a great deal that is new, and we will rediscover the value of vernacular traditions such as front porches, village squares, urban parks, corner pubs, bicycles, pedestrian-scaled communities, small and winding streets, local stores, riparian corridors, urban farms and wild areas, and well-used landscapes.

Finally, design practiced as a healing art is not a panacea for the egregious sins of the industrial age. However well designed, a world of seven to ten billion human beings with unlimited material aspirations will sooner than later overwhelm the carrying capacity of natural systems as well as our own management abilities. There is considerable evidence that humans already exceed the limits of many natural systems. Further, ecological design does not require building; the best design choices often require adaptive reuse or more intense and creative uses of existing infrastructure. And sometimes it means doing nothing at all—a choice that requires a clearer and wiser distinction between our needs and wants.

What ecological designers can do, and all they can do, is to help reduce our ecological impacts and buy us time to reckon with the deeper sources of our problems, which have to do with age-old questions about how we relate to each other across the boundaries and sometimes chasms of gender, ethnicity, nationality, culture, and time as well as how we fit into the larger community of life. Ecological design, as a healing art, is a necessary but insufficient part of a larger strategy of healing, health, and wholeness, which brings me to soul.

### Design for Spirit

For designers, it is no small thing that humans are inescapably spiritual beings, but only intermittently religious. Philosopher Erazim Kohak once noted (1984, 170) that "humans can bear an incredible degree of meaningful deprivation but only very little meaningless affluence." Most of us tend to grow and mature in the former condition, but come undone in the latter. This is not a call to deliberately incur misery, which tends to multiply on its own with little assistance, but rather one to underscore our inevitable spiritual nature, which is like water bubbling upward from an artesian spring. Our choice is not whether we are spiritual but whether our spiritual energy is directed to authentic purposes.

Much of the modern world, however, has been assembled as if people were machines without deeper needs for order, pattern, and roots. Modern designers filled the world with buildings and developments divorced from their context, existing as if in some alien realm disconnected from ecology, history, culture, people, and place. Ecological design, on the other hand, is a process by which we grow into a particular place, becoming citizens of the life and community in that place. It is a process by which dwellings and landscapes along with the uses we make of them become part of a larger story. As a kind of storytelling, design is a celebration of the life that connects us with the nature of the places in which we live and work, and grounds us in the still larger story of the human journey (T. Berry 1988).

Ecological design is not a formula but rather a complex process of adapting human intentions to ecological realities. It is art as much as science, ethics as much as economics, ecology as much as engineering. And it is a messy, uncertain, difficult, sometimes contentious process demanding a high order of competence, creativity, and goodwill. Properly done, it changes routines of institutional decision making and management. Rules of finance and budgeting, for example, that worked in the industrial era, when the natural capital of soils, forests, water, and climate stability was assumed to be free, no longer do. Designing ecologically requires the integration of expertise across many disciplines, perspectives, and professions such as energy specialists, ecological engineers, materials scientists, lighting consultants, ecologically adept landscape architects, engineers who understand buildings as whole systems, and those who will live and work there. It might also lead institutional managers to call on the considerable pool of faculty expertise and student energy to design sustainable solutions for problems of how to provision ourselves with food, energy, water, materials, shelter, health, and livelihood in a postpetroleum world.

Finally, beyond performance of the obvious functions such as durable shelter, usefulness, and beauty, what larger results do we want from our buildings, landscapes, and communities? Even to pose the question reveals how little we ask of the design professions and how much we should ask of them. We should want our buildings, neighborhoods, communities, and cities to honor the ecologies and cultures of the places in which they are built. They should promote rootedness, not anomie. They ought to foster an awareness of connections and ecological competence. They ought to make us smarter and more competent people, not dumb us down. They ought to be designed to regenerate natural capital and foster possibilities for real human engagement. They ought to be paid for fairly, not dump costs on others. But these, too, are means to still-larger ends.

**Box 3.1**
A designer's quandary

I was asked to attend a meeting with officials from Wal-Mart, the world's largest retailer at $300 billion in annual sales and growing. Wal-Mart is probably the most adept assassin of small towns and downtown businesses, working under the motto "We sell for less." And for those who think no further than the price of their toothpaste while overlooking the decay of downtowns, traffic congestion, the injustice of low wages, discrimination against women, decreased community life, and increased crime that accompanies the expansion of Wal-Mart, that slogan is a sufficient rationale. But by any reckoning, this is a false economy.

Company executives intended to improve their supply chain, thereby saving money and reducing their ecological damages. Working with Wal-Mart is like "dancing with the devil," as a colleague put it. Given the sheer size of the company, any improvement in efficiency would be a sizable gain, but it also adds to the profitability and viability of a force running roughshod over communities, workers, and environments in at least nine countries. During that meeting, company officials indicated that sales were enhanced considerably by good design practices such as daylighting. They wished to explore other design possibilities as well.

But should ecological designers work to improve the efficiency of companies such as Wal-Mart that stride the world like behemoths? On one side of the argument is the obvious leverage that such companies have. Any improvements translate into large reductions of environmental damage. The company operates the largest commercial truck fleet in the world and, by one estimate, could save 40 percent of its fuel use with a short payback time using readily available efficiency improvements. Further, at its scale, Wal-Mart could drive improvements in technology, like photovoltaics, to the next stage of efficiency and cost reduction. On the other hand, Wal-Mart is deeply entrenched with regressive political forces, and has a well-deserved reputation for exploiting its workers, its suppliers, and the communities in which it does business. It receives large public subsidies in part to compensate for the low wages and minimal benefits paid to workers while driving out small businesses. I presented the quandary to students in my ecological design class. Would they work with Wal-Mart? If so, under what conditions? If not, why not?

**Box 3.1** (cont.)

Some answered, "No way, no how," regarding the company as the epitome of evil—not an uncommon view. The majority of the class, however, was of the opinion that it would be appropriate to help Wal-Mart reduce its environmental impacts and become more energy efficient, if it was willing, in turn, to improve wages and benefits for its workers and suppliers, establish high environmental design standards, offset the economic damage it does to its host communities, and generally conduct itself with due penance. Some of these students would request no such quid pro quo in the belief that ecological design might over time exert a benign effect on the company. Those who would have refused to help Wal-Mart were generally of the opinion that doing so would debase the ecological design profession and the purity of its practitioners, and further, that some things, such as consumption and perhaps Pentagon planning, ought to occur in dark, dank, and miserable places.

The idea also surfaced that Wal-Mart, with a little imagination and guidance, might become a very different enterprise, selling reasonably priced products along with better ideas while paying fair wages. Could a retailer use its advertising and selling power to promote energy efficiency, life-cycle accounting, low-impact products, biodegradable packaging, or even products of service? Could a progressive retailer help to eliminate one-way containers and bottles? Could its stores become overt models of ecological design powered by current sunlight, discharging no waste, and fitting into local ecologies? Could employees of the company, its "partners," be paid fairly? Could a company become an exemplar of natural capitalism, improving its bottom line while enhancing the mindfulness of its customers? Could that company buy more at fair prices from local suppliers? But if it did these things, would it still be Wal-Mart?

# II

## The Building

# 4

# Origins

The system of education in this [Oberlin] Institution will provide for the body and heart as well as the intellect; for it aims at the best education of the *whole man*.
—*New York Evangelist*, 1833

Oberlin College was founded by an evangelizing preacher, John Jay Shipherd, in 1833. Having heard a sermon preached by the well-known evangelist Charles Grandison Finney in 1826, Shipherd had been caught up in the spirit of the Great Revival that swept over the United States and with his wife and two sons headed west from Middlebury, Vermont, to preach the gospel in the wilderness in 1830. His sojourn took him as far as the frontier settlement of Elyria, Ohio, where he became the pastor of a Presbyterian church. Elyria had been founded by one Herman Ely in 1817, and was little more than a few houses surrounded by "lands heavily timbered with chestnut, oak, white wood, hickory, maple, & beech, ash &c" when Shipherd arrived. However fine the land, Shipherd found the "moral condition" of the people "deplorable." But his efforts at improving what he termed "wolfish men" were met with whiskey-fueled indifference and, on at least one occasion, hostility punctuated by bullets. "Only two in this place to my knowledge have turned to God since I came here," he reported in a letter to noted evangelist Charles Grandison Finney (Fletcher 1943 1: 79). Shipherd's inability to "win over the impenitent to God" convinced him to resign in 1832 and endeavor to save other souls in a different manner.

His plan, formed over the course of a year, was to move nine miles south to the wilderness of Russia Township and create a settlement where "sin would not be allowed to get a start" (1: 85)—a modest (and as it turned

out, an imperfectly realized) goal—along with a school to train missionaries and schoolteachers. Moved by the example of Pastor John Frederic
Oberlin (1740–1826) in Ban de la Roche in the Alsace region of France,
Shipherd named this new colony Oberlin. Shipherd aimed to follow Oberlin's lead by creating a "manual labor institute" in which liberal education
would be joined with labor to properly equip students for a life of conse-
crated usefulness much as Oberlin himself had joined practical endeavors
with theology to improve the physical, economic, and spiritual lot of his
congregation. The Oberlin Institute would "provide for the body and
heart as well as the intellect; for it aims at the education of the whole man"
(119). The institute opened in December, on five hundred acres of donated
land. A year later, in 1834, the trustees proudly reported to their patrons
that:

its grand object is the diffusion of useful science, sound morality, and pure religion,
among the growing multitudes of the Mississippi Valley. It aims also at bearing an
important part in extending these blessings to the destitute millions which over-
spread the earth. For this purpose it proposes as its primary object, the thorough
education of Ministers and pious School Teachers. As a secondary object, the elevation of the female character. And as a third general design, the education of
the *common people* with the higher classes in such manner as suits the nature of
Republican institutions. (1: 130–131)

Nonetheless, the new institution was financially destitute after a year
of operations, and was rescued by a unique set of circumstances and
Shiperd's enterprise. Hard up for students, cash, and adequate professors,
Shipherd recognized a free speech crisis at Lane Seminary in Cincinnati
over the issue of slavery as an opportunity to attract expelled seminarians,
several professors, funding from the antislavery Tappan brothers in New
York, and the services of Finney as a professor of theology. The results as
they unfolded not only rescued the institute but shaped it along the lines
of the deal composed by Finney, by which the trustees agreed to "commit
the internal management of the institute entirely to the faculty, inclusive of
the reception of students," which in practical terms meant the admission
of persons of color (1: 175). At the time, however, the admission of African Americans was of less importance than the issue of freedom of discussion that had led to the expulsion of the Lane seminarians in the first
place. And whatever the motives, the decision reflected a keen appreciation for pecuniary advantage as well. Oberlin College thereafter became

an early leader in the education of women and African Americans as well as in the arts of faculty governance. As much as for any college in the United States, the founding DNA of evangelical zeal, concern for the oppressed, and participatory governance shaped the subsequent history of the college. The rationale and words may have changed, but the voltage behind the causes remained fairly constant.

Oberlin College evolved in the conjunction of its position on the moral high ground in the historical topography of the nineteenth century and its rather more bland geographic setting, formed by ancient seas, geologic uplift, and the glaciers that flattened the land of northern Ohio and left Lake Erie as the dominant feature of the region. An appreciation of this landscape, where the low ridges formed by earlier Erie shorelines are the highest point on the horizon, requires a subtle sense of geography (Sherman 1997). Yet a closer examination reveals more striking declivities cut by rivers flowing into Lake Erie, the Vermilion River to the west of Oberlin, and the Black River to the east, along with a remarkably diverse flora and fauna anchored by a few relict wetlands and remnants of the beech-maple climax forest that once stretched unbroken into Indiana. By the middle of the nineteenth century, the conversion of northern Ohio to farms and cities was virtually complete, stitched together by a dense network of railroads, roads, and interstate highways connecting the industrial cities of Cleveland, Lorain, and Elyria with other hubs of commerce.

In this place the college began to attract many good students, including Charles Martin Hall, who as an undergraduate discovered how to extract aluminum from bauxite and subsequently formed the Alcoa company. From that financially propitious position, Hall contributed heavily to his alma mater, thereby allowing for a considerable expansion of the college physical plant and program along with the creation of the thirteen-acre town square named for the Tappan brothers. For a time afterward architecture flowered on the Oberlin campus, including four notable buildings designed by Cass Gilbert, otherwise famous as the designer of the Supreme Court Building in Washington, DC, and the Woolworth Building in New York (Blodgett 2001a, 2001b). That era came to a close after World War II.

The architecture of the postwar campus was more starkly utilitarian, not unlike that built elsewhere. Because of a paucity of money and imagination, buildings constructed on college and university campuses in the latter half of the twentieth century were often designed to the same aesthetic standards as the strip malls and Kmarts of the time. The Oberlin campus, like most others, has a rogues' gallery of buildings from that era that were cheap to build, expensive to operate, and ugly, uncomfortable, and inefficient. Included in that genre are dormitories that were designed by architecture firms said to have been proficient makers of prisons for the state of Ohio. Add some razor wire, bars, and guard towers, and the results would be indistinguishable from any number of Ohio detention facilities featuring a different kind of curriculum, but at roughly the same cost per inmate. Oberlin College is not unique in this regard. I have seen similar or worse examples on other campuses around the country. The assumption behind the design of all such buildings is that the quality of thinking, purportedly our stock in trade, is unaffected by physical surroundings. Unsurprisingly, then, considerations of cost overwhelmed all others. The result was a kind of architectural barbarism—a war waged against the human psyche and physiology in the name of economics.

Ugliness aside, buildings built in the latter half of the twentieth century often shut out daylight, blocked natural air movement, and were filled with materials that off-gassed a witch's brew of volatile organic compounds that contributed to enough human health problems to fill a sizable medical textbook.[1] They also required aggressive foreign policies bent to the mission of providing cheap, uninterruptible energy supplies as a matter of necessity. The Oberlin College library, a massive, graceless, and unlovely cube said to nurture the capacities for thought and foresight, opened in 1973, the same year as the first oil embargo, and used one-quarter of the electricity on campus. It is said to have been built with a single light switch so that when the librarian went to check the mail on,

---

1. The seeming indifference of all who live and work in such places is striking. Beyond our own property, we seldom think of ourselves as active agents in the making of our surroundings and the places where we live, work, shop, and play. Democracy seems to stop were the built environment begins. Nor, typically, do we know much about the buildings and landscapes that we use—how they are made and maintained, and at what cost to whom. Such ignorance is instructive too. It tells us that a mindfulness of places and things about us is unimportant along with the effects of our actions on the world. It is ironic that studying in places intended to advance awareness, knowledge, and learning, we exist without the slightest awareness of their ecological and material underpinnings.

say, December 26, needing about thirty watts to light a desk surface, the entire building had to be lit like a Christmas tree. All in all, it is a rather consistent match of architecture and timing. But I quibble.

We did not set out to reform academic architecture. Our initial goals were limited to the problem of providing space for a small, but rapidly growing program in a liberal arts college long before those in charge had noticed that there was any problem at all. It started in fall 1992 with a yearlong class at Oberlin organized to examine the possibilities for creating an environmental studies center that would provide offices, classrooms, and working areas for students and faculty in the program. The class, which met every Saturday morning, functioned as a kind of scouting expedition. The format students chose was rather like that of a grand jury that subpoenaed leading green architects in order to grill them without mercy. Officially, we were supposed to meet on Saturdays until noon, but conversations between students and architects typically began on Friday night—when we picked our guests up at the airport—and extended through Sunday on the return trip. The first class in September 1992 met with Bill McDonough of William McDonough + Partners from Charlottesville, Virginia, in a windowless basement classroom in the bowels of Mudd Library.

In the field of green design, McDonough is a force, and he is not loath to say as much. He was once quoted as saying that he is not the edge of the wave in design; he is, indeed, the wave. Modesty at that scale creates disciples and enemies, of which he has both. The latter believe that he can suck all of the oxygen out of a room otherwise filled with brilliant minds and strong personalities. But few deny that the ego and incandescence are matched. I had heard of him in the early 1990s, and invited him to open the discussion about architectural possibilities for an environmental center at Oberlin. Over the drone of a poorly engineered ventilation system, McDonough's eloquence set the initial framework for the class in that year of 1992–93 and thereafter. Buildings, in McDonough's view, were more than "machines," as once proposed by Swiss architect Le Corbusier ([1931] 1986). They could be more like trees as part of a larger ecological fabric. McDonough is half Irish eloquence laced with blarney and half pure brilliance, and it is often hard to tell which brilliant half is which, but the fact is that the project was never the same again. He had set our sights on larger possibilities.

The college president at that time, an equal mix of charm, brilliance, and ego, however, was having none of it. "Orr's building," as he put it in a secret memo leaked to me by the dean, "has to be stopped." But his assurances to me were to the contrary. Walking across campus one cold December day in 1992, the president cheerily inquired, "How is the building 'project' coming?" My stammering response was more or less to say "slowly." "Well, don't let the bastards stop you," he replied. I did not have the presence of mind to do much more than smile and nod in the affirmative. Thankfully, more appropriate responses came to mind only seconds after he had walked away.

Through the year, the class met with a dozen other architects and designers at the frontier of the green building movement, including Robert Berkebile, Sim Van der Ryn, Gary Coates, John and Nancy Jack Todd, and Marc Rosenbaum. We first considered the possibility of renovating some existing building. On a chilly Saturday morning, the director of college operations took us on a tour of a half-dozen dilapidated houses owned by the college. Her assignment was to deflect, discourage, and defeat the enterprise, but the effect on the students was the opposite. Realizing that no suitable old building was available for renovation, the students quickly moved on to the job of designing a new one.

The class began with fifty students, but dwindled over the year to twenty-five and a hard core of half that number who believed that they'd found a way to save the world from certain ruin. The dozen or so who stayed with the project gathered steam and clarity, while the remainder lost interest to varying degrees, most having no affinity for chaos or, understandably, believing that the endeavor was entirely quixotic. In hindsight, I think few of the participants actually thought that anything would come from the effort; rather they supposed that, however noble, it was a labor in vain. By the end of the year, the class had assembled what architects would call a "preprogram" of goals, objectives, building standards, and possible building sites, and had developed a philosophical rationale that placed the project within the tradition of the liberal arts. We had also placed the project on the college agenda in a way that could not be easily ignored. The student newspaper had featured it prominently and frequently through the year. Student organizations discussed design ideas and solicited comments from the student community. Whatever else we had done, we had given the idea life, energy, a bit of clarity, a student following, and visibility in the community. More important, we had learned a great deal about possibilities. We were learning to ask about the life-cycle costs of materials and buildings, and to think of buildings as ecological systems within larger ecologies, not just as collections of isolated components. But we did not have authorization to do anything at all.

Academic politics are vicious, it is said, inversely to the stakes involved, and Oberlin College is no exception. Campus politics became unusually bitter in the early years of the 1990s. The causes were a combination of disaffection about salary levels along with real differences over how the institution ought to be managed and what it stood for. A presidential change occurred just as disgruntled members of the faculty were checking on the price and availability of tar, feathers, and well-splintered rails. The new president, a former dean at Vassar College, arrived on campus in summer 1994 to calm things down. Before moving to Oberlin, she had heard of our project in a rather roundabout way. I invited her to drive over from Poughkeepsie, New York, to attend the "Campus Earth Summit" organized by students at Yale University in February 1994. On a rainy Friday evening with students and faculty from several hundred campuses, the atmosphere in the Yale Law School auditorium was electric with enthusiasm, ideas, and idealism. The campus ecology movement was growing and, for the moment, this was ground zero. During the question-and-answer period following the panel discussion that evening, a student who had heard of the Oberlin design class asked me how the project was coming along. Like a batter served up a pitch the size of a watermelon, I swung from the heels. Later I was told that Teresa Heinz, sitting beside the new president, had nudged her arm and said, "Let him do it." True or not, the president became an early supporter.

In June 1995, in order to solve a problem of inadequate space, the Oberlin College trustees authorized the effort to build an environmental studies center. I was expected to raise money for the building within two years but without assistance from the college development office, which had other priorities. I was given a reduction of one course from my normal teaching load. My ancestors were all Scotch-Irish, the kind of folks who wore funny skirts, charged well-defended stone walls with gusto, and bludgeoned each other with fierce alacrity for microscopic causes. With Celtic blood flowing through my veins, I charged without fully weighing the odds of the enterprise, which the more rational could see were low. From the start, the politics of the process were awkward. The project depended entirely on the support of the college president, but the initiative originated in the Environmental Studies Program beginning with the class of 1992–93, not from the usual college planning process. The trustees had approved a building, but not explicitly a "green" one. We had originally estimated the budget to be $2.5 million, although quickly realized that the cost would be much higher, and the difference made the administration exceedingly nervous. The design process required collaboration between the college construction office (headed by an architect), the architect of record, an outside design team, and the Environmental Studies Program—a great many chefs in the kitchen.

These initial conditions influenced the evolution of the project. The fact that this was conceived and funded outside the usual bureaucratic channels was both an asset and a liability. Being somewhat independent of the college bureaucracy at the outset, the project developed with more ecological imagination than it would have otherwise. But that degree of independence came at a price: college "buy in" was inconsistent. The president's support did not necessarily translate into active assistance, or even the neutrality of other members of the administration or trustees. The separation between the vision behind the project and institutional power—a schism between responsibility and authority—made the process awkward at every stage. We had been authorized by the trustees and the president only to solve a space problem, not to design and build a green, high-performance building. As a result, the excitement of the design team, faculty, and students contrasted at times with skepticism and the fear of institutional embarrassment. Would it cost too much? Would all this novel technology work? Why were other colleges not building similarly? Students often asked why administrators did not attend the planning charrettes or respond to requests for ideas. We decided that we would approach such things as if they were data to be included in a study of institutional innovation.

Because of its idiosyncratic nature, the project was vulnerable to the vicissitudes of college politics, making successful completion contingent on moving quickly before the building could be undermined for reasons having to do with campus politics—that is, turf wars, changing institutional priorities, or budgetary problems. Constraints on the sources of money meant that the project would have to appeal to potential donors on grounds other than loyalty to the college. The building would have to attract support because it was intrinsically interesting, and because it set a higher standard for design and construction. It would have to be exciting enough to attract financial support from those otherwise unlikely to give to the college, but cheap enough to build—a middle ground on a continuum between lavish at the high end and dull and cheap at the other. The situation was paradoxical. Had we waited for the college to build an environmental studies center, we would still be waiting. On the other hand, had the college undertaken to do it, the likely result would not have been green. We began the endeavor, nonetheless, in the hope that the institution would eventually take full ownership of it.

In summer 1995, I made five decisions that shaped the design process. First, the programming phase would be open to students, faculty, and the wider community. In a world rapidly coming undone, this project would be an educational exercise in how to stitch landscape, materials, energy, water, and technology together in the context of a small building. I hoped, too, that participation would help to create an active constituency for the project. Skeptics warned me that this would be a formula for chaos and indecision, but Celtic by nature and Jeffersonian by inclination I persisted. A second decision was to make the building an example of the highest possible standards of ecological architecture. No other building would be worth the effort anyway, but neither would any other kind of building be interesting to potential donors without prior connection to the college. The third decision was to engage a team of designers including energy experts, ecological engineers, landscape architects, and a contractor to work with the architect of record. To professionals, this is known as "front-loading" the design process in order to better integrate the components of a building, optimizing the entire system rather than its particular components. A fourth decision was to hire John Lyle to facilitate the design charettes. John was a professor of architecture and landscape architecture at the California Polytechnic Institute in Pomona, and author of a classic in the design literature, *Regenerative Design for Sustainable Development* (1994). For a decade or longer, John led the effort to build a center on the campus at Cal Poly to teach what he called "regenerative design." After his death in 1998, the center was renamed the Lyle Center, a cluster of residential buildings and facilities housing seventy-five students that provides its own energy from wind and sun, grows food for residents, and cycles its wastes into aquaculture—the core of the curriculum John and his colleagues planned. In many ways, Lyle was McDonough's opposite: gentle, quiet, almost shy, and self-effacing. But in terms of talent, insight, and dedication, they were peers representing different yet complementary approaches to ecological design. Finally, to engage the campus community and coordinate details, I hired as project assistants two graduates from the class of 1993: Brad Masi and Dierdre Holmes. Brad's good-natured, workaholic, and disheveled passion contrasted with Dierdre's cool, buttoned-down, incisive competence, but they worked together with imagination and energy.

Since no one at Oberlin had ever designed a building in this way, we did not know what to expect. The first charette was planned for late September in what had once been the dining room for the Oberlin Seminary, which had moved to Vanderbilt University in the early 1960s. The day was overcast and rainy, but the attendance was higher than expected, including idealistic students, the dutiful who assumed that they ought to put in an appearance, one or two from the administration to keep an eye on things lest they get out of control, a scattering of faculty, and some who were merely curious. John patiently organized the effort of drawing useful ideas from the group as they warmed to the subject. Typical of design charettes, sheets of paper went up on the walls to document and organize the flow of ideas. As the charrettes went on through the fall, John artfully passed off the role of facilitator to others, doing what real leaders do: encourage the emergence of leadership in those around them. He continued, however, to play the part of guide, mentor, and critic, goading participants to ask larger questions and go deeper into possibilities. In other charettes and smaller breakout meetings, the preprogram took shape until the final session at the end of the fall semester.

If this project were a painting, the background for it would consist of the global trends of the final years of the twentieth century: population growth, the loss of biological diversity, climate destabilization, pollution, soil loss, urbanization, and technological dynamism—what is called the crisis of sustainability. The middle ground would have been the world experienced by the students—a world that has come apart in many ways: broken families, urban sprawl, community decline, and too much violence. The foreground of that painting would be the plans for the building and landscape. The project was making a statement, not about stopping things, although we knew that lots of things needed to be stopped, but about starting a revolution in building design, a solar movement on college campuses, and markets for green materials and sustainably harvested wood. We were caught up in the excitement of thinking that we were doing something better than it had been done before.

We were also making a statement not just about academic architecture but about both the substance and process of learning relative to the environment. Should environmental education differ from, say, the teaching of history or economics? If so, how? If not, why not? How do architecture, materials, and the organization of spaces and landscapes affect our affinity for nature? How do we learn across the artificial boundaries of disciplines, and how is that different from discipline-centric learning? Do values matter, or should we aim to be value neutral? Or is that an oxymoron? How do we step outside our small human interests to see a larger vision of nature? Are these separate things or parts of a larger whole? For that matter, what is "environmental studies," and how might that definition influence the places in which it is taught?

On such questions opinions varied. Some thought that environmental studies consisted mostly of a broad range of courses with some environmental content and yet minimal disruption of what they regarded as more serious coursework. Others believed that the subject ought to be conceived more radically, but were uncertain exactly how. Still others maintained the subject taken on its terms and logic would lead to a rethinking of the substance and process of education—a break from the confinement of disciplines and educational bureaucracies. Differences notwithstanding, we all agreed that the building ought to reflect our engagement with nature, and offer opportunities to learn in both intellectual and practical ways.

In the fall and winter of 1995 to 1996, the 250 students, faculty, and community members participating in the design charettes agreed to three basic principles. First, we decided to aim for a building and landscape that would cause no ugliness, human or ecological, somewhere else or at some later time. That standard required that the building be judged relative to its upstream effects at wells, mines, forests, and factories where the materials originate, and by its effects downstream on climate, biological diversity, and human and ecological health. If, at either end of the spectrum, the building were to impair human dignity or the integrity of ecological systems, to that extent it could not be judged a success or even beautiful. Like truth, beauty, and justice, however, that standard is beyond mortal attainment. After all, buildings are buildings, and their construction and operations are messy and destructive. We nonetheless decided that there was no other worthy standard. The college admissions office slogan of "Think one person can change the world?" was modified by students for publicity purposes to read, "Think one building can change the world?" And most believed that it could.

Second, we decided that the building and its landscape would be made active parts of the curriculum, not just anonymous places where education happened disconnected from place. We would aim to reconnect a mostly urban clientele with soils, trees, animals, landscapes, energy systems, water, and solar technology. The landscape, in other words, was conceived not as a decorative space between buildings but as part of a restored ecology and working landscape designed to instruct and connect.

Third, we decided to use the project to develop and apply new analytic tools such as least-cost, end-use analysis, full-cost accounting, and systems analysis, by which we might better appraise building performance and its full costs. The analytic tools of the industrial era, notably neoclassic economics and cost-benefit analysis, we believed were not appropriate to the goal of building societies that can be sustained within the limits of nature or to assessing the true costs of buildings. Having said that, however, we were not certain where to draw the appropriate analytic boundaries around the project or exactly how to measure its full costs. We thus set out with the goal of assessing the building by more inclusive and longer-term standards that show more accurately what it would cost over time, and to whom.

These three goals were just so many words, though. There was an actual building to design along with questions of how the project would fit within the academic life of Oberlin College. From the outset, no proposal or idea was considered to be too crazy for consideration. The results ranged from the absurd to the brilliant. One idea that surfaced early on was to enlarge the scope of the project in order to house an interdisciplinary research program along with Environmental Studies. The notion was to widen the conversations across often hermetically sealed disciplines, and to engage college faculty more fully in solving community and regional problems. The proposal involved selecting faculty each year in a competitive process to research a particular interdisciplinary topic of campus, town, or regional significance. The faculty selected would be paid an additional stipend, and their respective departments would be compensated to maintain the usual courses. The goal was to develop genuine and systematic cross-collaboration among the faculty, aimed at solving real problems that spanned two or more disciplines. Sprawl and farmland loss, for example, have become serious problems in the surrounding county, yet for the most part we at Oberlin are silent observers. But collectively as sociologists, biologists, psychologists, economists, artists, planners, and political scientists, college professors know a great deal about the causes and possible remedies for sprawl. Knowledge from many disciplines applied to real problems would bridge the gap between the college and the community, promote habits of cross-collaboration among academic departments, engage students as collaborators in practical research, and improve faculty morale. The challenge of giving architectural expression to the idea of practical, ongoing interdisciplinary collaboration would have changed the subsequent building design. But more important, it might have—in time—changed the college itself by encouraging wider collaboration, cross-disciplinary research and the application of that research, to real local problems. Whatever its merits, that idea died a quiet death, presumably because of cost and inconvenience.

The actual building program was much narrower, showing the influence of forces surrounding the project. Some faculty wanted a harder-edged building incorporating advanced technology, while others wanted a more earthy and frugal building. On such matters, the vice president for operations at the time was agnostic, concerned mostly about avoiding excessive costs. For my part, bringing the schematic design process to a timely conclusion was crucial because we were vulnerable to the shifting winds of campus politics and the vagaries of institutional priorities. The vice president for development, for one, regarded this project with a mixture of apprehension and creative antagonism. And typical of most projects, we were vulnerable to the possible loss of institutional commitment. I had two years to bring schematic designs to completion and raise the funds to build the center. But as it turned out, I did not have that much time.

Many, I'm told, regarded this as a quixotic effort not likely to amount to much. We quickly confirmed their worst suspicions by engaging the finer points of the human condition, such as alternatives to the modern propensity to mix drinking water with human waste—a subject that greatly amused the excrementally sophisticated. Blinded by zeal, we proceeded nonetheless, and the final building program, both ambitious and foolhardy, reflected twelve underlying objectives. First, participants wanted a building with lots of daylight that seamlessly engaged the surrounding landscape. Oberlin is located in one of the cloudiest parts of the United States, a reality felt acutely in the late winter months as severe light deprivation. Second, participants wanted a building that used energy and materials efficiently. Third, given a rising concern about the effects of climatic change looming ahead, participants wanted to power the building as much as possible by current sunlight. At some future date, perhaps a decade or longer, it was hoped that the building might become a "net energy exporter," generating more energy from sunlight than it used. Fourth, we decided to make the building a "zero discharge" facility—that is, drinking water in, drinking water out. Fifth, the materials used were to be screened to reduce toxics and volatile organic compounds. Sixth, we decided that the exterior would be landscaped to promote biological diversity, restore a portion of the original ecology, and be maintained as a working landscape with gardens, an orchard, and a greenhouse. Seventh, drawing from Bill McDonough and Michael Braungart, we decided wherever possible to use materials that would be leased from a manufacturer in a closed loop of "technical nutrients" that would not end up in a landfill. Eighth, other materials, including wood and fabrics, would be "certified" as having met the most stringent environmental standards possible. Ninth, the building would be designed to evolve over time. Most buildings begin their life with a maintenance and depreciation schedule. This one would also begin with a technology trajectory that would take it progressively to higher levels of performance. Tenth, this was not to be just a place where education happened but rather one that would be educational by the way it was designed, operated, and maintained. It would, in other words, serve as a laboratory for the study of ecological design. Eleventh, based on what we learned in this project, we intended eventually to raise larger questions about the application of ecological design to the entire campus. Finally, the performance of the building energy and water systems would be made transparent to the public, and evaluated by an authoritative agency independent of the college.

Beyond the specifics of architecture, the landscape around the building would be designed around three questions: What is the nature of this place? Where are we relative to the time and seasons of the year? What can nature and humans do in this place? Accordingly, the east side of the site would be developed as a wetland, pond, and small forest using native plants reflecting the biotic past of northeast Ohio. To the south, the landscape would be designed as a "sun plaza" featuring a large sundial marking the solstices and equinoxes. The north side would be a working landscape with an orchard and gardens built and maintained by Oberlin students under faculty supervision.

**Figure 4.1**
The building program

Maximize daylight
Use energy and materials efficiently
Use sunlight for electrical power
Export electricity—"as a goal to strive for"
Purify wastewater on site, that is, drinking water in drinking water out
Eliminate the use of toxic materials in paints, fabrics, and materials
Use recycled materials in office and classroom furniture
Promote biological diversity
Use certified wood and other materials
Design the building to evolve or "learn"
Design the building and landscape as an educational laboratory
Use the building as a model to develop a college environmental policy
Monitor performance

By January 1996, we had completed the preprogram that included the kinds of private and public spaces, the numbers of offices and classrooms, and the standards for the project. The request for qualifications was sent out from the college in September 1995, attracting submissions from twenty-six architectural firms including many of the best in the country. All indicated that their interest stemmed from the challenge in the building program to work at the frontier of ecological design. From that pool, we subsequently interviewed five firms and eventually selected William McDonough + Partners as the lead architects. In contrast to most college-architect relationships, this assignment required the coordination of a larger design team, work with Oberlin students, and research on environmentally benign materials and construction methods. During the spring, the program was further refined by the design team, which included engineers, ecological engineers, landscape architects, energy experts, lighting consultants, materials analysts, and a contractor. Design began in earnest in February 1996, and concluded when we broke ground in late summer 1998. The Lewis Center was completed substantially as described in the building program developed in 1995 and 1996.

# 5

## The Building

The art of building is the beginning of all the arts.
—Havelock Ellis

The physical organization of English universities at Oxford and Cambridge reflect the belief that scholars ought to be cloistered like monks in part, no doubt, to remove them from distractions, but also to protect them from irate townsfolk. The results were colleges facing inward, away from worldly temptations and physical threats. The Scottish universities at St. Andrews, Glasgow, Aberdeen, and Edinburgh, in contrast, were smaller than Oxford and Cambridge, more urban, and more like those on the Continent (Turner 1995, 15). Early American colleges reflected more of the English model and the belief that learning best occurs in the absence of temptation. They were located outside cities and typically designed around one large building with appendages to it in the fashion of a Palladian country house. Conceived as instruments to advance Christian piety, they were accordingly places of considerable austerity.

The idea of a secular college organized around a political philosophy was most famously Thomas Jefferson's idea as embodied in his proposal for an "academical village," which became the plan for Central College, later renamed the University of Virginia. Jefferson intended to equip the young for leadership in an agrarian democracy—a hope already foundering on Hamiltonian realities even as the college opened in 1825. Jefferson and his colleagues William Thornton, Benjamin Latrobe, and Joseph Cabell joined the buildings around a central space to symbolize a larger unity (Wills 2002, 51). The design is a combination of "the fixed and the free," reflecting Jefferson's proposal for an elective curriculum taught by master scholars (17). The college was arranged like a horseshoe around the lawn, "the soul of the place," a central opening of grass and trees that served as an open-air meeting space for great events, receptions, rallies, and commencements. The Lawn is surrounded by housing for students and faculty, classrooms, and an outer ring of hotels and service buildings. By proximity between students and faculty, Jefferson intended to promote dialogue and a more profound kind of learning reminiscent of his own experience at the College of William and Mary. Faculty quarters called pavilions were connected by an upper walkway to symbolize and facilitate the larger dialogue of ideas between the different branches of learning. Standing at the head of the lawn on higher ground, Jefferson made the library, patterned after the Roman Pantheon, the central focus, a symbolic statement about the importance of learning and research in this new democratic order (Turner 1995, 83). The omission of a chapel in Jefferson's plans underscored his view that this was to be a purely secular institution. The college was to be, in Garry Wills's words (2002, 59), "a complex teaching machine with parts interrelated." By the mixture of control with freedom, privacy with supervision, and inner housing with outer rows of functional buildings and hotels, Jefferson's design was also a model of sorts of the federal system (64). Jefferson intended his academical village to serve as a device to reinforce his larger goal of providing a broad, secular education that connected the fields of knowledge in a setting that used classical architectural styles as a reminder of proportion and harmony thought to exist in Sir Isaac Newton's clockwork world.

Jefferson's design for the University of Virginia is widely regarded as the greatest achievement of U.S. architecture. Much neglected in the nineteenth century, its influence on campus design grew steadily in the twentieth century. Jefferson's ideas on education, though, are now mostly forgotten, but they are still worthy of consideration. Jefferson recognized, however imperfectly, the potential synergy between architectural design and educational philosophy. Imbued with the optimism of the Enlightenment, he assumed that the impact and depth of education and scholarship could be enhanced by calibrating the setting, symbolism, design, and architecture of the university with the curriculum. Wanting to instill a sense of order and proportion in the minds of his students, Jefferson designed facilities that reflected the same qualities. Wishing to promote a large conversation that embraced all learning, he designed living quarters and the connecting corridors to promote conversation between students and faculty as well as between the different members of the faculty. Intending the university to be a place of research, he made the library the focal point to mirror what he presumed to be the larger unity of the world. Jefferson made the design of his academical village a visible manifestation of the philosophy underlying the curriculum—an educational tool that reinforced learning by the routines of daily campus life lived within a model of the larger order of things.

Jefferson was a product of both the Enlightenment and the agrarian frontier. His view of architecture reflected the order presumed to exist in an orderly world, and his university was aimed to preserve a democratic agrarian republic. In contrast, the designers of the industrial age seldom assumed that buildings were much more than reflections of function, fashion, and economic forces. When they sought a larger pattern, they found it in the machine and the faith in human mastery over nature. "When man begins to draw straight lines," as Le Corbusier put it ([1929] 1987, 37), "he has gained control of himself and . . . has reached a condition of order." Le Corbusier ([1931] 1986, 2, 227) thought that cities, like houses, were machinelike, problems solvable by geometry, concrete, mass production, and verticality. He and others of similar persuasion left their mark on contemporary academic architecture, which became a contest in rectilinearity, geometry, and ever more creative applications of prestressed concrete. Beneath it were assumptions that humans, armed with new materials, technology, and science, were masters of the universe, creators of their own harmony and patterns. In Le Corbusier's words ([1931] 1986, 272–286):

In these earlier ages, man ordered his life in conformity with what people call a "natural system". . . [but now] the modern age is spread before them, sparkling and radiant. . . . Everything is possible by calculation and invention, provided that there is at our disposal a sufficiently perfected body of tools, and this does exist. Concrete and steel have entirely transformed the constructional organization. . . . If we set ourselves against the past, we can then appreciate the fact that new formulas have been found which only need exploitation to bring about a genuine liberation from the constraints we have till now been subjected to.

For the modernists, greatly fortified by the optimism of concrete and steel, buildings were a signal of human mastery and power—an inadvertent pedagogy of sorts, but one nowhere aimed to instruct in natural harmonies or consciously buttress the curriculum.

The modern university, unsurprisingly, reflects more the assumptions of modernism than those of the agrarian world of Jefferson. There are no orienting principles and no agreed philosophy by which one might relate campus architecture with the curriculum. The university became in both physical design and education more like a factory than a mirror of any deeper reality. Each department has its own places and laboratories, mostly disconnected from those of other departments. The kind of conversations across disciplines that Jefferson wished to join by the easy access between professors' quarters and those of students happen less than one might wish.

Just west of the intersection of Elm and South Professor streets, the Adam Joseph Lewis Center stands amid an eclectic array of architectural styles and functions on a site once occupied by a residence house called May Cottage. The cottage was torn down decades ago, and the site had been used as an overflow parking area. To the south are two nondescript dormitories from the 1950s—rectilinear, square, holding pens. To the north, along Professor Street, are two unusual and handsome sandstone student residence buildings built in 1886. Running north-south is a space known as "Harkness Bowl," an open corridor once intended to visually connect the south campus with the central campus. West along Elm Street, past the Lewis Center, college buildings give way to vintage nineteenth-century housing, mostly built by college faculty to the architectural styles of a bygone era. North, adjacent to the Lewis Center, is Harkness Hall, another 1950s' dorm that has long served the housing requirements of students with a proud tradition of being different and reportedly with the highest maintenance costs per square foot of any building on campus.

Oberlin College has nine variants of its campus master plan, each apparently oblivious to its predecessor, but all equally encumbered with dust. Unsurprisingly, the decision to situate the Lewis Center where May Cottage once stood was not informed by any of these plans. The location was selected because the site was available and unobstructed, and it competed with no other proposed use. As an added benefit, it would mix an academic presence into a student housing area, in which college investment had been comparatively low. Some hoped that it would have a salutary effect on the dress and behavior of Harkness residents by some as yet undiscovered process of social osmosis—a vain hope as it turns out. The principal effect of its location, I think, has been that it physically separated Environmental Studies from other academic buildings, for better or worse.

It is said that 90 percent of building problems can be traced back to mistakes that occur in the first few weeks of the design process. True or not, the character and eventual performance of the Lewis Center reflected two decisions made early on. The first concerned the style of architecture: whether the building would be rustic or modern, or something in between. During the early charettes, we considered the possibility of timber-frame construction. Had we followed that course, the eventual building would have been considerably warmer, perhaps more sensually appealing, and more energy efficient. The use of straw bales for walls, for example, was considered because of their high insulation value and low ecological cost, but they were finally dismissed because of concerns about maintenance, fire safety, the difficulty of compliance with building codes, and the space required to accommodate the width of the bales. Eventually, however, the need to meet codes for public buildings, avoid unnecessary controversy, and expedite design, among other factors, pushed us toward a harder-edged, more contemporary style.

A second decision had to do with the level of technology used in the building. Some preferred to design the Lewis Center so as to avoid any dependence on advanced technology, such as photovoltaics, high-tech materials, and computers. Others, the majority as it turned out, believed such austerity to be unrealistic, perhaps an expression of nostalgia for a bygone era, and even hypocritical. The difference between the two views is rooted in very different assumptions symbolized by "deep ecology," on the one hand, and mainstream environmentalism, on the other. Beneath the discussion were concerns that the Environmental Studies Program would need to be more mainstream to be taken seriously. However interesting and important the debate, the project had to meet Ohio codes for public buildings and college standards for classrooms. After considerable discussion, we chose to use available (off-the-shelf) technology combined with state-of-the-art design. Even that approach, though, concealed markedly different building strategies. While agreeing with the use of contemporary technology, some wanted to invest considerably more in the building shell, increasing insulation in order to eliminate heating and cooling equipment as well as minimize computerized control systems. Others, including the engineers on the project and college officials, favored a more conventional and presumably risk-free application of heating, cooling, and ventilation equipment to accommodate existing expectations about indoor comfort. That decision led to others that made building controls highly centralized, hence less subject to management by its occupants.

Through the stages of design development, the massing and geometry of the Lewis Center evolved from a square building with a sawtooth roof for photovoltaics to one elongated along its east-west axis. The auditorium, located in the first schematic drawings at the rear of the building on the north side, migrated to the northeast corner. The flat roofline became curved, mostly for aesthetic, not functional, reasons. The location of the Living Machine wastewater treatment system moved from its original placement in the southeast corner of the first model to the front of the building on the south side, and finally, to the front of the auditorium on the southeast corner. The final 13,700-square-foot building is 70 percent brick and 30 percent glass.

The building is a passive solar design facing south across a concrete and stone plaza named for John Lyle that reflects sunlight into the building and marks the changing seasons. The shadow from a gnomon, or pole, at the center of the plaza moves in an arc throughout the year, falling on concrete forms in the ground that mark the solstices and equinoxes, a reminder of seasons and cycles. Most, I suspect, pass by either oblivious to such things or with interest much diminished by the superior belief that interest in solar cycles is an embarrassing remnant of druidic celebrations, unbefitting a secular academic institution in the twenty-first century. Looking back toward the building from Elm Street, passersby can see only the leading edge of the 4,700-square-foot roof that supports a 59-kilowatt rooftop array of monocrystalline photovoltaic panels. The south walls include conventional double-paned windows (R–3.3) in the classroom spaces and triple-paned, argon-gas-filled curtain wall (R–7+) surrounding the atrium. The curtain wall continues around the east facade, facing the pond and wetland. The original plans called for a trellis on the east wall to soften its appearance and provide summer shading. At right angles to the east wall the Living Machine faces south, also overlooking the pond. From the outside, the Living Machine appears as a tropical greenhouse. The east wall of the auditorium curves along its outer wall and downward along the top of the wall. An anaerobic digester, the first stage in purifying wastewater from sinks and toilets, is buried on the east side of the auditorium. The north side of the building is bermed to the second floor, providing a kind of thermal anchor to moderate temperature extremes along with a good location for an orchard of dwarfed fruit trees and small fruits. As one looks back from the northwest, across a second photovoltaic array covering the east side of the parking lot, student-maintained gardens, and an orchard, the building appears as a combination of greenery, curves, straight lines, and angles.

Inside the Lewis Center, the atrium dominates the building both spatially and visually. Surrounded on two sides by a glass curtain wall, it was intended as a meeting space as well as a source of light and lightness. In the early design charettes, students intended for this place to be the equivalent of a town square, open to the pond to the east and the Lyle plaza to the south. The atrium opens upward to a curving wood ceiling supported by laminated beams made of Douglas fir from the Collins Pine Company, harvested from forests certified for sustainable management to the standards of the Forest Stewardship Council (Malin and Wilson 2003). Prominent in the northwest corner of the atrium, a plasma display shows building performance data gathered every five minutes from 150 sensors placed in the building and landscape. We had originally intended for the display to be a digital presentation of building performance visible to people walking through the atrium, reporting data rather like McDonald's restaurants once reported the sale of hamburgers. But the rapid advances in Web technology permitted us to display data in the atrium as well as on the building Web site in a much more sophisticated, detailed, and informative way. The eastern corner of the atrium opens toward a glass-enclosed lab area and the Living Machine. The space is dominated by four large tanks, each 7 feet deep and 4.5 feet wide with support frames holding tropical plants whose roots penetrate the water column, pulling nutrients from the waste stream—a functional analog to a natural wetland. The water is returned through a gravel bed to a sump, sterilized with ultraviolet light and stored for reuse to flush toilets and irrigate the landscape. The technology of Living Machines is the brainchild of John Todd, a biologist and designer with a sixth sense for creation. Todd's particular genius was to recognize in natural wetlands the pattern for human-created systems that could process wastewater, and grow fish, flowers, fruits, and plants to be used for fuels and even anchor the economies of urban neighborhoods. His insight is brilliantly useful and a profound recognition that natural systems, evolved over 3.8 billion years, are a model for a post-fossil-fuel world. Ralph Waldo Emerson made the same point long ago, noting that we live mostly unaware in the lap of great intelligence.

Beside the Living Machine, on the northeast corner is a hundred-seat auditorium, an interesting juxtaposition of biological reality and human discourse. The auditorium is named for Richard Hallock and his son Jeff, both of whom died while the building was being constructed. As a decorated World War II hero in the European theater, Dick was an exemplary member of what Tom Brokaw has called "the greatest generation." A member of the 101st Airborne Division, Hallock became famous for his coolness and good judgment even after being wounded by enemy fire, and later as a fearless champion of Pentagon reform—a role that cost him at least one promotion. I knew Dick late in his life and witnessed the same quality of courage under different circumstances as cancer ravaged his body. Like most genuine heroes he didn't talk much about himself, and never of his bravery when others were counting on it. Jeff was similarly blessed with courage, but cursed for much of his life as an invalid. Eventually he died of Lou Gehrig's disease, although not before he had shown all who knew him how to die by inches with grace and humor. Both men were heroes of different sorts, yet both would have laughed at the suggestion that they were any such thing.

The auditorium that commemorates their memory is a comfortable, warm space for lectures and classes. The acoustic paneling on the side walls is made from compressed wheat straw, giving the space the slight aroma of a barn. The seats are covered with materials made without carcinogenic, mutagenic, or endocrine-disrupting chemicals. The wood paneling on the stage and ceiling is made of Forest Stewardship Council–certified maple harvested from forests in Pennsylvania. The flooring is from Interface, Inc., in Atlanta, and will be returned to the company as a product of service, a feedstock to be remanufactured into new carpet. All

First iteration of the Adam Joseph Lewis Center

David Orr, William McDonough, and Kevin Burke, 1996

Peter B. Lewis and Adam J. Lewis

Lewis Center under construction, 1999

Students transplanting species from nearby Camden Bog, 2000

David Benzing

Student gardens

Class at east side of building, Fall 2004

59 kilowatt rooftop photovoltaic array

100 kilowatt photovoltaic array over parking garage

Living Machine facing south

Living Machine facing west

Atrium

Hallock Auditorium

Classroom

The Lewis Center at night

in all, the auditorium is a small gem of a place graced by the names and legacy of a father and son who, in different ways, exemplified courage and good heart.

West from the atrium the hallway passes a kitchen, bathrooms, a maintenance closet, and mechanical rooms on the north side and two classrooms on the south side. In all classrooms and offices, a plenum between the floor and a subfloor houses all of the wiring and plumbing. Hallways and classroom floors are covered with carpet tiles also leased from Interface, Inc., as products of service designed to be recycled back into new carpet. Ray Anderson (1998), the founder of Interface, reports being converted after reading Paul Hawken's book *The Ecology of Commerce,* which hit him like "a spear in the chest." As a result, he set about to transform his company and its legacy. His goal was to power the company by solar technologies and make useful products leased as products of service that would not end up in landfills. The company has eliminated 54 percent of its greenhouse gas emissions while expanding production over the past decade (Interface, Inc. 2004). As McDonough points out, consumer products are either part of an ecological metabolism or are technical nutrients that should be returned to the manufacturer to be remade into new products. The difference is whether the materials can be broken down by natural processes or not. The distinction is revolutionary, affecting product design, manufacturing, and distribution while closing industrial nutrient cycles and eliminating waste.

The second floor of the Lewis Center includes seven offices, two classrooms, one small conference room, and remarkable views in all seasons of the pond and wetland to the east and the surrounding buildings in four other architectural styles. From that vantage point, the feeling is one of openness to the nature beyond—light in all seasons. I've stood on the balcony above the atrium in tropical comfort and watched snowstorms raging around the building. My office, on the contrary, is small, and because it is overstuffed with the academic detritus of books, papers, and journals, can be claustrophobic—a self-inflicted penalty of an unreformed bookaholic. Daylight from the atrium, clerestory windows below the roofline to the north, and windows all around eliminates the need for artificial lighting on most days. Sensors detecting motion or carbon dioxide that indicate human presence are deployed in classrooms and commonly used spaces to turn lights and heating, ventilation, and air-conditioning systems on only when needed.

Materials in the building were selected to minimize the use of toxins so that the indoor air quality is exceptionally good. All of the office and classroom furniture is made from certified wood or recycled materials manufactured by Herman Miller, Inc. Thomas Moser, Inc., a Maine firm, crafted a table for the conference room and furniture for the program office from Pennsylvania maple. Four sections of what had once been a bowling alley are incorporated as shelving in the main office and student library.

We intended to create a building that evolved or, as Stewart Brand puts it (1995), "learned" over time. Typically, however, buildings are assumed to be complete when the contractor hands the keys to the owner. Thereafter, the life and usefulness of the building result from the tug-of-war between maintenance and depreciation. In contrast, buildings designed to evolve, or learn, will anticipate changing technology and uses from the beginning. High-performance buildings are complex systems that require ongoing adjustments and tinkering, and change in the behavior of users after the initial commissioning (Malin 2000, Malin and Boehland 2003). They ought to be flexible enough to accommodate improved technology as it becomes available, and to adjust to refinements in the art of building management and use. They require what in the trade is called "continuous commissioning," a process of constant calibration of controls, structural changes, and technological upgrades.

The actual use of the center is greater by perhaps half than we originally estimated. In the first few years it was the site for one wedding and one funeral, and lots of dinners, poetry readings, and other public events. The president became fond of holding official dinners in the atrium with a string quartet playing from the balcony above and wine bar below. On at least one occasion, the remainders of an unguarded wine bar lubricated what turned out to be one of the more lively classes I've ever taught.

The actual building represents, perhaps, 80 to 90 percent of what was possible to achieve in the design and construction world of the late 1990s. Some things proved to be unworkable. A few, including the idea of the interdisciplinary center, were simply ignored, while others were deleted because they were thought to be too expensive. A few good or even necessary items were "value engineered" out, ostensibly to save money. In 1997, the college hired an outside firm to manage the physical plant and construction. That firm, in turn, brought in another firm to analyze plans for the Lewis Center in order to eliminate any unnecessary and excessively costly features. To my knowledge, they did so without setting foot on the campus or talking to any member of the design team, but they did so with considerable exuberance nonetheless. Among the design elements cut were venting skylights in the Living Machine that will have to be installed later at a much higher cost, a 400-square-foot seminar room overlooking both the atrium and the campus to the north—what would have been the finest meeting space on the entire campus—easily operated windows in the classrooms, and a substantial chunk of the southwest corner of the building. For this vandalism, the college reportedly paid fifty thousand dollars to reduce the quality of the building without improving its engineering, performance, utility, or aesthetics. The reasons had to do with the fact that those charged to do value engineering and those who hired them were carefully insulated from the designers and originators of the project.

Three features of the building have received considerable interest and scrutiny: the energy systems, including the photovoltaic system; the Living Machine; and the building monitoring system. Assessing overall building energy performance is a complicated mix of intentions, architecture, engineering, actual use, and the quality of maintenance and management. The building program for the Lewis Center included six categories of goals, the fourth of which was to "maximize energy efficiency while meeting as much of the energy needs for heating, cooling, lighting, and electrical power from renewable sources as possible" (Adam Joseph Lewis Center, Project Goals and Principles, April 19, 1996). Becoming a "net energy exporter" was described as "a goal to strive for" over the next decade or so as technology and management improved. But energy models (DOE-2 simulation software) based on early building designs suggested better performance than was subsequently achieved. Between the potential and the actual building were a number of problems, the most important of which was the substitution of an emergency boiler in the place of a heat pump to supply heat via a radiant floor system to the atrium. In the final construction documents, the engineers retreated to the least risky though most energy-intensive option for heating the largest space in the building. But neither the architects nor the college personnel overseeing the project noticed the change, which was buried in the details of the final construction documents. The difference would have been discovered had the college run a final energy simulation based on the actual construction documents. Yet in order to save money it did not. As a result, energy use in the winter months was considerably higher than necessary until subsequently corrected in 2003.

Energy use in the Lewis Center reflected a number of different loads. Initially, 12 percent of the center's energy use was consumed by processing its wastewater, and another 3 to 5 percent went to outdoor lighting and small uses such as heating hydraulic fluid for a seldom-used elevator and an oversized transformer. An air-lock entry on the west side, removed by the value engineers, was later expensively added to reduce air infiltration. The design of the mechanical system, however, proved to be the largest problem. Some of the heat pumps deployed in the building were not as efficient as they should have been. They were selected, however, because I assumed, erroneously as it turned out, that they would be donated to the building. Further, the building was designed to use 100 percent fresh air, which improved indoor air quality but required more heating energy in cooler months. Most of these problems were solvable at a fairly low cost.

The differences over energy engineering stemmed from real differences in opinions about: the cost-effectiveness of superinsulating the walls and ceiling of the building; the aesthetic and psychological value of daylighting, particularly from the east curtain wall, which worked against the goal of energy efficiency; and questions about the risk entailed in relying on newer technologies, including ground-source heat pumps that extract or dump heat from twenty-four wells, 280 feet deep. Midway in the design process we decided not to tie into a college steam line from a coal-fired power plant on campus—a considerably cheaper alternative, but one that would have connected us to an umbilical cord stretching back to central Ohio coal mines. That decision was based on the belief that the future power systems for buildings would be predominantly electric, provided by a combination of efficiency and building-integrated photovoltaics and fuel cells, and that the cost of these and related technologies would fall rapidly while becoming steadily more efficient and reliable. That remains, I think, a good bet.

The actual energy performance of the Lewis Center is impressive, if lower than early models predicted. Energy use is calculated as either that used specifically in the building (site energy) or in the entire energy chain back to primary energy used at power plants (source energy). Given the inefficiency with which fuels are rendered into electricity and the line losses incurred in moving fuel from a power plant to end use, source energy is typically a little over three times that used on-site. When the Lewis Center opened, the site energy performance in the first year was estimated from utility bills to be 47.5 kBtu/ft.$^2$, and the source energy was estimated to be 148 kBtu/ft.$^2$ (Pless and Torcellini 2004, 112). In the third year, after several refinements and engineering changes, the respective numbers dropped to 29.8 and 53 kBtu/ft.$^2$. Subtracting production from the photovoltaic array, the net energy used on site in years two and three was, respectively, 15.7 and 16.4 kBtu/ft.$^2$. For comparison, the national average site energy figures for classroom and office buildings generally was reported to be 90 kBtu/ft.$^2$, and federal standards for new construction is 55 kBtu/ft.$^2$.

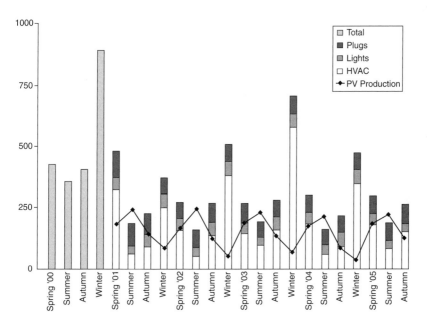

**Figure 5.1**
Oberlin Lewis Center Monthly Energy Performance, January 2000–Fall 2005

**Table 5.1**
Measured Whole-Building Results: First, Second, and Third year of Operation

|  | Measured site use intensity kBtu/ft.² (MJ/m.²) | Measured PV production intensity kBtu/ft.² (MJ/m.²)[1] | Percent of building load met by PV |
|---|---|---|---|
| First year (from utility bills) | 47.5 (539) | 1.6 (18) | 3% |
| Second year | 30.6 (348) | 14.9 (169) | 49% |
| Third year | 29.8 (338) | 13.4 (152) | 45% |

1. PV production normalized by building floor area for comparison to site use intensity

The best academic building operating in roughly similar weather conditions uses an average of 36.7 kBtu/ft.², according to scientists at the National Renewable Energy Laboratory (Pless and Torcellini 2004, 4). In the first four years of operation, the rooftop photovoltaic array provided roughly half of the energy budget for the building. The same scientists estimated that the Lewis Center, fully optimized and well managed, would provide up to 85 percent of building energy loads (113).

What this means depends on what one wishes to find. Postconstruction, the energy performance of the building was evaluated by three separate engineering teams, and they reached somewhat varying conclusions. All agreed, however, that the building would require the changing of mismatched or inappropriate heating, ventilation, and air-conditioning equipment, the recalibration of building controls to better accommodate actual use, and other changes in equipment and ducting to approximate its potential. As one engineer put it, the Lewis Center is "a very good building, performing badly." Further, all were in agreement that the Living Machine and east curtain wall, both architectural decisions, were obstacles to reducing energy use, whatever their other benefits. The postcommissioning studies diverged sharply, though, on the extent and cost of modifications as well as the overall potential of the building. The most authoritative of these, by Ron Perkins of Supersymmetry, Inc., showed that with reasonable and fairly inexpensive changes, the building ought to function plus or minus 10 percent of 20 kBtu/ft.² not including photovoltaic production

**Table 5.1**
(*continued*)

|  | Measured net site use intensity kBtu/ft.² (MJ/m.²) | Measured source use intensity kBtu/ft.² (MJ/m.²) | Energy cost intensity $/ft.² ($/m.²) |
|---|---|---|---|
| First year (from utility bills) | 45.9 (521) | 148.1 (1,682) | 1.21 (13.02) |
| Second year | 15.7 (178) | 50.6 (575) | 1.17 (12.59) |
| Third year | 16.4 (186) | 53.0 (602) | 0.85 (9.15) |

(Malin and Boehland 2002, 13). A Pittsburgh engineering firm was even more optimistic, concluding that with reasonable modifications in the mechanical and control systems, the goal of becoming a net energy exporter "was not impossible at all" (Tower Engineering 2003, 3). Even the most pessimistic analysis showed that "significant energy savings" were possible with a redesign of the mechanical systems (Scofield 2002).

Compared to other new academic buildings constructed at the same time, energy use in the Lewis Center is quite low, but it could have been lower still. The difference between potential and actual performance is a complex story. In the building program, energy efficiency competed with other goals—such as education and aesthetics—that are important in their own right. Second, the college prolonged the design process for nearly three years, which did not help morale on the design team and, in turn, diminished the quality of the final building design. Third, college oversight of the project was complicated by a change in management midway through the design phase, which affected continuity and commitment to the original goals. Fourth, mistakes in the design of the mechanical systems resulted in a suboptimal integration of the geothermal system, heat pumps, occupancy sensors, ducting, fresh air, and heat-recovery systems with the actual use. Fifth, the computerized controls were not optimized to maximize performance. Finally, like all high-performance buildings, the Lewis Center required better and more consistent management by the college facilities staff, which was stretched thin by institutional budget cuts.

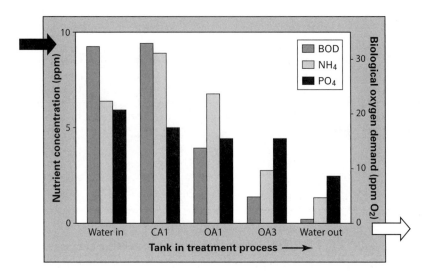

**Figure 5.2**
Living Machine Performance

   The performance of the Living Machine was less controversial, although a few critics seized on the fact that the system was designed to handle twenty-three hundred gallons of wastewater per day while the actual use has been a small fraction of that number, and sometimes considerably less. It became known, too, that starting the system required the use of outside nutrients—in this case, dog food. The resulting rumors circulated around campus that we had to feed dog food to the system in perpetuity to keep it going, confirming critics' worst expectations. In fact, since it was established, the system has worked well, processing only human waste, thriving even at reduced flow rates, and producing exceptional water quality without the use of chlorine or aluminum salts.

   It has been proposed to expand inputs to the system by capturing the wastewater output from an adjacent residence hall. (Were that to happen we would be, I think, the first academic department ever to seek out and purify human excrement, rather than deliver it.) More important, the system functions as a laboratory for the study of ecological systems—a way to learn biology by using microcosms that replicate the workings of larger natural systems—and it is a reminder of the reality of waste and the possibilities in nature for purifying polluted water in ways that are productive and beautiful.

A third unique feature of the building is the data monitoring system. In the early design charettes in fall 1995, as mentioned earlier, we decided to make building performance data publicly available, displayed digitally in the atrium. But given the advances in technology, the idea evolved from a digital display in the atrium to a Web site with real-time data from 150 sensors located throughout the building and landscape. Developed by faculty colleague John Petersen and his students, the result is perhaps one of the most sophisticated building monitoring systems yet deployed. The intention is to provide quick feedback on energy use, display related environmental data graphically, and increase awareness of the relation between the building and natural systems.

The Lewis Center was conceived as a place to experiment with the application of technologies and design strategies in a particular place as a part of an environmental curriculum. We assumed that the building would never be entirely finished, but would change with technology and be modified as our concepts of education changed. After all of the effort, how was the building perceived by those closest to it? The building elicited complex reactions from members of the administration and trustees. Understandably, they enjoyed the favorable publicity that surrounded the project, but some were inclined to disappear at the first hint of criticism. Few showed any interest during the design process and so the intentions behind the building, including its potential as an instrument of instruction and research, eluded many of them. The idea that the building would never be entirely completed and would require continuous commissioning challenged their belief that buildings ought to be finished once and for all. For those charged with management and maintenance, the Lewis Center was a special challenge, requiring mastery of new technologies and complex control systems. For one or two, the building was a failure because it did not immediately meet all of its long-term goals, including those we had assumed to be years into the future. Judging by the number of visitors from hundreds of colleges, universities, architectural firms, development companies, and businesses beyond the Oberlin community, the building stood out elsewhere as an attempt to set a new standard for both design and education. A considerable number of buildings on other campuses have been influenced by the example of the Lewis Center—a few of which, such as those at Yale and Stanford universities, will be far better as a result.

Finally, the professional response to the Lewis Center was dramatic. The building received two awards from the American Institute of Architects in 1999 and 2002, for design pedagogy and overall environmental performance, as well as others from the Chicago Atheneum, the state of Ohio, the General Contractors of Ohio, and the National Convention of Associated General Contractors. It was also described by the U.S. Department of Energy as one of thirty "milestone" buildings of the twentieth century, such as Frank Lloyd Wright's Fallingwater.

Henry David Thoreau said that he went to Walden in order "to drive life into a corner, and reduce it to its lowest terms," where he might study it more thoroughly. Similarly, the Lewis Center, was intended to drive some of the problems of living sustainably into a 1.25-acre laboratory where they might be studied on a comprehensible scale, helping to equip students with the skills, abilities, and wherewithal that will be necessary in the post-fossil-fuel world ahead. The building and landscape were intended, in other words, to be part of an ongoing dialogue about the arts of inhabitation involving the complex interplay of nature, people, place, technology, landscape, and building. That expectation has not disappointed. But beyond this one small building are larger questions that Jefferson, were he alive now, would have understood. How might college buildings and entire campuses come to harmoniously reflect the ecological order of their places? How might ecology come to inform building design, landscape management, and material flows? How might colleges and universities foster a dialogue between humans and nature as part of an ecological enlightenment? And how might we prepare a generation, not of yeoman farmers, but of ecological patriots.

# 6

# Landscape: Monologue to Dialogue

The ecological view requires that we look upon the world, listen and learn. The place, creatures and men were, have been, are now and are in the process of becoming. We and they are here now, co-tenants of the phenomenal world, united in its origins and destiny.

—Ian McHarg

My first notions of landscape were formed in the rolling hills of western Pennsylvania on the edge of the Allegheny Plateau. The town of New Wilmington—nestled below "Furnace Hill," on which we lived—is ringed by gently sloping higher ground on all sides. To the east across the Little Neshannock Creek, the hillside slopes to its crest perhaps three miles distant from our home. This was a well-ordered landscape of farms, fields, and country lanes that I'd come to know well in my teenage years as a part-time farm laborer, and with somewhat more alacrity and imagination in the full bloom of courting. Further east and north, most of the farms were owned by Amish families, who lived by agriculture, forestry, and craft work, and were known for a sharp but honest eye for their pecuniary advantage. To the north of the town other hills ringed the horizon with woods, farms, and the remnants of the great wetland that once stretched nearly to Lake Erie, seventy miles distant. Our family spent summer vacations at a cottage situated on forty acres of hemlock forest on the banks of Mays Run, one mile from the Allegheny River and four miles from the riverside village of Kennerdell. The land around the cottage was once the site of a small, hardscrabble farm and gristmill along the logging trail leading down to the river. A previous owner, a man known to me only as "Mr. Brady" from Pittsburgh, had converted the barn into a modest house with two large fireplaces and with knotty-pine paneling throughout.

Immediately behind the house a steep hill was covered by a mature hemlock grove and large rock formations, which we, with youthful imagination, gave names like "Shipwreck" for one that looked to us like the Titanic going down.

Close by an old house foundation were the decrepit remnants of a wooden springhouse that still stood guard years later over a spring never known to go dry. The water came out from under a sheer rock face rising thirty feet or more above. Many years before, the Mays family had built a springhouse on a square sandstone basin as a natural refrigerator with year-round forty-degree water. I can testify that that water would keep a watermelon ice cold on a hot summer day and quench more than just thirst anytime. Above the spring were more towering hemlocks and massive rock formations decked out with ferns and dark green moss. Through the woods beyond were the remains of an abandoned apple orchard in a rocky glen along with a depression with mossy banks made by an old logging road that led back to the top of a ridge that jutted toward the Allegheny River like a giant thumb. My image of paradise still includes hemlock trees, giant rocks, ferns, moss, and springs that flow clear and cool.

I do not recollect family, friends, or teachers talking much about the ecology and natural history of the land of western Pennsylvania, or our place on it. Paradise, when it was discussed, was described as some far-off place rather like a perpetual old-time Sunday spent doing things that boys find indescribably torturous: singing hymns, strumming harps, and the like, sufficiently reprehensible to have once called down the wrath of Mark Twain. I remember no curiosity about the function of the town dump that stood on the banks of the Little Neshannock Creek, beyond an interest in the muskrats to be trapped thereabouts. I recall thinking of the strip-mining machinery visible on the southeast horizon as a desecration, but one unconnected to the electricity we used or the lives we lived, and I was oblivious to the damage we caused by how we lived. Mostly, I just thought the machinery was ugly. I had a vague sense of foreboding as I left New Wilmington at the age of twenty-one about the future effects of Interstate 80 being built four miles north of the town and Interstate 75 running at north-south seven miles to the east. But I was off to greener pastures and didn't dwell on such things. I was to discover, however, that the same things were happening to greener pastures elsewhere.

I lived on Long Island for one year before going to graduate school at the University of Pennsylvania in Philadelphia. In a dense urban setting for the first time in my life, I felt claustrophobic among so many people, roads, and buildings, and so much noise and pollution. I recall a brief trip that my wife, Elaine, and I took to New Hampshire and Vermont in the fall of that year rather like a journey of a thirst-crazed traveler to an oasis of green, hills, and what I took to be undefiled nature, which of course it wasn't. The following year I returned to graduate school, but chose to live as far away from Philadelphia as possible while still being able to catch the mainline express train into the city from Harrisburg to the 30th Street Station.

Even though I was a graduate student in the international relations program, I still managed to cross the campus at every opportunity to attend classes or public lectures by Ian McHarg, chair of the Department of Landscape Architecture. McHarg, a legendary character, was in full stride and that was something to behold. The time was full of controversy, violence, and excitement. The environment was fast becoming a national issue that could not be ignored—even by Richard Nixon. Professor McHarg was a powerful and vocal national presence. His masterpiece, *Design with Nature,* published in 1969, illuminated the terrain like a bolt of lightening on a dark night. "The Plight," chapter 2, is still one of the finest environmental polemics ever written. But McHarg's point was more than castigation, although he was a master of the art. Picking up where Frederick Law Olmsted and Jens Jensen left off, McHarg proposed a marriage of ecology with landscape architecture. His intention was to discipline human purposes and economic growth with a thorough understanding of natural processes and form. It is a lesson we are still struggling to learn.

McHarg's forthright energy, vision, clarity, and hopefulness, and that of others like Phil Lewis at the University of Wisconsin, were an antidote to the anger and despair of the time. Under their tutelage, landscape architecture was becoming a scientific discipline centered around the notion "that the ecology of a region or extensive landscape could be analyzed, synthesized and graphically presented," in Robert Thayer's words (2003, 156). This was more than an academic theory; McHarg offered method and direction driven by the passion to do something beyond rearranging the flowers. More than a few of his disciples, like Frederick Steiner, Pliny Fisk, and Ann Whiston Spirn, intended to use ecologically designed landscapes to transform society along more ecologically sane lines. Any talk by McHarg was full of ribald humor and trenchant perspective, and included a summons to act with ecologically informed intelligence toward nature. McHarg helped reorient and ground my interests and passions for life.

After graduate school, I invited him to present to the "Atlanta Environmental Symposium" that I had organized with a colleague at Agnes Scott College. McHarg kept a large crowd spellbound for an hour and a half about the ecological limits to human expansion. But no amount of good sense about proper land use and the costs of sprawl could prevent Atlanta from becoming what it was in the process of becoming, which was a great deal less lovely and resilient than it might otherwise have been. Six years later, McHarg helped to shape the plans for a nonprofit educational center I'd cofounded with my brother on fifteen hundred acres in the Ozarks. Even on this scale, his eye picked out the details and context of the landscape with great clarity.

McHarg was a chain-smoker and nonstop talker, but there was at least one moment in his life in which I know for certain that he stopped both. He had asked to go to the top of a ridge six hundred feet above the valley floor to see the lay of the land along the three miles of Meadowcreek and the gorge of the middle fork of the Little Red River beyond. But there was no easy way to climb what was called "pinnacle peak." Given the state of our equipment and roads at the time, the best way to get there, other than by an arduous hike, was on a narrow logging road that climbed the side of the precipice, with two perilous switchbacks, in a 1929 Model A Ford Roadster pickup that my brother, Wil, had modified with a Mercury overdrive transmission, giving it sixteen forward speeds and four in reverse. The thing could have climbed the side of a barn. As we approached the first switchback, the road narrowed to the width of a cow path and the ground on the left became a precipice overlooking the hollow several hundred feet below. McHarg was uneasy, but kept on smoking . . . and talking. Yet when the path angled up to forty degrees or so as we approached the first switchback, he uttered a fervent "Oh my God" in his heavy Scottish brogue with more than a hint of desperation. Aiming to free both hands for what he deemed an emergency, and subconsciously thinking that the gas cap was an ashtray, he reached through the empty windshield frame to tamp out his cigarette. I tried to say, "Don't do that!" but like a bad dream when things move in slow motion, as if in molasses, the words would not come out. Ashes mingled with gas sloshing around the cap, but God had apparently heard his invocation or wasn't ready to meet him just then, and nothing exploded. Hanging on with a degree of ferocity given only to Scotsmen in dire straits, McHarg remained silent as we backed up to the second switchback and went forward again to the top of the ridge. He was a somewhat lighter shade than I'd recalled seeing just minutes before and rather more humble, a remarkable thing itself. After surveying the lay of the land and confessing the need for a wee bit of exercise, he chose to return to the valley below on foot.

My last memory of McHarg is from a course we co-taught as visiting lecturers at Ball State University in 1995. He was no longer affiliated with the firm of Wallace, McHarg, Roberts, and Todd, or the University of Pennsylvania, but he was still irrepressible, irreverent, and full of good ecological sense. In his last decade, McHarg (1996, 334) took on other, smaller, opportunities and continued gamely, as he put it in his autobiography, to "maintain dignity, act with generosity and perhaps with wisdom, continue to seek and solve problems, recover from assault and insult." His legacy as a theoretician, organizer, teacher, writer, speaker, and practitioner is larger than can be easily reckoned. He prepared several generations of students to be able and imaginative practitioners of ecological design. For his reading and listening public, McHarg was a provocative thinker and communicator. His contributions to the field of landscape ecology and our general understanding of how humans might fit harmoniously with nature are very large indeed.

McHarg's stature notwithstanding, designing with nature is still the exception and we ought to ask why. Along with other monumental figures of the middle years of the twentieth century such as Rachel Carson and Aldo Leopold, McHarg worked against the tide of technology, population growth, economic expansion, and the exuberance of an automobile-saturated society. Leopold's call for the adoption of a land ethic ran against the culture of capitalism and the belief in the human duty to dominate nature. The chemical industry's opposition to Carson's *Silent Spring* was rooted in a kind of technological fundamentalism and willful denial with a tincture of criminal intent. The reaction to McHarg was more complicated. As both theoretician and practitioner, he took pains to show that designing with, not against, the ecological grain was advantageous in every way; his was the language of practical self-interest. Why did the appeal often fall on deaf ears, and why is it still not heard?

McHarg himself thought that one reason was the hold of reductionism on the curriculum of the academy and hence on the minds of its graduates (McHarg and Steiner 1998). And to this day, we mostly conduct education and research in boxes called disciplines. Our main product is specialists—experts ill-equipped, and often disinclined to see patterns, systems, and causes at a distance from their effects. A second reason stems from our ambiguous feelings about land. On one hand we celebrate "America the Beautiful," while on the other hand regarding it mostly as real estate, a place to drive through on the way to somewhere else, and a means to get rich. Cheap land for speculation, mining, forestry, and farming—extractive uses—was the original appeal of the New World, along with the freedom to do as one pleased. This vandalism persists, amplified by global corporations and thinly disguised by the ideology of the market. McHarg's words (1969, 25) sadly still ring true: "We have but one explicit model of the world and that is built upon economics. . . . Money is our measure, convenience is its cohort, the short term is its span, and the devil may take the hindmost is the morality. . . . Neither love nor compassion, health nor beauty, dignity nor freedom, grace nor delight are important unless they can be priced." Competent affection for the land, disciplined by the ecological realities of places has not yet taken a firm hold on the U.S. mind. If it ever does, we will owe that great achievement to the likes of McHarg, Leopold, and Carson.

There is a third reason for the resistance to McHarg's appeal to design with nature and that is the feebleness of U.S. government when confronted with systemic, long-term problems. But there was a time when we might have charted a different course. Between 1968 and 1980, republicans and democrats worked together to lay the foundations for a national environmental policy that included the National Environmental Policy Act, the Clean Air Act, the Clean Water Act, and the Endangered Species Act. But they stumbled in 1973 in rejecting the idea of a national land-use policy—a portent of worse to come. From that time to ours, the cause of environmentally decent land use has lagged. The very idea is anathema to that end of the political spectrum that calls itself "conservative," yet finds little to conserve other than the rules of the game by which a few are greatly enriched. The courts have been of little help, preferring instead to emphasize the private rights of landowners to the exclusion of both other rights and a broad definition of the public good (Freyfogle 2003). McHarg's vision of humankind and nature working in harmony, on the other hand, will require a higher level of national maturity, ecological wisdom, and foresight—a genuine patriotism. I believe that some day we will reach that level and that optimism, too, is part of the legacy of Ian McHarg.

Located fourteen miles south of Lake Erie, the town of Oberlin was designed on a grid pattern, the dominant feature of which is a thirteen-acre Central Park–like square named after New York abolitionist and financier Lewis Tappan. Most of the college buildings were once located on the square, but were later removed due to the insistence and philanthropy of alumnus Charles Martin Hall. Typical of many midwestern towns, the square is surrounded by a church on one corner and college buildings on three sides. The south side of Tappan Square is the main business district, a row of buildings that stand in need of imaginative renewal. A stream that used to run diagonally through the square on its way to Plum Creek was buried many years ago. Tappan Square features a variety of large native oak, ash, and maple trees as well as some exotics like a dawn redwood and smaller decorative varieties. On a warm spring day, it is full of students lounging on the manicured grass, a few professors holding forth, and sometimes an itinerant preacher of questionable sanity haranguing a crowd of taunting students about their many sins, most of which have to do with sex. Predictably, both work themselves into fits of opposing self-righteousness. On summer evenings, band concerts draw several hundred town residents and their children along with and visitors to bask in camaraderie, music, and the glow of the Ohio twilight. Each May graduating seniors, depending on their politics, march through or around the arch on the west side of the square built to commemorate the sacrifices of Oberlin missionaries to China. Tappan Square is a defining feature of the town landscape and perhaps of the mindscape of Oberlin's residents.

While thoroughly pleasant and bucolic, Tappan Square is interesting, too, for what it reveals about our attitudes toward land and landscape. Nothing in the square exists except by human permission. Every tree, shrub, and carefully sculpted flower bed is the result of human selection. The uniformly trimmed, dandelion-free grass is the result of the use of fossil energy imported from some distant place in space and time in the form of fuel for lawn mowers, and as the chemical substrate for herbicides. There are few clues about the forest and meandering creek that once existed in this place, the wildlife that once lived here, the seas that covered this region hundreds of millions of years ago, or the ice sheet that covered it as recently as twelve to fourteen thousand years ago. Passersby learn neither about the geologic forces that changed it and will do so again, nor about the Miami and Shawnee who once hunted the dense forests that existed here or the lives of the settlers who displaced them. The place tells no story of the forces of geology, evolution, ecology, and human history that shaped it. Nor does it reveal the human ecology now being played out in this place. No story, that is, except that of human domination, and no clue why we ought to wonder about the intersection of geology, ecology, history, human ecology, and landscape. In a word, it is a monologue maintained by a vast infrastructure supplying temporarily cheap derivatives of ancient sunlight used to hold wildness at bay, or maybe it is a kind of willed ecological amnesia.

That we find such places pleasing is a different sort of relationship between our evolutionary past and culture. Some believe that we are predisposed by evolution to prefer open, savannah-like places because they allowed our ancestors to avoid ambush by enemies and predators. For a small, slow, upright mammal lacking fangs, claws, and speed, but blessed with fair eyesight and an oversized frontal lobe, such places were safer than the deep forest or jungle. Or so the story goes (Bormann, Balmori, and Geballe 2001, 10). Certainly our preference for particular landscapes is also a cultural preference honed over centuries. The word landscape entered the English language in the sixteenth century from Dutch and Germanic origins. Originally *Landschap* in Dutch or *Landschaft* in German meant a jurisdiction or unit of human occupation, but in the hands of the great Dutch landscape painters the word came to mean "a pleasing object of depiction" (Spirn 1998, 16; Schama 1995,10). In either language, land meant both a place and the people living there, while *skabe* or *schaffen* meant to shape (Spirn 1998, 16). The equivalent for Italians, as Simon Schama notes (1995, 10), was known as *parerga*, a sort of pastoral idyll.

The great English landscape painters such as Joseph Turner and John Constable depicted a comfortable relationship between people and a settled, prosperous countryside. For Americans, a more graphically minded people, the paintings of Thomas Cole and the photographs of Ansel Adams helped to propagate the idea of a majestic wilderness devoid of human presence, a promise of things to come or a separation of humans from nature, depending on what one wishes to see.

Inspired by eighteenth-century landscape painters who depicted original nature as a kind of arcadia and repelled by the ugliness of emerging industrial cities, British landscape architect William Kent (1685–1748) developed seamless landscapes in which the manipulated, grass-covered foreground flowed smoothly into a distant and untrammeled nature (Bormann, Balmori, and Geballe 2001, 15). The invention of the lawn, however, is commonly attributed to another English landscape architect, Lancelot "Capability" Brown (1716–1783). With an unbounded "penchant for planes of grass," Brown covered vast lawns with grasses adapted to the English climate (Elizabeth Rogers 2001, 247–251; Bormann, Balmori, and Geballe 2001, 16). The landscapes Brown created for the great estates of those like the Duke of Wellington at Blenheim Palace were pastoral scenes where sheep grazed in a supposedly benign nature of short grass, scattered trees, and lakes–a blend of art, artifice, and landscape. In the words of one study, the success of Brown's landscapes "cemented the lawn as the great icon of late eighteenth-century British Society." Olmsted incorporated Brown's ideas into U.S. life, notably in the design of Central Park in New York City, among others. But Olmsted had been to Yosemite and had a different vision of the U.S. land. Instead of mirroring the purely pastoral landscape, he designed Central Park as a kind of antipastoral to preserve as much of the original "easy, undulating outlines, and picturesque, rocky scenery" as possible (Schama 1995, 569). The result, evident in much of Olmsted's work, was a blend of two versions of arcadia: the wild and the pastoral.

The idea of the lawn, however, flourished in United States, where it became a prominent feature of Washington's Mount Vernon, Jefferson's Monticello, and the famous Lawn at the University of Virginia. The mowed lawn was the chief attraction of the suburbs built in the nineteenth century. Edwin Budding's invention of the lawn mower, in 1830, made it possible to maintain large spaces in mowed grass, giving rise to what has grown into a thirty billion dollar per year lawn-care industry selling equipment, adornment, and the chemicals necessary to eliminate competing species. The "industrial landscape" of uniform species and height is the standard across an area in the United States the size of the state of Pennsylvania, some 27.6 million acres, of which 21 million acres are private lawns (Bormann, Balmori, and Geballe 2001, 48–51).

Highway 58, a busy thoroughfare for traffic between Amherst and Lorain to the north and central Ohio destinations to the south, runs along the east side of Tappan Square. The daytime traffic is dominated by commuters, shoppers, and an endless line of semitrailers. County planners have long intended to widen the highway and bypass the town altogether. All around Oberlin the land is sprouting starter mansions on five-acre lots like mushrooms after a summer rain. To the south, Wal-Mart is building a store where it deems the sprawl and traffic patterns to be sufficiently dense to provide a good cash flow and add further to the congestion. Nearly everywhere in Lorain County, farms and farmland are either under considerable pressure from changing land-use patterns, or have become derelict and untended—their owners, some in resignation and some with anticipation, waiting for the inevitable development.

Whatever one's preferences or opinions, we've known for a long time that sprawl is not only ugly, it is expensive and it is killing us (Frumkin, Lawrence, and Jackson, 2004; Burchell et al. 2005; Council on Environmental Quality 1974). In economic terms alone, the costs of sprawl include those of electric lines, water, sewers, roads, and schools as well as providing police services to more and more dispersed locations. It requires more driving and hence more gasoline, and more wars to protect our sources of oil. Automobile dependence dictated by sprawl has contributed to making us the fattest people on Earth, waddling toward future epidemics of diabetes and heart disease. It has reduced the quality of our air and water along with biological diversity. For good reasons, the people who study such things connect sprawl to a growing sense of isolation and loneliness in suburban populations and the decline of what political scientist Robert Putnam (2000) calls "social capital" in our communities. The costs of climate destabilization, a by-product of the burning of fossil fuels, loom ahead, but no one can say with authority how large that economic expense will be or whether that is even a useful way to understand what it will do to us. Not the least, the paving of prime farmland will one day be seen as an extraordinarily stupid thing for a country with four to six hundred million people to feed.

It is all of a piece: the serene and bucolic prettiness of Tappan Square, the traffic jams, the sprawl, and the fragmentation between rural and urban, wild and domesticated. We, Americans, live on landscapes mostly without dwelling in them. Remove cheap fossil energy, and much that we've built and assume to be permanent would collapse like the proverbial house of cards. Often devoid of competence, affection, and foresight, our landscapes are shaped by illusion, wishful thinking, and increasingly, excess, the roots of which extend back through federal and state tax laws as well as subsidies for oil, highways, and sprawling development. Go a bit deeper and there are historical, cultural, and deeply embedded psychological forces, some unique to Americans and their history as a "people of plenty" feasting on the last large chunk of unexploited temperate real estate on Earth. For those inclined to inquire, there are still deeper causes, rooted in our ancient predispositions formed in a world of danger and scarcity (Whybrow 2005).

If buildings are educational, by the same logic landscapes are as well. And what is being taught by the history of land use and particularly that of the past half century? Without anyone necessarily intending as much, we've taught generations of young to think of land mostly as the space between a starting point and a destination, valuable primarily for its wealth-generating potential, not as a community of life shaped by time, water, wind, biota, and human hands. The lesson, in a word, is that of human domination. We've subdivided, clear-cut, mined, bulldozed, paved over, and polluted a good portion of the 2.2 billion acres of the United States, destroying the underlying logic of its organization by watershed, geology, and ecology. Aside from that small percentage protected as wilderness, we just haven't gotten to yet. In the process, we've shown generations that order, beauty, and ecological functions do not matter relative to those of short-run economic expediency mostly benefiting a few. Every scientific study of the U.S. land, as a result, reports the same trends of degradation in its various forms: a decline in biological diversity, the loss of farms and open space, the pollution of water, the effects of acid precipitation, and now the effects of changing climate (Heinz Center 2002; U.S. Department of the Interior 1998).

To believe that such sweeping changes in ecological organization do not also affect our minds and souls is beyond fatuity; it is a kind of collective insanity. Landscape and mindscape, too, are of a whole cloth. Whether consciously aware of it or not, we are diminished by outright ugliness, commercial uniformity, ecological dysfunction, and blight. Living in landscapes rendered uniform for the convenience of commerce, stripped of beauty, memory, and the capacity to nurture mindfulness and ecological competence, we become autistic to the nature and even human artistry that once existed there, and to the potential that might yet be realized. The price of such mindlessness is an atrophied sense of being rooted in a place, what Simone Weil (2002, 43) once described as the most basic of human needs. Being physically displaced or, worse, deplaced—having no sense of roots—was seen by Weil as "by far the most dangerous malady to which human societies are exposed, for it is a self-propagating one. For people who are really uprooted there remain only two possible sorts of behavior: either to fall into a spiritual lethargy resembling death . . . or hurl themselves into some form of activity necessarily designed to uproot, often by the most violent methods those who are not yet uprooted" (47).

McHarg's was a powerful voice for the recovery of place, landscape, and time, but he was not alone. Others equally eloquent have emerged in agriculture, forestry, urban planning, community design, and river preservation. Across the spectrum of issues, scales, and regions, a movement to reinhabit North America is gathering steam. It goes by various names, such as sustainable agriculture, community supported agriculture, smart growth, planned unit development, historic preservation, eco-cities, holistic resource management, permaculture, community forestry, or trails to rails. By whatever name, however, the goal is to ground human communities and aspirations into a larger, storied harmony, perhaps a kind of homecoming.

From this flowering of ecological imagination, a theory of reinhabitation of sorts is emerging (Thayer 2003; F. Steiner 2002; Beatley 2004). Nature and natural processes are the bedrock—the measure and the standard of human dwelling in a "lifeplace" (Thayer 2003), not just an inert some-thing to be bulldozed into submission. As Wendell Berry puts it (1987, 146), "What has nature done here? What will nature permit here? And what will nature help us do here?" The questions are both practical and philosophical. At one level, answers would inform us about the condi-tions, materials, natural energy flows, soils, biota, topography, history, and culture of the particular places in which we live and work. Berry's ques-tions also root us in a different set of values that does not begin and end with human needs and desires but places us within a community of life stretching far back in time and forward to the far horizon of imagination.

If nature is the standard, it follows that human activities on the land ought to conform as much as possible to the flow of energy through natu-ral systems. The industrial landscape has been shaped by our ability to ex-ploit, for a brief time, solar energy stored as oil, coal, and natural gas. Nature, a ruthless bookkeeper, will eventually require that the books be balanced, forcing us to live within our means of current solar income, which is infinite and free. But that free energy is also dispersed and not eas-ily stored with our current technology. And selling the equipment to har-vest free energy does little for the vendors of coal and oil—a considerable political obstacle to a rational transition reinforced by armies of lobbyists.

Third, living within our energetic means requires that we expend energy no faster than we harvest current sunlight. The exploitation of fossil en-ergy permitted a rapid but brief escalation of the clock speed of civiliza-tion, increasing the velocity of energy, materials, water, money, people, and waste moving through the landscape. This is as difficult for us to see as for the proverbial fish to imagine the water in which it swims. Godfrey Reggio has captured this quality of the pervasively invisible in a brilliant film, *Koyaanisquatsi*. By taking the scenes of ordinary life from streets, airports, factories, and malls, and speeding these up to the rhythms of mu-sic by Philip Glass, Reggio portrays the insanity of the high-speed, fossil-fuel-powered world that most of us have come to accept as normal. By exceeding the speed limits of natural systems, however, the result has been ecological disorder, cultural disintegration, and violence. Having ex-hausted most of our own sources of ancient sunlight, we have the choice of trying in vain to perpetuate our profligacy or learn to live within our means. Yet, since speed is addictive, establishing speed limits for civilization is as much a psychological matter as one of rational choice.

Fourth, living on current solar income at nature's pace means that we will have to become a great deal smarter about how we provision ourselves with renewable energy, food, and materials, and how we recycle our waste. The thousands of services of nature—pollination, water purification, oxidation, insect control, fertilization, and waste cycling—have to be protected and enhanced within the context of economies designed to be sustainable. The end of the extractive economy means protecting and enhancing the natural capital of soils, aquifers, forests, wildlife, and ecological systems. We do not know yet the full extent of what this means or what it will require of us. Taken far enough, though, one can imagine the outlines of a new economy designed with nature as partner and mentor. But how will we learn the skills and aptitudes necessary to create and sustain that economy?

The challenge to schools, colleges, and universities is to equip generations of young people for the great work of building an economy and civilization that can prosper within the limits of natural systems. That task rests on the proposition that the disorder of landscapes and ecologies reflects a prior disorder of mind, and is therefore a test for those people and institutions purporting to improve minds. Meeting that challenge will require a revolution in the substance and process of learning and in those places in which formal education occurs.

Walking west from Tappan Square along College Street one passes through a neatly manicured and decorative landscape. Turning south past Talcott Hall, the north side of the Lewis Center intrudes on what was once an extended green or bowl area that visually connected the south campus with the main quadrangle. A manicured lawn gives way to a different landscape. The east side of the Lewis Center appears to be overgrown with weeds, wildflowers, willow trees, and a scattering of other trees and shrubs. From a slight rise on the north side, a swale curves around the east side of the building, ending in a shallow pond on the south directly in front of the Living Machine. Rainfall flowing from the slightly higher ground to the north is the primary source of water for this small replica of the Black Swamp that once extended for nearly one hundred miles from the west side of

Cleveland past Toledo along the south shore of Lake Erie. Ninety-five percent of Ohio's wetlands have disappeared in the past century and a half, drained for agriculture, roads, and housing. Many of their species, too, have disappeared or are endangered. The trees and shrubs that ring the swale were selected because they were once native to that vast wetland forest, prior to the arrival of European settlers.

Looking to the north side of the building, an earthen berm is planted with dwarfed apple and pear trees. Across a sidewalk are three raised garden beds, a large garden arranged in a circle, and a composting bin. The landscape was designed by Andropogon, a landscape design firm in Philadelphia, along with John Lyle, and David Benzing, a distinguished Oberlin biologist. It is maintained by Benzing, Oberlin students, and Don van Dyke, a retired physician and full-time public servant. It is harvested mostly by passersby from the community. Tomatoes, beans, squash, cucumbers, and flowers give testimony to nature's fecundity and the possibility of rejoining labor and learning in working and instructional landscapes.

Next to the garden area and small vineyard, a hundred-kilowatt photovoltaic array covers the east end of the parking lot—a solar harvest of a different sort. That energy, like the rooftop array, is grid interconnected. It provides power for the building; the surplus is sold back to the Oberlin Municipal Light and Power Company at the prevailing market rate. Connected to the array, a small recharging station supplies power for electric vehicles on campus.

On the south side of the Lewis Center, surrounding the Lyle Plaza is a landscape of young oaks and fruit trees. On the southwest corner, students from my design class have proposed locating a forty-seat amphitheater named for Lyle. Their specific assignment was to honor the man's life and work in a way that would instruct future generations of students about what he'd called, as noted earlier, regenerative design. After reading his writings and visiting his home in California, the students arrived at a proposal to build a small amphitheater of three levels in a spiral of the same ratio as the Fibonacci sequence, the same ratio evident in the spiral of galaxies and snail shells (1, 1, 2, 3, 5, 8, . . . each number, starting with the third, being the sum of the previous two). Down one side they envisioned a cascading stream of water in what is called a flow form powered by a

photovoltaic cell that would work only as long as the building is exporting power onto the grid. The design reflects Lyle's desire for an amphitheater in the landscape, which had been value engineered out.

Lyle's imprint, however, is evident throughout the entire landscape design. The landscape is intended as a blend of a working landscape, a small
restoration of what had once existed on this site, and a space designed to
orient visitors to time and sunlight. It is a landscape designed to harvest
sunlight for heating, electric energy, and food production as well as to
maximize biodiversity, featuring plants and animals native to this region
prior to European settlement. It is also designed to slow the rate at which
water leaves the site. Roof water is diverted into a holding tank to be
used later to recharge the wetland during dry weather, while the pond
and wetland holds surface water runoff, allowing the wetland to act as a
catchment basin to the slow runoff of heavy pulses of storm water. The
landscape of the Lewis Center is a tiny island surrounded by hundreds of
acres of conventionally managed urban and college land. Reactions to
it have been mixed. A college official is reported to have once called it
"ugly," meaning, I suppose, that the restored wetland on the east side does
not look like the landscape of a country club. But others find the diversity and seasonal changes of the wetland appealing and interesting. The
mowed part is maintained by a combination of student and volunteer
labor using a solar-powered electric mower and is sometimes slightly un-
kempt by the manicured standards of suburban lawns. Similarly the gardens and orchard, sources of interest and food for some, are unsightly
intrusions for others.

We intended the landscape, however, to be instructive about the biological past of the site, the art and science of ecological restoration, and the
practical arts of horticulture, gardening, and wise landscape management.
But these are matters of interpretation. The biological past of this small
place, assuming that we have restored it accurately, more or less, means relatively little if one assumes that the human conquest of northern Ohio, including the destruction of most of the wetland communities that once
existed here, is a good and permanent thing. The region is now heavily
dominated by remnants of declining industry and chaotic urbanization—
a crazy-quilt pattern of highways, agriculture, malls, and housing tracts.

**Figure 6.1**
John Lyle's Original Landscape Design for the Lewis Center

So what purposes are served by a small and fairly expensive restoration on this site? One answer is strictly utilitarian: wetlands are useful to filter water, preserve species and ecological systems that provide necessary services to humans, protect habitat for species that give us pleasure, reduce loads on city sewage treatment systems, and provide visual relief from a tawdry and ecologically mismanaged landscape. If wetlands are necessary to the ecological health of our landscapes, they are essential for humans as well. It follows that advancing the art and science of restoration is justifiable solely on the grounds of self-interest and utility, if one's moral periphery extends no further. And if such projects are useful to further human purposes otherwise unobtainable, then the expense they incur is also justifiable.

Ecological restoration is potentially useful, also, as a hedge against future changes in our preferences or our larger circumstances. If future generations decide that such an extensive network of highways, malls, and factories is dispensable or a liability that can no longer be maintained, they will need to know how to reset the successional clock, and rehabilitate and restore degraded lands to a semblance of their prior condition. There are possibly larger changes in our circumstances in the years ahead. The end of the era of cheap fossil fuels, for one, will drive up the costs of commuting by car and could thereby make dense, in-town development far more desirable. Historian Kenneth Jackson (1985, 304) believes that "by 2025 the energy-inefficient and automobile-dependent suburban system of the American republic must give way to patterns of human activity and living structures that are energy efficient." James Howard Kunstler (2005, 1) is even more forthright, saying that the looming end of the age of cheap oil "is an abyss of economic and political disorder on a scale that no one has ever seen before." For others, climate change will increase the value of restored lands as carbon sinks to mitigate some of the worst of what may lie ahead.

At a community scale, the restoration of degraded lands can help to bring people together across the divisions of politics, class, and culture to enhance the beauty, prosperity, and ecological resilience of their bioregion (Higgs 2003; Thayer 2003). "Restorationists," in the words of Eric Higgs (2003, 157), "create stories through their actions, which accumulate and prepare the way for a richer interpretation of the place"—stories written in the sweat, blood, and dreams of people who make landscapes a kind of collective portrait. The effort to restore degraded ecologies can educate us about ecological relationships otherwise unseen in the uniformity of the dominated and chemically manipulated landscape. It can enhance our ecological competence and the skills with which we manage natural systems. As well, it can enhance prosperity by taking advantage of the services of healthy natural systems for water filtration and storage, pollination, pest control, the maintenance of biological diversity, fertility preservation, and climate modification (Daily 1997). Restoration can spark our ecological imagination, helping us to rethink our relationship with the natural world and the standards by which that relationship is judged. Ecological restoration as a community effort allows us to make storied landscapes, places of meaning and memory. As landscape architect Ann Whiston Spirn puts it (1998, 262): "Now is a time for telling new tales, for retelling old dilemmas: how to live in the world *and* preserve it; how to sustain tradition *and* foster invention; how to promote freedom *and* cultivate order; how to forge identity *and* value difference; how to appreciate the parts *and* grasp the whole." The story of how humans first degraded and then restored landscapes is more than an interesting possibility; it is a noble and inspiring tale relevant to a world where perhaps half of our arable lands are now degraded and tens of thousands of acres are now classified as derelict brownfields. This, too, is a story of human values justified by a larger standard of economy and usefulness.

Moving to the boundary where self-interest and altruism become blurred, restoration places us in a larger story about the evolution of the community of life in which all parts are ecologically codependent and deserve protection. Human mastery in this larger narrative is often self-defeating. An ecologically enlightened self-interest leads us in other directions, toward the recognition of the possibility that other species as citizens of the community of life have interests as well. But protecting the interests of other members of the community on which we depend is also an act of self-interest. And not the least, the restoration of degraded ecologies may help us root our affections on the very ground on which we stand—the ultimate patriotism.

The working landscape of an orchard, raised garden beds, a grape trellis, and a compost bin is also part of a larger story. Long separated from our agrarian roots, we've come to believe that our agricultural problems have been solved once and for all—a premise seemingly confirmed by every visit to a well-stocked supermarket. It takes an informed and courageous imagination to foresee the possibility that one day those well-stocked shelves may be empty, and that future famine is a real threat. How could this happen? Food now travels, on average, some fifteen hundred miles from where it is grown or produced to where it is eaten, requiring by one estimate sixteen to seventy calories of fossil energy to put one calorie of food on a plate (Kunstler 2005, 241). By contrast, peasant agriculture requires only one calorie of human or animal labor to put fifty calories on a plate, but at a much lower volume. Energy-intensive, industrial agriculture is possible as long as oil is cheap and can be burned with few adverse environmental consequences. But we are coming into a new time in which oil will become increasingly expensive, including the costs of fighting oil wars and dealing with the resulting antagonisms. It is not at all inconceivable that terrorists will impair the infrastructure necessary for the long-distance transport of food, requiring us to dust off and rediscover the arts of ecological competence. And we know that climate destabilization will change virtually everything we now take for granted about our present food system. The casual abandonment of Ohio farms to asphalt, malls, and housing development will some day be a cause for great regret. Yet there is another side to this story.

Each year over six billion dollars are spent in northeast Ohio on food, but farms in the region supply only about two hundred million dollars of that amount. A renaissance of local agriculture would preserve open space, and serve as the foundation for economic development that is resilient in the face of higher energy costs, economic uncertainty, and climate disorder. There are few, if any, other areas in which investment and education could yield as much as that spent to reestablish a strong local agricultural base. But the average age of farmers is over sixty, and young people see no good future in farming.

Agriculture as a subject of study, moreover, has been relegated to land-grant institutions where it is rendered into a series of technical disciplines and research mostly in service to agribusiness. But what subject or discipline could be more central to the liberal arts curriculum than one having to do with food, health, land, landscapes, ecology, animals, water, the politics of land distribution, and rural communities? In fact, agriculture ought to be regarded first and foremost as a liberal art with technical aspects, not the other way around. Those relatively few liberal arts colleges that have included agriculture and food issues in the curriculum typically find students interested and eager to experience farming. We intended the landscape around the Lewis Center to demonstrate a truce in our war against the land, and show good possibilities for creating working, productive, and attractive landscapes, growing food, and stretching the ecological imagination and competencies of our students.

# The Gift Must Move: Reflections on Costs, Economics, Giving, and Receiving

There are nothing but gifts on this poor, poor Earth.
—Czeslaw Milosz

The cost of a thing is the amount of what I will call life which is required to be exchanged for it, immediately or in the long run.
—Henry David Thoreau

Not including the building endowment, the total project cost of the Lewis Center was $6.5 million. Of that, the architectural, engineering and research costs were $1.1 million. The construction costs were $4.1 million or $299 per square foot including $402,000 for the photovoltaic array, $400,000 for the Living Machine, and another $155,000 in site preparation costs. Since most buildings do not have their own power plants or wastewater treatment facilities, a more useful comparison suggests a cost closer to $240 per square foot at the high end of the average for classroom/office buildings of a comparable size built in the region at the same time. But the fact is that no comparable buildings were being built here or elsewhere, and that virtually every building is unique, not easily compared to any other. The Lewis Center was an early prototype of a high-performance building designed to be an educational tool to equip students with some of the skills necessary for solving the big problems of the twenty-first century.

Had we known at the beginning what we knew afterward, it would have been possible to build the same building for a great deal less money. Some research and design expenses could have been reduced. The costs of investigating the use of alternative materials like straw and reclaimed timber could have been eliminated. The design process could have been streamlined and better integrated, reducing both delays and costs. I think we could have built the same building or a better one for $.5 to 1.0 million less, or less by $35 to $70 per square foot. Ironically, worries about cost overruns and possible mistakes tended to increase costs and decrease morale in the design team, and led to more inadvertent mistakes that had to be expensively fixed later. Value engineering, mentioned above, cut necessary components that had to be (or will have to be) added expensively later.

Is it possible to build green at, near, or even below, the price of conventional construction? Based on a growing body of experience the answer is yes. One analysis of the costs of fifty-two green academic buildings found that the relation between those seeking LEED certification from the U.S. Green Building Council rating and conventional buildings was low (Adamson, Matthiessen, and Morris n.d., 19). Sustainable design goals could be achieved within the "initial budget, or with very small incremental funding" (25). Gregory Kats, with Capital E, Inc., similarly found that the cost premium for thirty-three green buildings in California was 2 percent, or $4 per square foot, while the financial benefits of green design were $50 to $75 per square foot, over ten times what they cost. The often-overlooked benefits cited in the Kats study (2003, 85) include "lower energy, waste, and water costs, lower environmental and emissions costs, lower operations and maintenance costs, and savings from increased productivity and health." The benefits are likely to be even larger when designers master the art of what Amory Lovins (2002) calls "tunneling through the cost barrier," by planning the building and its components as a unified system. Typically, the costs of extra insulation, better windows, daylighting, and more efficient equipment are added to the base cost as if they were so many options added to the list price of a new car. The difference, however, is that they offset the expenses of other things such as heating, ventilation, and air-conditioning equipment while reducing ongoing costs for maintenance, operations, energy, and equipment replacement, even as they also improve productivity and the morale of people who enjoy working in well-designed and well-lighted places. Lovins's point is that the true cost of efficiency and good design taken to its logical conclusion and measured in the aggregate drops to zero or below, and functions more like an endowment than a cost.

Collateral benefits of green building are also frequently overlooked because they are difficult to quantify and we fail to look for them. A true estimate of the economics of well-designed, high-performance buildings ought to subtract collateral benefits from the building costs. Specifically, the Lewis Center brought a great deal of favorable publicity to the college. It was the only college building, for instance, mentioned in *Time* magazine's "planet earth" issue (August 26, 2002). The U.S. Department of Energy selected it as "one of thirty milestone buildings" of the twentieth century. It was also the subject of several hundred newspaper stories, television reports, and magazine articles. The fact that the college made no attempt to estimate the financial value of national publicity made the collateral benefits no less real. A related benefit of publicity was increased giving to the college. One gift of $2.75 million and another of $1 million, among others, came as a result of the Lewis Center. A third benefit was an increase in prospective students' interest in the college and environmental studies. But most important, the Lewis Center provided an extraordinary laboratory for student research on the problems of sustainability. What would otherwise be abstract academic problems were grounded in the reality of the landscape, the Living Machine, the energy systems, and the larger subject of ecological design. Building costs and economics also became a research focus. For example, a senior honors project on the payback from the photovoltaic array showed that the array displaced the carbon dioxide caused by its manufacture in 3.7 years and recovered the energy embodied in the equipment in 7.3 years, but that the financial investment would not be recovered in the lifetime of the array unless the calculation included the "external environmental and health costs of the displaced fossil fuel" (Murray 2004; Murray and Petersen 2004).

Green buildings also have other benefits no less real because they are overlooked and often difficult to quantify. Research shows that worker productivity and morale is higher in green buildings (Kellert 2005, 23–25). Properly landscaped, green buildings reduce the heat-island effect common to urban areas. Because they use energy efficiently, such buildings reduce air pollution and thereby promote health; they lower emissions of carbon dioxide, thereby reducing the risks of climate change; and to the extent that they use local sources of renewable energy and incorporate locally sourced materials, they help to build sustainable regional economies.

By minimizing their demand for water, green buildings reduce the need for expensive infrastructure to supply and reclaim water. The use of local materials is an incentive for local entrepreneurs. Similarly, the use of environmentally certified materials provides an incentive for companies to move toward sustainable resource use. In other words, green buildings promote community, health, prosperity, and the kind of resilience that reduces vulnerability to economic downturns, terrorism, accidents, and acts of God.

How much life did we exchange in the construction of the Lewis Center? How much ugliness, human or ecological, did we incur somewhere else or at some later time? The unavoidable truth is that we damaged the world in some measure. The Lewis Center was built from steel (recycled), brick, metals, plastics, wood, and worst of all in terms of carbon emissions, concrete. Typical of all construction projects, the building site looked like a war zone. But all buildings are built in the faith that on balance, the good effects outweigh the bad over time. Beyond generalities, however, we do not know much about the damage we incurred because the material supply system that connects wells, mines, forests, and manufacturing facilities with the construction of buildings is largely hidden from view. In the global economy, it is all but impossible to track the thousands of materials that go into a building back to their sources or downstream to their later effects. It is somewhat easier to estimate the ecological costs of the fossil energy required to power a building once it is built. Even so, the fact is that we are largely ignorant of the true costs of the built environment—costs that must be measured over decades and centuries. Beyond the difficulties of knowing such things in a complicated world, we are ignorant of the costs because our economic theories do not require an accounting of the full ecological and human costs, and we permit those ideas to unduly influence our decisions. This is a larger problem rooted in the separation of our notions of wealth and well-being from the health of natural systems.

A philosopher once proposed to an interdisciplinary group of which I was a member that we ought to organize a conference on the theme, "The State of the World and the Adequacy of Our Knowledge." Everyone was enthusiastic except for the economist in the group, who responded by saying that this was a good idea for the rest of us and the disciplines that we represented, but not for economists because their knowledge "is perfectly adequate" to the world and its further improvement. So instructed, the rest of us departed, humbled and greatly edified.

No theology has ever had a stronger hold on the minds, imaginations, and behavior of any group of believers than neoclassic economics has today. Its principles, illuminated by abstract mathematical models, are said by its disciples to be an accurate description of how humans behave and how, were they perfectly rational, they would behave. It purports, in other words, to both describe and prescribe, to blend science and theology. And on such presumptions, armies of businesspeople, government officials, and economists since Adam Smith published *The Wealth of Nations* ([1776] 1965) have bestirred themselves considerably to remake the world in the image of the free market. Few doctrines have ever secured such devoted conformity in such a short span of history. A handful of renegade economists, theologians, and others occasionally fire broadsides at this juggernaut, but in the minds of its beholders the received doctrine has been largely immune to criticism, however trenchant, and the corrections in thought and behavior that would otherwise have been required of the faithful. The simultaneous and related rise of technology came at an inconvenient moment for the critics, since the miracles so wrought by the union of capitalism and technology appeared to confirm the faith that humans could master the physical world and become rich.

With the disappearance of the rival ideologies of communism and socialism, the doctrines of the free market are now the blueprint for organizing the world. Its institutions—the World Bank, the International Monetary Fund, and the World Trade Organization—rival or exceed the power of governments that have come to measure their performance by neither the well-being of those in their care nor the standards of justice, but merely the abstractions describing the growth of the economy. "It's the economy, stupid," has become a kind of shorthand to remind us of the really important priorities in our public affairs, which are not to be confused with loveliness, fairness, or the longevity of the human enterprise. At the individual level, it is widely assumed that self-interest is best measured by pecuniary gain and that money is the strongest of all possible motivational forces, the examples of suicidal terrorists and equally zealous

Christian missionaries notwithstanding. Even my most progressive students will commonly assume self-interest and selfishness to be one and the same thing. The behavior, then, of both Mother Teresa and Kenneth Lay can be explained by saying that they're just "doing their thing," whatever that may be, and no further explanation is assumed to be necessary. The alert will recognize the confusion of fundamentally different categories. As sentient beings we cannot help being self-interested, but as moral creatures we have choices about how and how broadly we define our self-interest as well as how we chose to act on it. But distinctions are lost on those who have too eagerly accepted the convenient myths of pervasive self-absorption found at the core of standard economic doctrine (Schwartz 1994, 139).

Whether or not this image corresponded with the original revelation as delivered to Adam Smith is a separate, but not unimportant, issue. Smith would have had good reason to wish for more attentive readers and fewer disciples. Befitting a professor of moral economy and successor to the chair occupied previously by the famous philosopher Thomas Hutchinson, Smith's first major work was *The Theory of Moral Sentiments* ([1759] 1976). Like Hutchinson, Smith argued that the bonds of sympathy between humans were stronger than those of self-interest as a matter of fact and morality. Yet he is best known for an entirely different assertion in *The Wealth of Nations*, drawn from Bernard Mandeville's *Fable of the Bees*, that narrow self-interest promotes the collective welfare as if led by an "invisible hand." Humanity has a "certain propensity," as Smith put it ([1776] 1965, 13), "to truck, barter, and exchange one thing for another." That being so, he famously observed, "It is not from the benevolence of the butcher, the brewer, or the baker, that we expect our dinner, but from their regard to their own self-interest." Smith accordingly maintained that "we address ourselves, not to their humanity but to their self-love" (14). Had Smith inserted the word "only" in the first clause between "not" and "from," as Kenneth Lux speculates (1990, 87), he might have saved later generations from considerable mischief. But Smith did not. Here and elsewhere in his masterpiece, Smith came "within a hair's breadth" of preventing "immorality from finding its intellectual and theoretical justification in the name of economics," notes Lux (90). Even slight modifications in Smith's prose would have cautioned against the simple primacy apparently given to self-interest and invisible hands that supposedly transmogrify selfishness into a public benefit. Ironically, Smith believed *The Theory of Moral Sentiments* to be his better book, and in his final edition of this work in 1790, Smith, increasingly skeptical of "the depleting moral legacy" of commercial society, expanded his earlier warnings against the unbridled pursuit of wealth (Lux 1990, 107, 121).

Imagine, as well, that the discipline of ecology had arrived on the scene before Smith wrote, and that he'd undertaken to link his economic ideas with those of biophysical health along with the need to preserve the natural capital of soils, forests, wildlife, and ecosystem services. Were that the history, economic thinking early on would have been greatly improved by the habit of keeping the accounting boundaries wide enough to subtract the drawdown of natural capital from the gross national product to arrive at a truer estimate of our wealth. But no such linkages were made, and with notable exceptions, economists have been indifferent defenders of ecology and resistant to the idea that there are any limits whatsoever to economic growth.

Smith's sympathy for the plight of workers, and the debilitating effects of the division of labor and unchecked avarice in capitalist society notwithstanding, his legacy is presumed to be otherwise. A caricature of his views has been used ever since to justify the global effort to remodel societies, cultures, and the biophysical world to coincide with the imperatives of markets in a manner that would have greatly astonished and perhaps dismayed Professor Smith. For the first generation of industrialists, *The Wealth of Nations* was a godsend, presumably giving moral sanction to what was already well underway. Charles Darwin's writings a century later on evolution would be distorted even more fervently by the social Darwinists to justify the gross inequities arising from the excesses of the robber barons. In our own time, the mainstream of the discipline continues to give considerable aid and comfort to only slightly refined barbarities presumed necessary to the further advancement of the material conditions of humankind and its financiers, but with little concern for the distribution of wealth or the longevity of the human experiment. In the darker recesses of Chicago and Washington, economic doctrine functions as a surrogate religion applicable to virtually all human decisions toward the end of blessed salvation via economic growth in the by and by (Cox 1999).

More than any other body of thought, economics has shaped our assumptions about the world, and about what's rational and what's not, but its flaws are deep. Mainstream neoclassic economics is constructed on the presumption that the economy can grow without limit in what ecologists know to be a finite ecosystem. The economy is quietly presumed to operate independent of the laws of thermodynamics, which physicists know to be inviolable. The theory presumes humans to be rational, selfish, and insatiably acquisitive, which psychologists know to be simplistic and theologians know to be morally depleting. It further presumes the primacy of private wants over public goods, which political economists know to be corrosive of the public good; that human societies consist of only atomized individuals, in ways that most sociologists know to caricature a far more complex reality of interdependence; and the supremacy of concepts like utility, which logicians know to be circular. The theory also presumes that people know what they want and need, can distinguish between the two, and understand the market possibilities by which to satisfy these. But that faith ignores the effects of pervasive advertising, and bears little resemblance to what we actually know and how we actually behave. And the theory describes and prescribes self-aggrandizement as rational in a way that stands no good test of history, morality, or even daily experience. Taken to its extreme, this is a worldview mostly devoid of genuine altruism, kindness, cooperation, community, public good, and the possibility of higher purpose—a world in which what is economized, as one economist put it (Schwartz 1994, 193), is love. Some believe that economic calculation is an adequate guide for human behavior in the areas of marriage and childbearing, and as a replacement for the standard of justice in courts of law. Its limitations and flaws notwithstanding, the paradigm of economics is thoroughly ingrained in the contemporary world.

Ideas, conservative philosopher Richard Weaver once said, have consequences. The reigning economic ideas are particularly consequential. In the name of free-market economics, we are witnessing the largest transfer of wealth from the poor to the rich in human history (Gates 2002, 2003). Because it is assumed to be uneconomic, we have thus far refused to take the obvious steps to prevent possibly catastrophic climate change and a massive loss of biological diversity. To further oil-powered economic growth at all costs, we have declared our right to launch Armageddon (the Carter doctrine), initiate preemptive wars (the National Security strategy of George W. Bush), and poison our souls and bodies alike. This is held to be common sense serving the goal of progress, which no one can clearly define. When stripped of its veneer, it is an enterprise much given to accumulation, speed, and death, or as the Buddhists would have it, to illusion, greed, and ill will.

Can the theory and practice of economics be improved? One way to do so would be to extend the logic of capitalism to properly value all forms of capital: financial, material, human, and that of nature in the form of soils, forests, and healthy ecosystems. Paul Hawken, Amory Lovins, and Hunter Lovins, in their seminal book *Natural Capitalism* (1999, xiii), convincingly argue that "the world stands on the threshold of basic conditions of business. Companies that ignore the message of natural capitalism do so at their peril. . . . [T]he move toward radical resource productivity and natural capitalism is beginning to feel inevitable rather than merely possible." One difficulty with this view is simply that financial and material capital operate mostly by the laws of greed and smartness, while human capital and our willingness to protect that of nature work mostly by the laws of affection and foresight. The authors of *Natural Capitalism* assume that the transition to a better economy will be driven by market logic, the pressure to become more efficient, consumer preferences, and enlightened self-interests. There is, in fact, a growing movement in business circles, led by corporate visionaries like Ray Anderson at Interface along with companies such as 3M, STMelectronics, and British Petroleum, to eliminate pollution and reduce carbon emissions. My skepticism about how far this will go on its own is of the sort described by philosopher Mary Midgley (1996b, 126): "At this range, enlightened calculations tend to be too indirect to have much force, and ordinary, unenlightened sectional selfishness usually works quietly in their shadow. If prudence on this scale is to be effective, it needs to be supplemented by a much more direct spontaneous moral feeling—in fact by a sense of outrage." So, when I reach the part of my environmental policy course dealing with such things, in addition to requiring my students to read *Natural Capitalism,* I hedge my bets and also require them to read Joel Kovel's counterargument in his *The Enemy of Nature* (2002, 6), a vigorous Marxist dissent to the effect that capitalism "is incorrigible . . . it cannot be reformed: it either rules and destroys us, or is destroyed, so that we may have a lease on life." On the question of whether capitalism can, without government direction, render itself into natural capitalism, and in time to prevent the worst that lies ahead, or whether we need some other kind of economy, I am of a mixed mind. On Mondays, Wednesdays, and Fridays I think capitalism can reform itself, while on Tuesdays, Thursdays, and Saturdays I most assuredly do not. On Sundays I rest.

While there is no simple relationship between economic doctrine and architecture our ideas of worth, wealth, and economy are important factors about where, how, and what we build. For example, if land is valued only for its development potential and not for its ecological functions, then sprawl is a likely outcome, on the one hand, and urban decay is equally likely, on the other. If our notions of time go no further than those of the accountant's horizon, we will preserve no historic landscapes or places of memory. If nature is presumed to consist only of inanimate objects, which is to say dead "resources," we are free of any obligation to honor the life force they represent. We are more likely to exploit land and labor, if we do not value ecosystem integrity and the dignity of people remote from us. If we assume economic expansion to be the highest goal of public policy, we may take whatever resources are necessary to that end. Moreover, if we assume, as some commonly do, that whatever becomes scarce can be replaced by a substitute, we are more likely to build without thrift and innovate without caution. If we assume the world to be infinitely forgiving of human insult, we will pay scant attention to the ecological costs of buildings and their operations. Also, if we presume to judge our work solely by the calculus of financial costs and benefits, we will account for only those costs that can be easily counted, which leaves out a great deal. If we discount the future, as we typically do, our prices will not tell the truth about the full costs that our children and their children will pay if things go badly. If we assume ourselves to be made in the image of the rational economic man, the built environment becomes a mirror of our acquisitiveness, smartness, and individual accomplishment. And if we magnify desire and greed, we will "kindle envy and outstrip reason" (Whybrow 2005, 38)—that is, we will become a meaner and dumber people.

If we educate the young only for success in such a world, the buildings most appropriate to that goal will be designed to accommodate fragmentation by disciplines aimed to focus time and attention in order to promote the kind of specialization that best maximizes lifetime earnings. If it is assumed that the price of energy derived from fossil fuels and nuclear power is accurate, fair, and relatively permanent, then we will not build to maximize energy efficiency and the use of renewable energy; we will compromise the ecological health and climate stability of the world our students will inherit. We will build without honoring our grandchildren and protecting their prospects, on the assumption that cheapness is the deciding criteria for buildings and materials, Similarly, if we surround our buildings with chemically drenched and sterile landscapes, we teach other lessons about our presumed mastery of the world without anyone having to say as much. If we assume that the distribution of wealth in a highly inequitable capitalist society ought to correspond to the distribution of power, then we will surrender our role as active agents in the making of our world. The lessons taught are those of hierarchy, on the one hand, and passivity, on the other.

## A Digression on the Economics of Neighborliness

Holmes County, fifty miles south of Oberlin, is home to the largest Amish community outside of Lancaster County, Pennsylvania. The Amish are mostly farmers and highly self-sufficient, but probably no more so than typical farmers were a century ago. They are a horsepowered people, which limits the size of their farms, the speed and range of their wanderlust, and the impulse to shop. In Amish society, the horse functions rather like the governor on a machine to limit its performance within some preset range. By contemporary standards, the Amish's needs are minimal. Male elders rule mostly, but women are not taken for granted. Domestic violence is rare in Amish communities. The Amish adopt technologies only after first considering their impact on their communities. A decision to refuse a technology is based on the belief that its effects would be deleterious to the community even though it might be profitable or useful. The Amish do not accept social security, welfare, or insurance, except that

**Box 7.1**
True wealth

For too long we seem to have surrendered personal excellence and community value in the mere accumulation of material things. Our gross national product now is over $800 billion a year, but that gross national product counts air pollution, and cigarette advertising, and ambulances to clear our highways of carnage. It counts special locks for our doors and the jails of people who break them. It counts the destruction of the redwoods and the loss of our natural wonder in chaotic squall. It counts napalm, and it counts nuclear warheads, and armored cars for the police to fight the riots in our city. It counts Whitman's rifles and Speck's knives and the television programs which glorify violence in order to sell toys to our children. Yet, the gross national product does not allow for the health of our children, the quality of their education, or the joy of their play; it does not include the beauty of our poetry or the strength of our marriages, the intelligence of our public debate nor the integrity of our public officials. It measures neither our wit nor our courage, neither our wisdom nor our learning, neither our compassion nor our devotion to our country. It measures everything, in short, except that which makes life worthwhile. And it can tell us everything about America except why we are proud that we are Americans.
—Robert Kennedy

provided by their own community (Kraybill 1989). After a devastating tornado, I once witnessed Amish barns rebuilt and stocked with hay in a matter of weeks by Amish crews from three states, while the debris from the "English" farms was still strewn across the land and their owners were still waiting for their insurance checks. Amish children do not attend school past the eighth grade, but many become avid lifelong readers. Community barn-raisings and collective farmwork are the norm. On Sunday the Amish worship in each other's homes. It's not perfect, but the Amish life is as close to a practical model of sustainability and community as exists in North America. On weekends, the roads of Amish country in central Ohio are choked with SUV-driving tourists with their digital cameras and credit cards, eager to acquire tangible evidence of a saner life.

What writer Gene Logsdon (2000) calls "Amish Economics" is a blend of Christian charity, common sense, frugality, practical competence, and community self-reliance. One Old Order Amish said to me that farming is both his livelihood and what he does for pleasure. He does not belong to a health club and, vanity not being in style, is an unlikely candidate for the South Beach Diet. The Amish's lives are sufficiently balanced to dispense with psychiatrists, consultants, experts, and economists alike. A typical Amish dairy farmer can earn three to five times per cow what a conventional farmer can, much to the distress of agricultural economists who believe such numbers to be impossible. The Amish dress in a common and simple garb, and are mostly immune to commercial advertising. As businesspersons, they are known for doing quality work and charging accordingly. The Amish are highly buffered from the ups and downs of the larger economy. But they are subject to what they consider to be a higher level of economy that begins with the injunction not to lay up for themselves treasures on Earth, where moth and rust consume and thieves break in to steal. They are invariably kind, hospitable, restrained, and nonantagonistic, even when persecuted. And their communities offer a useful model for a more permanent kind of economy.

In quite different circumstances, other examples of economies exist to promote fairness, just distribution, participation, ecological health, the widespread ownership of capital, and stable communities without violence, militarism, or the exploitation of workers, and without undermining the prospects of future generations. The Mondragon Cooperatives, for example—the work of Father José María Arizmendiarrieta-Arrieta (Arizmendi)—is a network of over one hundred worker-owned cooperatives in the Basque region of Spain that has established a democratic basis for a prosperous economy (Whyte and Whyte 1988). The radical economic development in the Kerala region of India is another instance in which better economic thinking expanded peoples' rights, raised the condition of women, and established widespread literacy and prosperity in an area of considerable poverty (McKibben 1995; Franke and Chasin 1991). Similarly, the Grameen Bank in Bangladesh similarly, has loaned over three billion dollars, 95 percent of which is in the form of microloans to women and women's cooperatives (Yunis 1999). Its success is measured, in part, by a repayment rate of nearly 100 percent and a sharp improvement in the economic independence of women in Bangladesh.

From time to time, we've come close to forging the bonds of a better economy in this country. For example, in his State of the Union address on January 11, 1944, Franklin Delano Roosevelt proposed an economic bill of rights including the right to useful employment, adequate food, a decent home, medical care, education, and old-age security (Sunstein 2004, 243). According to legal expert Cass Sunstein, the United States was moving toward the adoption of Roosevelt's "second Bill of Rights" until derailed by the election of Richard Nixon in 1968. Seymour Melman, William Grieder, and Jeff Gates, among others, have proposed sensible reforms that would lay the foundation for a fair, stable, and decent capitalism. Others, such as John Cobb, Herman Daly, Paul Hawken, Amory Lovins, and Hunter Lovins, propose even deeper economic reforms to include full-cost realities. Clearly we do not lack for better ideas. Our lack is deeper.

One clue as to the depth is found in our language. We, the richest people ever and marinated in convenience, live in a kind of unspoken terror of scarcity and have no concept of enough. When, for example, will the economy be large enough? Apparently never, since every president runs on their ability to make it even larger, and not to do so is regarded as the ultimate political failure. When does any one of us have enough wealth? Some societies that we regard as "primitive" had no word for scarcity and lived as "actors in natural cycles . . . [knowing] that what nature gives to us is influenced by what we give to nature," a kind of gift exchange. (Hyde 1983, 19). The abundance of the forest, for one, was "a consequence of man's treating its wealth as a gift," in Lewis Hyde's words (). In a "gift economy," scarcity appears only when wealth "ceases to move freely when all things are counted and priced. . . . [W]hen the market moves mostly for profit and the dominant myth is not 'to possess is to give' but 'the fittest survive,' then wealth will lose its motion and gather in isolated pools" (22–23); "gifts that remain gifts do not *earn* profit, they *give* increase" (37). Work, an intended activity done by the hour for pay, is distinguished in gift economies from labor, which has "its own interior rhythm, something more bound up with feeling, more interior, than work" (51). Labor is the working out of gratitude in an awakened soul, and gratitude "requires an *unpaid* debt" (51). In contrast to commodity exchange, a gift becomes a bond between two people.

At its worst, the exchange of deceptively defective commodities becomes a license to kill. Ford Motor Company executives once decided not to redesign the gas tank of a car called the Pinto that was prone to explode in rear-end collisions, thereby predictably killing some of their customers. Instead, they reasoned that it was cheaper to kill a few hundred customers and settle lawsuits than to redesign the car. Gifts, on the other hand, properly given and openly received, are aimed to increase plenitude and health, and mirror the gifts of sunshine, rain, fertility, the seasons, animals, the dependable rhythms and balance of nature, the night sky, sunrise, and sunset, which come to us by a benevolence we cannot comprehend.

## Asking

Everyone ought to have to do it some time in their lives—raise money, that is. One can wear out a lot of hat brims and knee pads in the process, but the supplicant's posture changes one's perspective considerably. But I've also served as a trustee of four foundations that give money away. Between the two experiences, I am persuaded that it is indeed more blessed to give than to receive. Giving money away is easy, but giving it away to good effect is not so simple, only less nerve-racking. Properly done, philanthropy is hard work requiring investigation, discernment, a gambler's intuition about people and their projects, and the ability to say no without impairing the initiative and self-worth of the supplicant. Philanthropy well done and to good effect is, I think, rare. The chief executive of a large national foundation, for example, once told me that he'd never funded "a mistake," meaning that he'd given a lot of money only to safe and prestigious organizations not likely to embarrass, and perhaps equally unlikely to do anything very imaginative or even useful. Playing it safe can be another and larger kind of mistake. "New truth," Aldous Huxley once said, "begins as heresy and ends as superstition." A decent philanthropic portfolio ought to include a lot of heresy. And sometimes failing for the right reasons is a higher kind of success.

The besetting sins of philanthropy include giving in order to bask in the reflected glory of the recipient's prestige. Another is to use philanthropy as a way to subtly or sometimes not so subtly control recipients. A third is the false sense of self-importance that arises from having people always return your phone calls and laugh at your sorrier jokes. In such circumstances, it is possible to believe that being sought out means that one really is important and therefore one's ideas are superior. A fourth is inconstancy:

"The environment? We did that last year; now we fund widget research."
A fifth is the desire to make the world over on the basis of some warped,
procrustean, late-night totalitarian vision of how things ought to be.
Right-wing foundations are said to have spent over three billion dollars
between 1970 and 2004 in order to resuscitate the public spirit of the
nineteenth-century robber barons, restore the moral sensitivity of the social Darwinists, and promote the vision of Calvin Coolidge, and we are a
poorer and meaner nation to the extent that they have succeeded. At their
worst, protected charities can be drivers for some really nutty ideas, of
which there are a few outstanding examples in the past two decades. All
good philanthropy is a letting go with no strings attached. The gift must
move and that requires a discerning mind and a good heart.

On the other side of the philanthropic equation, a great deal of the little
that I know about the art of raising money I learned from my dad, who
was the best salesperson I've ever known. He never sold anything that he
would not buy, and would not ask anyone to give to a cause to which he
had not given both cash and effort. As the president of a small Presbyterian college, he sold Christianity along with possibilities of what could
be with a little foresight and hard work. I once asked him how he raised
money. He thought awhile and finally came up with six rules: never let a
conversation with a potential donor get to a "no"—that is, keep the door

**Box 7.2**
Giving can be scary

---

In spring 1982, the *New York Times* reported the following story: "(1) Two
men seeking to promote their adult-education school [the Learning Annex]
announced that they would throw $10,000 in dollar bills from the 86th floor
of the Empire State Building. (2) Two other men chose the same time to hold
up the Banker Trust branch in the building, and after firing a shot found
themselves pursued up 34th Street by plainclothesmen. . . . (3) The suspects
were tackled and disarmed in one of the most heavily photographed arrests
of recent times. (4) The promoters, unaware of the commotion, got out of a
taxi on 34th Street with five clear plastic bags full of money. (5) After some
understandable confusion about the loot from the bank and the bags of
money, the promoters were denied admittance to the tower." After being
roughed up by the assembled crowd, some of whom helped themselves to
the free loot, one of the entrepreneurs from the Learning Annex was quoted
as saying that the experience was "scary," vowing never to attempt it again.

open; don't ask anyone to give unless you've given first; always express appreciation on the same day that a gift is received; don't ask for anything you don't really need; don't be afraid of failure; and get up earlier, work harder, and stay later than your competition. He also ran a tight fiscal ship and had rock-solid integrity. Many years after his retirement one of his trustees, a former federal judge, told me that my father was the hardest man to give a raise to that he'd ever known. There was always some other college priority he considered more critical than his own salary. When he created a retirement program for the faculty and other administrators, he exempted himself because he did not want it to appear to be self-serving. A lifelong tither, he retired on funds accumulated the old-fashioned way: by thrift.

In one of my first ventures into raising money, I received a letter of refusal from the president of a Chattanooga-based foundation saying that his trustees did not give west of the Mississippi River. Reaching deep into the bag of desperation I wrote back thanking him for his consideration, but I wanted him to know that "Every reputable geologist that I know believes that Arkansas is sliding toward Chattanooga at the rate of an inch each millennium and so soon—as God measures time—we'll be neighbors. I'm certain that your trustees would not like us to be poor when we get there." He responded by return mail, saying, "I'll alert my trustees that you all are on your way. Please leave the Razorback fans at home, but do bring plenty of wild rice." He forgot to include the check. On another occasion I approached the legendary Whit Stephens, founder of Stephens, Inc., in Little Rock, who'd started his considerable fortune by selling belt buckles in the Depression years and using the profits to buy state bonds for pennies on the dollar. Eventually, he used the sizable profit to buy oil and gas properties, politicians, and lots more. By the time I met him, his financial net worth was estimated to be well over a billion dollars, but no one knew for sure. His secretary did not warn me that he was in a bad mood that particular day, and so I entered his office with my three-point sales pitch ready for everything but his question snarled out between teeth firmly holding the remnant of an unlit day-old stogie: "What the f— do you want with me?" I don't recall what I said, but I do remember stammering it out thoroughly flummoxed, a mere puddle of quivering postpotential protoplasm. I've been prepared for that question ever since.

I don't think I was ever impolite to a potential donor, yet from time to time I was on the edge. In response to one of the country's most lavishly privileged sons of wealth, who said that flying over the country in his Learjet he could see no evidence of soil erosion, I responded by saying that he was looking from the wrong altitude. No check there either.

Since the Lewis Center was to be funded from unlikely sources within two years and with no help from the college development office, speed was imperative. But as design progressed, the budget increased from the first estimates of $2.5 million to $7.2 million (including endowment), causing great consternation in high places. But I was focused more on what we would build than what it would cost. A double-wide trailer would have been cheap enough, but try to sell that to a prospective donor whose name will forever be blazoned on it. Somewhere between a double-wide and yet short of the Taj Mahal, we wanted to build the first thoroughly green building on any college campus in the United States. For that goal, cost was not the most important factor—ideas were.

I spent about one-third of my time over the next two years working with my colleagues on design issues and another third raising money. Buildings are hard to sell to prospective donors, especially if you cannot play the card of institutional loyalty. On average, about half of the money for new academic buildings must be borrowed. The problem, often, is not that donors will not fund buildings but that the vision in which the building purportedly fits is either weak or nonexistent. During a meeting with a well-known Texas donor who'd paid for a few buildings in his time, I asked what he'd funded that really excited him, to which he responded, "Not one damn thing; it's all boring as hell!" The lesson is that you sell not buildings but ideas crystallized into a built form. Saying to a potential donor that a project fits somehow into a campus master plan is a weak card, as is the argument that other colleges have better facilities. The purposes ought to go deeper. What is the larger pattern? What is the problem for which a building is the solution? What will students learn in this facility? What will they do with what they learn? How will that improve the human condition? How will the design, performance, and use of this facility fit into the largest issues on the human agenda, all of which in one way or another have to do with the sustainability and fairness of the human enterprise? How will the project stack up against the problems of global warming, deforestation, biotic impoverishment, soil erosion, toxic pollution, and global poverty as well as the growing problem of inequity? What is the institutional commitment to sustainability and to equipping its students to be of use in that transition?

Shortly after construction began on the Lewis Center, the college started to design a fifty-five million dollar science facility. This would have been a good opportunity to extend what we had learned about ecological design to a larger and more complex building, and also to ask deeper questions about science and its relation to the challenges of the twenty-first century that our students will face. What kind of biological science is appropriate, for example, for a world hemorrhaging biological diversity? Given the toxic legacy of the industrial age, what kind of chemistry ought we to teach? Given the fragmentation of disciplines, what kind of building would help launch a larger conversation about science and the human prospect? Is there any relation between the architecture of science buildings and what some believe to be the hubris of modern science? The prospect of building a new science building would allow us to combine architecture with a more integrated and farsighted curriculum. And aiming higher would make this project more appealing to prospective donors, thereby also making it easier to raise funds.

I put the case for a green science building into a short paper with the title "The Architecture of Science," and sent it to scientists at Oberlin and other universities (Orr 2002). No one quarreled with the logic or the conclusions, but all said that it would be unpopular. When the paper was later circulated to the administration, it was clear that there was no support for the idea, and the subject of a green or even energy-efficient science building was dropped, as was any conversation about larger issues. The college proceeded to build a good twentieth-century science facility that opened in the twenty-first century—a building that uses perhaps twice as much energy as necessary. And it had to borrow most of the money to do it.

Philanthropy, at its best, is a gift exchange between equals, not a form of begging by one party or manipulation by the other. One side offers an opportunity, and the other side supplies the means by which it can be realized. But even the most mundane request ought to fit into a larger vision.

For grant writers, the right question is always, what might this do in the world that really needs to be done? In my experience, grant writers most often fail, sometimes even when they succeed, because of a poverty of vision. The challenges of our time call for a larger vision by both the givers and receivers of philanthropy. We have been given a great deal and much will be expected of us. Still, it is axiomatic in a commercial culture to take more than you give, and that practice is killing us and destroying the health of the world we will leave behind. There is only one true model for philanthropy, and it is found in the fact that we live by the grace of sunlight, water, and ecological fecundity, a benevolence given with only the stipulation to use it well.

# III

## Evaluation

# 8

## The Politics of Institutional Change

Assemble a cluster of professors in a country town, surround them with scenic grandeur, cut them off from the world beyond, and they will not have much trouble congratulating themselves into curricular torpor.
—Frederick Rudolph

You're afraid, aren't you?
Yes, sir.
Don't be.
—a dream

### Flashback

The nursery school met in the basement of the New Wilmington United Presbyterian Church, an oppressively cavernous prison for a five-year-old incarcerated therein. We made our break during the afternoon nap time. I stacked a chair on top of a table to reach the height of the casement window at ground level, crawled out, and summoned my buddies toward freedom, probably saying the five-year-old equivalent of "You have nothing to lose but your chains," or maybe it was "You have nothing to fear but fear itself." Most likely, however, it was just "Come on, let's get outta here." We headed for the corner store a block away and pooled our nickels for ice cream all around. A short time later, we were discovered by the nursery school police in the second booth from the front door, happily oblivious to the long reach of the law and returned forthwith to the big house. Some thought I was merely rebellious; I preferred to think of myself as a victim of oppression, and a liberator from arbitrary and incompetent authority and dark basements—a freedom fighter with a taste for ice cream.

From that day forth I have had—oh, how to say this?—an interesting relationship with authority. On the continuum between absolute order and
possibility, most of my life has been spent pushing toward the latter, placing me in an uneasy relation with those who believe it their duty to maintain the status quo. In my second year of college teaching, a colleague and
I spent a summer organizing and fund-raising for a national conference in
Atlanta that would feature speeches by twenty of the most prominent
voices on the environment and the limits to economic growth. The event
was to consist of three days of presentations on campus and downtown at
places like the Federal Reserve Bank. We secured financial support from
the major banks and businesses in the town along with endorsements
from the mayor and the governor. We met with the dean, who'd earlier
given her approval, to describe what we'd done and arrange details on
campus for the event still eight months distant. When we finished, there
was a long silence after which she earnestly inquired whether we had
"checked to see that the organ in the auditorium will not be in use on those
days?" Indeed, we had not.

The political organization of Oberlin College is believed to have originated either in a compact between Charles Grandison Finney and the
trustees or in the lower reaches of hell, depending on your perspective
(Fletcher 1943, 668). Whatever its origin, that arrangement, henceforth
known as the Finney Compact, served as the basis for a system of strong
faculty governance and relatively weak presidents from that time nearly
to the present. By the terms of the compact, matters of curriculum, hiring,
firing, and promotion were left to the faculty, safely out of the hands of
the administration and trustees. A wit once compared the Finney Compact
to a car with four drivers, four steering wheels, four brake pedals, and
three reverse gears. However arranged, college politics, as noted, are particularly bitter because the stakes are so incredibly low.

Those surrounding the design, funding, and construction of the Lewis
Center were no exception. But they are of no importance except as they illustrate more generally the difficulties of innovation in organizations and
some aspects of a larger problem that philosopher Bruce Wilshire (1990)
once described as "the moral collapse" of higher education. I think that is
particularly true regarding our orientation to the issues pertaining to "the

long emergency" ahead. Institutions of higher education are still unde-
cided about whether and how "to address the underlying intellectual issues and moral imperatives of having responsibility for the earth, and to
do so with an intensity and ingenuity matching that shown by previous
generations in obeying the command to have dominion over the planet"
(Pelikan 1992, 21). It is fair to say that relative to the job of educating and
equipping a generation adequately to face that challenge, colleges and universities are underachievers. They have, for the most part, allowed bureaucratic routines to dictate purposes and sap creativity, an overblown sense
of rigor to cloud vision across boundaries, finances to eviscerate larger
purposes, and unnecessary paperwork to swallow the most valuable time
and energies of faculty and administrators.

## A Few of the Players

The Lewis Center originated in an unusual arrangement between a new
president, the committee governing the Environmental Studies Program,
the trustees, and myself. The terms, previously described, gave me two
years to raise the funds for the building and complete the schematic drawings. I was required only to report to one member of the administration,
the director of sponsored programs, who in turn reported to the president.
The director was a person of unusual intelligence, a survivor of college politics with a vivid sense of humor and an eye for creative possibilities. From
the outset, the project was hampered by the division between institutional
authority, on the one side, and the vision for the building and fund-raising
responsibility, on the other. Not having originated in the college planning
processes, the project existed tenuously at the margin of institutional
power, but with the support of the president.

Oberlin students from the first have been known for their passion about
matters of fairness, poverty, and justice. A learned visitor from Harvard
once remarked that they were "suffocating in their idealism." True or not,
it is to be expected that virtually any endeavor at Oberlin will be attacked
by a few on the grounds that it speaks insufficiently to the needs of the
poor as well as to the cause of rectifying poverty and injustice. The Lewis
Center, alas, was no exception. Even before its approval by the trustees,
several students launched an attack in the campus newspaper, proposing

that the funds to be raised could be better spent to hire faculty whose responsibility it would be to further elucidate the needs for justice in the world. A later group of students, having forgotten that their peers had decided two years before that nonnative plants were to be removed from the building site, spent a considerable amount of energy to deposit a large section of a particularly invasive nonnative mulberry, recently removed from the site, in front of my office door with a sign identifying me as a tree killer in creatively graphic terms.

Idealism is an endearing and sometimes irritating trait. But the students' conviction that the world ought to be made a better place than it is helped to launch the Environmental Studies Program in the late 1970s and energized the effort to build the Lewis Center. Specifically, it caused us to consider issues of ecological design as a means to promote justice, fairness, and sustainability by giving due care to the supply chain for materials and their effect on employment, pollution, and the long-term external effects of the building. Before it was fashionable elsewhere, Oberlin students proposed to join ecological design and green building with larger issues of fairness, health, and environmental justice.

Oberlin faculty, if more restrained in their enthusiasms, are similarly inclined. But to the extent that they thought about it at all, I think they regarded this project with a mixture of enthusiasm, skepticism, and perhaps pity. Most, understandably, observed from the sidelines while a few became indispensable to the planning and execution of the project. Others helped to run interference and clear administrative obstacles. One or two conservatives attacked the project with some vigor for its more quixotic aspects, evident, they thought, in its flawed design, faulty technology, and a less than rigorous philosophical orientation. All in all, the Oberlin faculty members are an amiably contentious bunch. Yet were it to require a consensus, I have heard it said that the faculty would be unable to agree on whether and how to leave a burning building. Some, it is alleged, would argue that doing so would show cowardice in the face of danger and thus set a bad example for the students; others might say that we deserve to suffer and should remain; and still others would quarrel about the order by which we might recess until well roasted.

For its part, the administration was not of one mind about this endeavor. The project was conceived without benefit of legitimate parentage in the formal planning process and without the imprimatur of the development office, the director of which regarded it as a rather mixed blessing at best. He was a nattily dressed extrovert on speed. Having once reportedly secured a gift of fifteen million dollars for another institution, he was, in his own modest estimation, the most adept fund-raiser since King Midas: a self-assured hail-fellow, well met; a compulsive bloviator; and a charmer— not an altogether unlikable combination. He once began a meeting on the Lewis Center by saying that he had to get something off his chest. Turning to the president, he proceeded to announce, "You are a great president! No, no don't stop me, I just have to say this. I go all over the country and meet with hundreds of alums and all kinds of people, and you are regarded by all as a really great college president," and so forth. The president's beaming smile showed a combination of gratitude tinged with embarrassment and befuddlement. His head was where, as a country song once put it, the sun don't shine. I once heard him expound on the theory and technique of what he called "deep listening" to the inner needs of prospective donors, presumably a key to his success as a fund-raiser. The beneficiary of his wisdom on this occasion was a college trustee, an attorney known as a good cross-examiner, who drew him forth with a combination of flattery and puffball questions, while listening no doubt bemused behind the poker face of a good lawyer.

Later, when it became clear that we were about to receive what in development jargon is called "the naming gift"—the funds that make the project possible—he called me into his office at 7:00 a.m. to instruct me on the proper way to nail down the gift, as he put it. He looked at me intently for a moment, leaned forward in his chair, and said in a low confidential tone, as if sharing a profoundly important secret: "David, are you a fisherman?" "No," I said. "Well," he continued, "let me tell you as one who is, how to reel in the big gifts." He proceeded to describe how an adept fisherman casts, jiggles the line just right to attract the fish's attention, hooks it with an ever-so-subtle movement of the wrist, lets it run out a bit, and then reels it in. He leaned back in his chair, greatly pleased, hoping that I would invite him to help reel this one in, adding another trophy to his wall. I glanced at my watch; it was 7:20 a.m. Instructed in the finer arts of fishing, I departed.

Colleges, by and large, seldom hire those with an entrepreneurial disposition into administrative positions. To do so would invite chaos, upset the routines of paperwork, and violate procedural normalcy. In a lifetime spent in and around higher education, I have seldom heard an academic officer encourage anyone to innovative, bold, or courageous action that

**Box 8.1**
From *Book*, by Robert Grudin (1992)

From the start of his academic career, J. Thoreau Marshall had shown professional qualities of an unmistakable character. Fresh out of college, with a Big Ten degree and a kaleidoscopic gamut of graduate options at his disposal, he had chosen as his heart's desire the field of business statistics. Set in this course, he then proceeded, from his dissertation years on through a brace of assistant professorships, to produce a succession of timid, shortsighted, derivative articles, couched in muddy meandering wearisome style. Marshall's comportment as a teacher was equally distinctive. Terrified of being at a loss for words, he wrote out his lectures which, sauced with redundancy, seasoned with non sequitur and served up at a metronomic pace in a pained nasal monotone, induced narcosis in all who heard them. In committee meetings he was notably inarticulate, dead to nuance and phobic to original ideas. His other relationships were of a similar ilk. To his students he was autocratic and unfair, to his advisees distant and obtuse, to his colleagues earthbound and hollow.

It was eventually apparent that these characteristics, displayed consistently and noted by all, ideally qualified Marshall for academic administration, and before long he was welcomed into a confraternity whose members, by and large, shared his talents and propensities. Yet so far did he exceed his colleagues in these regards that he speedily rose to the summit of his profession, leaving the ranks of department heads and deans to become vice president for academic affairs, or provost. . . . [I]n this office he observed with unflinching purpose the timeworn obligations of his profession: bullying his subordinates and cringing before his superiors, stifling talent and rewarding mediocrity, promoting faddishness and punishing integrity, rejecting the most impassioned and justified individual plea yet acquiescing to every whim of political interest; avoiding confrontation, whenever possible, with the naked truth; shirking decisions and articulating such decisions as had to be made in memos so vague, oblique and circumnavigational as barely to deserve the name of language. For these persistent efforts to maintain the standards and security of a great institution he was rewarded with the reverence of the faculty."

might threaten established procedures or even parking permits. So selected and groomed, administrators are ill disposed to do much to discomfit the academically comfortable or disturb the deep torpor of the rigorously complacent. No, they emerge from the womb with a wet finger stuck in the air. They are mostly tame and civilized folks—decent people really—sent to patrol the boundaries of normalcy and vigorously prosecute infractions of procedural regularity. The spirit of J. Thoreau Marshall reigns.

The explanation for this state of affairs, I think, begins with the fact that the field of academic administration has increasingly tended to attract ambitious careerists, people eager to rise in the hierarchy of higher education. Any mistake, even for a good cause, would blemish their record, thereby removing rungs on the ladder of upward mobility. By virtue of both disposition and self-regard, they tend to approach risk rather like oil regards water. And careers in academic administration offer great public esteem, stable indoor employment, and travel to exotic places where they and their peers solemnly congregate to contemplate the deeper arts of administration, all at a goodly salary.

For their part, presidents and trustees needing ever-more money to meet the rising costs of buildings, laboratories, libraries, technology, scholarships, and salaries are similarly loath to risk alienating their financial benefactors. Thus it is that a tone of conservative self-congratulation sometimes pervades the upper reaches of the industry of higher education. Financial exigencies mean that some departments with something to sell are regarded as more essential than, say, departments such as classics, dismissed as purveyors of ancient and dusty things. It is reported that on occasion, entire institutions are similarly for sale to the highest bidder (Washburn 2005). Derek Bok (2003, 201), a former president of Harvard, warns ominously that "universities may not yet be willing to trade all of their academic values for money, but they have proceeded much further down that road than they are generally willing to acknowledge." What is known for a fact is that corporate giving to higher education grew from $850 million in 1985 to $4.25 billion a decade later, and with it a considerable control over the directions of research and hence the evolution of entire disciplines (Newman, Courturier, and Scurry 2004, B7). But I digress.

The flanks of the Lewis Center project were haunted by a few cranky old men, who took it on themselves to stop the project as a matter of honor and to rescue the good reputation of the college. One offered a sizable gift early on to get things moving, and having done so, decided the time to be propitious to reorganize much of the college better to his liking. He proceeded to attach many fairly bizarre conditions on the use of his money, indicating a considerable need for personal therapy. But every time the college met one objection he would raise yet another, taking, one might surmise, perverse delight in the consternation he'd caused. One long, soul-searching letter written in the dark of night would arrive, soon followed by another. In response, drafts of carefully worded letters would circulate between the president and the college attorney, with the intention of finding the right words to reassure with a minimum of enforceable obligation. But all to no avail. I understand that there is a clinical name for this kind of attention-getting behavior, but I have at my all-too-ready disposal a more graphic and satisfying vocabulary. After a year or so of futile letters back and forth, the gift, minus that already spent, was returned in exchange for this donor's agreement never to bother his alma mater again.

Yet another cranky old man, an alumnus from a distant time before the discovery that Earth had a biosphere, regarded the building and environmental studies generally as fraudulent, perhaps even a form of religion. We traded letters pro and con about global warming in the local newspaper until I realized that he had nothing else to do in his retirement but make trouble and was a large time sink for those with whom he dueled. Not willing to spend my remaining years in dubious battle to no good purpose, I stopped responding. Without a jousting partner, he resorted to posting flyers around the campus bearing the title "A Physicist Questioning Authority," presumably confusing me with authority. Below the heading would be the most half-baked, crackpot analysis since Bishop James Ussher proved that Earth was created on a Saturday afternoon, December 22 in 4004 BCE, all to prove that global warming was a hoax perpetrated by liberals like me. Flattered by the power ascribed to me to have caused worldwide concern over global warming, I basked silently in what I presumed to be the envy of my colleagues. In hopes of scuttling the building project, the alum wrote the college trustees to vilify the project and similarly to donors, who, in sympathy I suspect, contributed another $250,000 to the building fund. It remains on my "to do" list to send him a letter expressing my gratitude and to inquire whether he might have time to strike yet again.

## And the Politics

The origins of the Lewis Center, to repeat, are unimportant, except insofar as they illustrate problems of innovation in educational institutions and in other organizations, and how they affect our educational mission. The way colleges and universities spend, build, plan, reward, and punish speaks loudly to students about our real priorities, and hence is a powerful, if unspoken, form of education. The experience of the Lewis Center—what worked, what did not, what we did well, and what we did poorly—properly analyzed, might be useful as a case study to improve decision making here and elsewhere. It remains to be explained why the college, having played a major role in initiating the green building movement in higher education, would have reverted to a lower standard in two subsequent building projects that were designed with less concern for energy efficiency and environmental impacts, and with barely a nod to the LEED standards. Reasons are to be found, I think, in the culture of the institution, the dispositions of those involved, and the specifics of history. In my view, the story shows that the construction of high-performance buildings on institutional campuses is not so much a problem of technology, engineering, architectural design, or even cost but more likely one having to do with the scope of institutional vision, personal relationships, timing, and above all, leadership or its absence.

The fact that the Lewis Center was built at all is a considerable achievement for a small liberal arts college without lavish resources. The credit for that accomplishment goes to several dozen people, including the president under whose auspices we worked, the donors who paid for it, the architects who stayed with it when they had good reason not to, and several staff and faculty members who continued to believe in it when others did not. The process of innovation was much harder than it should have been, although that is not an uncommon problem in any organization. I once heard an executive of a major corporation say that his company suffered from a "deficit of joy," a revealing combination of economic and spiritual words to say that they just weren't having much fun. The phrase captures a quality of many organizations that have confused mission with maintenance, performance with paperwork, and seriousness with stuffiness. But why should this be?

British philosopher Mary Midgley (1989, 67) once said that the fundamental rule governing higher education is make no mistake. I think she's on to something. The fear of making mistakes corrodes institutional purposes, personal relationships, and our openness to larger possibilities. At the faculty level, even behind the shield of tenure and the relative safety of the learned world, fear in its various guises of being found wrong, out of step with one's colleagues, taking risks, not being taken seriously, professing with too much emotion, being too far in front, or too far behind is a strong incentive to herdlike behavior. Many outside think the professoriat to be rather like Visigoths before the gates of Rome, eager to rape and pillage, when in fact they pose no more threat to established values and culture than, say, Girl Scouts at your front door selling fat-laden cookies. Most are, in Robert Grudin's words (1990, 169–170), "constitutionally wary of undertaking social criticism or making value judgments in general. [We] have been nursed on an academic tradition that prizes technique and distrusts values. . . . [T]his state of affairs discourages bold advances and disciplinary self-questioning, instead encouraging conservative projects, patriarchism, faddism, and groupiness." We, the learned class, work not in an open forum of wild and dangerous ideas, as commonly thought, but "in a bureaucracy of letters, a vast system of categories, departments, and subspecialties devoted to narrow and formalized discourse, inimical to questions of wholeness, and resistant to any evolution except the incremental proliferation of its own complexity" (169). It is a system that often methodically kills enthusiasm, a word meaning "a god within." We professors are, as philosopher Robert Solomon put it (1992, 45), "all but incapable of getting excited, or getting other people excited; indeed we tend to look at excitement as a sign of charlatanism." Perhaps so. To that extent, we have made ourselves a toothless bunch, marinating in the sauce of self-importance. Occasionally, however, we bestir ourselves to combat in monumental battles over miniscule issues, the significance of which we would be hard put to describe in plain English down on Main Street (Graff 2003).

It is the fear of making a mistake, I believe, that dictates the glacial clock-speed by which we do our business. If so, this may explain why the first response to a proposed change oftentimes is a recitation of the many reasons why it cannot be done and could never be done, with scarcely a nod to why it should be done.[1] The resulting sense of urgency can sometimes make the inch-by-inch retreat of the Laurentide Glacier, which twelve thousand years ago covered this land, look like a high-speed event. Fear disguised as a concern for thoroughness explains why we are otherwise inexplicably willing to spend many of our most creative hours on the most trivial of bureaucratic tasks that require documenting the obvious in great detail when a convivial conversation over coffee would be better. Educational institutions generally, I think, are overmanaged and underled. The result is a system long on rules and routines, and short on direction and perspective—"busy work on a vast, almost incomprehensible scale," in the words of historian and onetime university president Page Smith (1890). The system requires ever-more-elaborate evaluation procedures, the expenditure of large amounts of time, and detailed documentation, thereby complexifying things of no great import. If one cares to add them up, the costs of the system are sizable. It generates long-standing animosities; diverts us from larger purposes having to do with ideas, education, and the relation of ideas and education to the world outside; drains our imagination; and induces the narcotic habits of timidity and tinkering, and always the fear of being out of step in the slightest. We at Oberlin spend untold hours, for example, evaluating each other for salary increases and promotions, and then evaluate each other on how well we evaluated each other. Worse, our fears infect those who come to us to learn, to learn how to learn, and to acquire the wisdom to discern the difference between the important and the trivial. What they learn, more often than we would care to admit, is that success means making no mistake.

1. The Danish Work Psychology Department at the Technological Institute of Denmark has assembled a list of "Proven and Effective New Idea Killers," including: let's think more about that, LATER; I know it's not possible; we are too small/big for that; we have already tried that, and it will be too expensive; that will mean more work; we have always done it this way, so why should we change now?, let somebody else try it first; we have no time for that; it sounds fine in theory, but how will it work in practice?, and we are not ready for this idea yet.

The fear of error pervades academic administration where the stakes are much higher than those for the faculty. Administrators from time to time actually get fired for screwups. College presidents and deans mostly live in fear of budget overruns, tuition shortfalls, rising costs, falling market shares, and their institutional position in the annual *U. S. News and World Report* rankings. Fear has a number of faces. One of these shows in the tepid language of the administrative memo, the bureaucrat's way of avoiding contamination between the personal and the professional, as we live life in fragments. I once received a memo that read, "As it happens, this office doesn't have a copy of your most recent book. I'd be grateful if you would favor us with a copy." A phone call saying, "I'll buy the coffee, you lunkhead, and in return I want a copy of your lousy book, which I don't intend to read," would have been funnier, more honest, and a lot more human. Distance beyond arm's length, the fear of encountering each other as persons. We purport to teach writing skills to our students while writing to each other in comatose prose. E-mail has become yet another way to avoid personal contact and further degrade the language. Even on the same hall, we e-mail more and talk face-to-face less and less, and presume the difference to be the essence of efficient communication, without asking, "Efficient for what?" Some will say irate and careless things by e-mail that they would not dare to say face-to-face, and then copy half of the known universe. E-mail allows us to write and proof documents collectively, and so words multiply and wordiness triumphs over discernment about what's important and what's not. Means become ends, and in the confusion we've lost sight of what education is for.

Fear has a certain style about it, which is often tepid and emotionally hamstrung. On December 6, 1996, for example, the architects and Lyle presented the "schematic design" for the Lewis Center to a select meeting of the college senior staff and a few trustees in a dismal upstairs room of the Oberlin Inn—a 1950s building with low ceilings and lots of right angles, or a plausible justification for the selective use of nuclear weapons. McDonough led off with a typically incandescent description of the basic design philosophy of buildings being metaphorically like trees. The audience sat unmoved. Lyle followed with a presentation of the center's landscape design, featuring a restored wetland with native species, gardens, an orchard, and a small amphitheater. In their different styles, Bill and John made a compelling case that Oberlin had an opportunity to set a new direction in academic architecture and demonstrate leadership in the emerging ecological design movement. A long and awkward silence followed. Finally, a member of the senior staff boldly inquired, "How will we wash the windows on the east side?" Predictably, another asked about costs. A few other perfunctory questions came next. The tone was one of condescension with the faint aroma of boredom. A gem had just been laid in their laps and they seemed to regard it as if it were a piece of gravel. The meeting adjourned with few signs of enthusiasm, interest, gratitude, or engagement. No one seemed to get the point of the project, or comprehend its potential for the institution or anything beyond. "Is this how they always respond?" Bill inquired as we packed up the building model and drawings. "No," I said, "they aren't usually that wild and crazy." In truth, however, most of those present did get it, but the unstated rules of engagement required that they show little or no enthusiasm, make only innocuous and thereby safe remarks, express no gratitude for fear of I'm not sure what, and take cues from superiors—a chain of angst beneath the thin veneer of polite managerial competence.

Close to institutional finances and priorities, fear takes on a harder edge, which is understandable. In this case, the design effort was shot through by the worry about cost overruns. The college had had a recent history of building projects exceeding projected budgets and having to be paid for from the endowment, an excellent way to irritate trustees and be shown the exit door. Accordingly, the vice president for operations had her marching order, which was to bring the Lewis Center in on budget, period. Her efforts notwithstanding, and to the dismay of the senior staff, the project budget grew steadily. As the person in the financial hot seat, my attitude was sadly in keeping with Admiral Farragut's philosophy of damn the torpedoes, full steam ahead. This was hardly a popular view among the more practical minds of the administration. The architects, unsurprisingly, were fully willing to spend all that was available and then some. It came to a head on August 26, 1996.

The day began with a 9:00 a.m. meeting with the vice president for development to review the progress on fund-raising, followed by a 10:00 a.m. presentation to his entire staff. He had been instructed to investigate my fund-raising plan. My plan, not to put too fine a point on it, was to find people with money and ask them for it. But for this occasion, I presented a slightly more formal version with actual names and details. He seemed assuaged, and even impressed. Yet I'd heard through the grapevine that the administration had serious misgivings about the entire project, and that the vice president for development was saying that he'd have to be called in to rescue the effort like the cavalry riding over the hill in a Western movie. If so, his introductory comments to his staff at the 10:00 a.m. meeting were disingenuously effusive, laced with words like "exciting," "leadership," and at the "forefront" of one thing or another. He could sell ice to the Eskimo, as they say, and at a considerable markup. His staff listened attentively and asked a few good questions. The meeting was upbeat and positive, giving no hint of what was to follow. At noon I was told, not asked, to attend a meeting at 3:00 p.m. in the administration building with the president and her senior staff.

The conference room of the main administration building is a gloomy and foreboding place. The room is elongated with east-facing windows looking out onto Tappan Square. From dark, paneled walls the somber visages of various past presidents peer out, some appearing to be undergoing a colonoscopy during their portrait sessions, but without the benefit of anesthesia. Even on a sunny day it is not a place where celebration, humor, and joy are likely to happen without a lot of planning. The purpose of this meeting was not revealed in advance. After perfunctory pleasantries, the vice president for development began by noting what he believed was a serious lack of success raising funds for the building. Contributions were stagnant, he said, but the estimated costs for the project were rising quickly. In fact, as he knew, the fund-raising was well ahead of our expenses and pretty much on target. He also knew that I'd identified major donors for the project with no prior connections to the college and that we finally had the schematic drawings to show. Since I had that very morning talked through the effort with him and he had assured me that things were fine, I was caught off guard. Encouraged by my obvious discomfort, he demanded to know the names of the people I was approaching for funds. I responded by saying, "You've already been told these names." He demanded that I repeat the list. It was alpha male showtime. Offended by his tone and what I took to be his intentions, I dug in and refused, saying that I was obliged to report only through the director of sponsored programs to the president. "I find it absolutely extraordinary," he nearly shouted, "that the vice president for development does not know who is being asked for funds." The others around the table sat in silence, enjoying my discomfort. Past presidents hanging about glared down at the scene. I repeated that he'd already been informed and pointed out that we had more than enough funds to complete the schematic design phase, at which time we would have something tangible to sell to the prospective donors that I had been cultivating over the past year. Playing to the president, he lamented the prospect that he would have to rescue the effort himself just, as he'd thought all along. I said that it was clearly understood that if I could not raise the money, the building would not be built. I asked for a private meeting with the president to discuss this further. We adjourned to her office to talk, but it was evident that her support for the project had been undermined behind other closed doors.

Two weeks later, on September 17, with a few extra minutes before a meeting with a prospective donor in Washington, DC, I called the architects on what I thought was a routine matter. Kevin Burke and I talked for a moment, before he said, "Oh, you must not have heard; the project was canceled yesterday." Indeed, I had not heard. On the flight home that night I thought what an idiot I'd been to work on this for fifteen months and have it all collapse now. By the terms of my agreement with the college, I had two years to raise the funds and develop the design for the building. I went to the president's office the next day and in the course of a tense discussion discovered that the project would be officially terminated at the next trustees meeting, purportedly for lack of funding. Arguments that we had the funds necessary to complete the design and good prospects ahead were of no avail. In the past year I'd developed good funding contacts in a half-dozen states and now it was time to test the level of their interest. Since I had been forbidden to approach the foundations that fund buildings, these were all individuals with substantial wealth who I'd met, or who knew of the project from friends, family, or business associates. In between classes and other academic duties, I spent the next two days making phone calls to schedule appointments with the best dozen prospects I had for the naming gift. Quickly, I had a half-dozen meetings between New York and California set for the following week. Each had been contacted multiple times and so knew of the project, and each had expressed interest in knowing more. On Monday morning, September 24, before setting out for the airport for the first visit in San Francisco, I received a call from Adam Lewis asking me to dinner with his father, Peter. The next morning I had confirmation of the naming gift. A week later a second large gift arrived from the prospective donor in San Francisco. Reassured of the financial viability of the project, the president put the building back on track. The schematic designs were completed in the following month and we knew we were under way. The events of those weeks were never mentioned again.

In the first year and a half of the project, the administration's reigning fear, I suppose, was that the fund-raising effort would come to nothing and the pressures to build an environmental center would force the college to pay for a building from its endowment. Later, as the design progressed, the administration feared that technologies such as Living Machines and photovoltaics, which were key design features, would prove to be embarrassing mistakes. Some, no doubt, feared that the entire project would look foolish in a world of cool, button-down management consultants coming to be dominated by biotechnology and the financial optimism of the dotcom bubble of the late 1990s.

It soon appeared that their worst fears would come to pass. In the final stages of construction, and before we had analyzed and tested building systems (a process known as commissioning), a faculty member with considerable zeal for contention set out to prove that the Lewis Center would never live up to the expectations that had been widely publicized as well as sometimes inflated by the architects, the press, and the project's enthusiasts. Immediately after occupancy, and while the building was still a construction site, he discovered that the building was using more energy than had been forecast in energy simulations run by Steven Winter Associates. For the next year and a half, he analyzed in minute detail every design mistake he could find (see chapter 5) as well as every statement ever made about the building, including erroneous quotes by newspaper reporters. He scrutinized discrepancies between early projections and the project's performance in elaborate detail to document what he alleged to be incompetence and fraud.

Had it been done constructively, some of his analysis could have been helpful for building commissioning and subsequent corrections. Alas, it was done with the religious zeal of a self-appointed Torquemada intent on exposing what he deemed to be fraud. Over the next eighteen months he relentlessly attacked what he thought were building mistakes in letters to editors, public presentations, and a few right-wing national publications. The effect was to distort the context and larger purposes of the project while generating a considerable fuss over problems that are typical of new buildings. The building, he asserted, could never live up to its billing as a "net energy exporter," even though the program had listed that as one goal among many, and only as "a goal to strive for" over the longer term. Since drawing and quartering had fallen out of fashion, he proposed that the college merely sue the architects and engineers, and do all in its power to publicly embarrass all of us involved in the project.

Aside from the emotional cost and wasted time, the ensuing spectacle raised four issues, the least important of which was actual building performance. As mentioned above, the Lewis Center did not immediately perform as designed and required commissioning and correction. This we already knew from the reams of data being gathered daily. But we also knew with equal certainty that most of the issues, once identified, were fairly easily fixed, and further, that this is a normal process for new buildings. The second issue had to do with the accuracy of statements various people made about energy performance prior to completion. Since the building design had evolved through at least four different models, each having somewhat different energy performance projections, one could sift through the public record and find a range of opinions about how the building would eventually perform. The third issue was more complicated. Since the extensive building data-gathering system called for in the building program was installed partly as a research project by a faculty member in the Environmental Studies Program and paid for by money raised by the program, the question arose as to who had the right to analyze and publish performance data on the Lewis Center. Nevertheless, the issue had nothing to do with censorship as he'd charged, because the building data was to be publicly displayed on building monitors and a Web site, as had been decided in 1996. The question was whether the data on the energy performance of a college building were open to anyone and everyone, or specifically to those who'd designed, installed, and funded the data-gathering system and thereby had a considerable professional stake in it. If regarded as wide open, how would that standard square with those for other privately gathered research data in, say, the physics or chemistry department? A fourth question was whether there were any proper bounds to the extent, scope, and duration of attacks on other faculty and members of the administration; in other words, at what point does such behavior constitute professional harassment? However one chose to answer these questions, it was apparent that the furor would not die quickly. Whatever the intention, one of the lasting effects was to reinforce institutional fears about undertaking any further innovation in design and construction.

Until the data-gathering system was in place, however, we could make no effective response and so battened down the hatches to ride out the storm. Once completed, the system gave us reliable raw data on building systems, though. Working with scientists from the National Renewable Energy Lab, among others, faculty member John Petersen converted the data into a progressively more sophisticated analysis of building behavior and a tool for improving performance. In the meantime the barrage of negative reports and distortion continued. Several of us requested administration help early on to establish a Web site on which to portray information about the building in its full context: goals, standards, history, projections, and actual performance. We were flatly turned down and told that we were on our own. Walking out of that meeting, a senior member of the faculty council described it as "the most insulting" moment of his long career at Oberlin. He later wrote to the administration, saying that "the meeting was chilly and stiff, even disrespectful." The college would often use the Lewis Center for publicity when it was convenient do so, but sometimes excused itself when controversy arose. The ownership of the building, or the vision behind it, had not yet been transferred.

The controversy over energy performance began to recede after the National Renewable Energy Laboratory scientists, who had been contracted to help analyze building performance, met with the president, the dean, and the senior staff on January 4, 2002. They had assembled and studied one year of peer-reviewed data on the Lewis Center, which showed that flaws and all, the center used about one-third of the source energy of a typical new classroom/office building. Subtracting the energy produced by the photovoltaic array, the net was less than a quarter of that for comparable new buildings.[2] There was an audible sigh of relief from the administra-

2. Letter from Paul Torcellini to Nancy Dye, January 9, 2002.

tors, but they showed no curiosity or interest about the larger issues raised in the commissioning process. Our chief critic became noticeably quieter thereafter, but did not disappear.

From the history of the early years of the Lewis Center, what can be learned relative to the way innovations occur in higher education and organizations generally? First, institutions of higher education have been generally slow to recognize the seriousness and scope of environmental issues, and to respond to them with alacrity and imagination. Innovations are most often confined to the unquestioned application of ever-more-advanced technology aimed to preserve things as they are but more efficiently. We boldly experiment with "cultural diversity" while filling institutions with people whose worldviews diverge hardly an iota. We presume that our underlying paradigms, frameworks, methods, and "preanalytic" assumptions are beyond reproach. In the meantime, our bills are underwritten by investments in the kind of economic growth that often jeopardizes the ecology, social resilience, and security of the world in which our students will live. This is to say that higher education is complicit in the problems, in the ironic way in which George Orwell (1977, 120) celebrated the enlightened of his times: "We all live by robbing Asiatic coolies, and those of us who are 'enlightened' all maintain that those coolies ought to be set free; but our standard of living, and hence our 'enlightenment,' demands that the robbery shall continue." Thomas Berry puts it this way (1999, 73):

The university prepares students for their role in extending human dominion over the natural world, not for intimate presence to the natural world. Use of this power in a deleterious manner has devastated the planet. . . . [S]o awesome is the devastation we are bringing about that we can only conclude that we are caught in a severe cultural disorientation, a disorientation that is sustained intellectually by the university, economically by the corporation, legally by the Constitution, [and] spiritually by religious institutions.

Second, the specific institutional culture of Oberlin evolved while forging a distinguished human rights record on issues of race, gender, ethnicity, and sexual orientation. In its curriculum, faculty, and facilities, Oberlin is one of the truly great U.S. liberal arts colleges. As an institution, though, it had been slow to recognize the relation between environmental destruction and its core mission and values. Moreover it was not much given to entrepreneurial ventures of the sort described here. Neither shortcoming is exceptional among institutions of higher education, however. It is fair to say that for most of the trustees, senior staff, and faculty, environmental problems were just another item on a long list, not yet a lens through which to see other problems or a linchpin that connects them to any larger biophysical or moral framework. In truth, few had thought much about environmental problems or what they meant for the operations and management of the college.

Third, while the project proceeded with the blessing of the president, the concept of a high-performance building did not have visible "buy in" or enthusiasm from others on the senior staff. The vice president for operations at the time interpreted her role as one of keeping costs down, but otherwise showed little passion for any larger, green vision. The dean, who had once been vaguely hostile to the project and the Environmental Studies Program, remained scrupulously neutral. Other college committees, including those charged with construction and planning, were seldom heard from. But the facilities manager was an early and energetic supporter until he departed in 1997. His replacements initially had neither the expertise nor much interest in ecological design, nor the rationale for it.

Because the project had originated from the Environmental Studies Committee, not through the normal institutional channels or with the usual college imprimatur, we were caught in a paradox. Had we worked through the usual process by which the college makes decisions about capital projects, we would have been in direct competition with other and more powerful interests, and thus would have been rejected outright. We were a small program at the margin of the institution with one full-time faculty member in an institution that had shown only intermittent interest in matters pertaining to global change or environmental deterioration. In this particular instance, the project could not have happened in any other way: outside the bureaucracy and without taking funds from any other priority. That is not to say, however, that the Lone Ranger approach is the right one. It has a lot going against it, not the least because it does not foster much institution-wide learning.

Fourth, the decision-making structure did not allow for ample communication in and feedback from the wider college community, a dreary way to say that it did not much change who had lunch with whom. Early on, the college rejected the idea of forming a wider decision-making group around the project. On December 18, 1995, for example, I had requested the creation of a larger structure aimed to bridge the chasm between the design team, college administration, and faculty. The idea was dismissed, and the gap between the designers, the program, and the college community was never effectively closed. As a result, we did not learn all that we might have in what is otherwise a learning community. The ideas and excitement about, and the commitment to, the project did not permeate much beyond the design team and the faculty and the students directly involved. The effect was to corrode relationships between the design group and the administration. To my knowledge, no one on the senior staff ever expressed gratitude to the architects or college staff who put in long hours on the project. The operational culture of the college made relationships with outside contractors antagonistic, not cooperative. Bills were often paid late. Relationships were strictly business, seldom lubricated by camaraderie, humor, or personal engagement. With any member of the senior staff present at design meetings, levity was rare, yet morale in the design group was high nonetheless. After the building was completed, the college did not undertake a debriefing to analyze what worked, what did not, and what might be learned. Two years after occupancy, I brought the members of the design group and program committee together to do that at our own expense.

The overall institutional response tended to marginalize both the substance and educational implications of ecological design. The most visible evidence was that the new science building constructed two years later incorporated few of the standards for green buildings, as discussed earlier. Its energy use, according to one of its designers, is twice what it should otherwise have been with better technology and with three- to five-year paybacks. The college thereby increased the building's long-term operating costs, and lost the opportunity to extend the logic of ecological design from the Lewis Center to a larger and more complex building. It also lost the chance to set a new benchmark for high-performance science facilities along with the possibility to explore curriculum at the intersection of science, ecological design, and the challenges that our students will encounter in the twenty-first century. That would have been a more demanding design challenge, but it would also have resulted in a more exciting building—and one far more attractive to many potential donors.

Colleges and universities have tended to become risk-averse organizations, yet we had embarked on a project that involved (or was perceived to involve) some risk. Colleges, like most industrial-age bureaucracies, are organized as separate fiefdoms. To create a building like the Lewis Center, however, required a high level of integration across divisions of curriculum, finance, operations, communications, admissions, and development. We set out to design and build with an eye toward the long term, but colleges and universities orient to shorter time horizons, particularly in matters of budget and finance. Colleges are hierarchically organized, but the energy for this project, as distinct from its authorization, did not come from the top. From John Henry Newman to the present, liberal arts colleges have de-emphasized the practical arts, yet the design and construction of the Lewis Center required the marriage of theory and intellect with practical application. We designed the center to evolve over a period of years, but that requires organizational learning as well. Buildings as evolving, not fixed, assets require a longer view, patience, growing technological skill, and an ecological vision of the built environment.

In sum, the technical challenge of designing a high-performance building, complicated as that can be, proved to be much easier to solve than the human and institutional aspects of the design process. When we stumbled, or nearly so, the cause almost always had something to do with human dynamics, and most often the failure or refusal to communicate across the divisions of outlook, assumptions, rank, and officialdom. This was true between the college and the architects as well as within the design group over practical and philosophical differences.

# 9

## Planning to Learn: A Digression on Institutional Learning

Herein lies the core learning dilemma that confronts organizations: we learn best from experience but we never directly experience the consequences of many of our most important decisions.

The most accurate word in Western culture to describe what happens in a learning organization is . . ."metanoia" and it means a shift of mind.

—Peter Senge

The experience of the Lewis Center highlights one of the more remarkable, but consistently less agreeable features of humankind.[1] When we join together in organizations of all sizes and purposes, our collective intelligence is less than the sum total of that of the people involved. While we often speak of smart people, we seldom refer to smart organizations, and for good reason. Mostly, they aren't. Organizations of all kinds have great difficulty in learning so that the collective behavior of government agencies, private corporations, and private organizations often falls short of any reasonable standard of intelligence. Smart people working in dumb organizations create shoddy products, self-perpetuating conflicts, ecological ruin, boredom, inequality, idiotic doctrines, and sometimes persecution based on gender, racial, ethnic, religious, or national stereotypes. We do things in organizations that no one would do, or admit to doing, as individuals. Is it possible to create smart organizations that learn?[2] If so, what might this mean?

1. This chapter is adapted from David Orr, "Planning to Learn," *Planning* 31, no. 3 (March–May, 2003), 77–81.

2. Peter Senge (1994) defines a learning organization as one "that is continually expanding its capacity to create its future" by "developing people who learn to see

Intelligent people, for starters, learn to size up situations and contexts. Smart organizations ought to have the same capacity, which is to say the ability to foresee and act responsibly in light of the larger historical, ecological, and moral landscape. Mostly, organizations situate themselves relative to the competition for market share, political power, or influence. This is inconvenient, however, if the entire herd is headed over a cliff. People in organizations capable of learning ask whether the game is worth playing at all. For the captains of the global economy, for example, it would be worth asking, in the words of an IBM advertisement, whether the world needs more clever ways "to sell more stuff to more people more of the time." Some of this stuff is lethal in parts per million; some of it contributes to climate change and biotic impoverishment; and some of it causes obesity and human incapacitation of various kinds. Most of it is produced, packaged, and consumed wastefully. But I doubt that individuals in any legally chartered corporation really intend to kill their customers or the planet, even if by inches. Rather, I think they seldom stop to ponder such things. One might hope that learning for organizations would include the openness and opportunity to rethink what they do as well as how they do it relative to a larger standard of human and ecological health. And there are a growing number of examples of learning at this scale.[3] Real organizational learning is not just a matter of doing more efficiently and happily what should not be done in the first place. It is a deeper and more honest process of seeing patterns that connect what people in organizations do to and for people along with their prospects elsewhere.

According to Peter Senge (1994; Senge et al. 1999), organizations that learn relative to the rapidly changing world in which they exist have three characteristics. First, they are oriented to what people "truly care about," and not on daily crises. In learning organizations, people build shared visions that require skills of "unearthing shared 'pictures of the future' that foster genuine commitment and enrollment rather than compliance" (Senge et al. 1994, 9). Second, conversations in learning organizations promote "charity, enthusiasm, communication, and commitment" (Senge 1994, 227). People do not just "talk at one another, engaged in never-

---

as systems thinkers see, who develop their own personal mastery and who learn how to surface and restructure mental models, collaboratively."

3. One notable instance is that of Interface, Inc.; see Anderson (1998).

ending win-lose struggles." The process of genuine learning, in other words, changes the substance of what we say to each other. Third, organizational learning requires the capacity to understand complex systems and to see how structures of which we are unaware hold us prisoner" (Senge 1994, 94).

Can organizations that purport to advance learning themselves learn to recalibrate their mission and operations, not just to increase their portion of a market share, but more important, in relation to the larger facts of global ecological change? The obstacles to doing so are significant. Remove computers, and the amount of real innovation in education over the past half century has been unremarkable or worse (Oppenheimer 2003). Higher education has tended to fashion itself into an industry beholden to other industries (Press and Washburn 2000; Washburn 2005), and is thereby complicit in larger societal and global problems. In Thomas Berry's words (1999, 4), we have fostered "a mode of consciousness that has established a radical discontinuity between the human and nonhuman." And we take great pride in equipping our students to do well-paying work in an unsustainable economy. Many administrators and faculty acknowledge larger global environmental trends, but they have yet to adjust institutional behavior or curriculum accordingly.

The fear of failure or appearing unprofessional shackles imagination and creativity in the very places where such qualities are said to be highly valued. On a continuum between suffocating orderliness and utter chaos, most institutions tend toward the former. They often have little vision beyond that of being just like some other notable place that is itself trying hard to be like some still-more-notable place. At the very top, one finds as likely as not the proud assurance that comes with bulletproof complacency. But fitting the organization to larger ecological realities requires a willingness to run risks, work across boundaries, and account for full costs. Colleges and universities are, in the main, risk averse, segregated into departments and administrative divisions, and tend to count costs narrowly. They are often strongly hierarchical and highly conservative organizations. Innovation is mostly confined to tinkering at the margins. Decisions having to do with the design of buildings, landscapes, and energy and materials flows are the jealously guarded prerogatives of the management. Whole systems design, on the contrary, works best when participation is encouraged, initiative is rewarded, innovation is valued, new ideas are appreciated, the tolerance for risks taken for the right reasons is high, and administrators are competent. It is far easier, too, when social interaction is regularly lubricated by all of the little things that reduce interpersonal friction: respect, informality, camaraderie, and gratitude. Finally, ecological design—and lots of other things as well—works best when people share a common vision and understand what they are attempting to do in a larger ecological, moral, and historical context. This necessitates more than the usual narrow expertise required of faculty and administrators, though. The culture must be one in which people read widely, think imaginatively, confront core assumptions, and recognize concerns larger than those of institutional survival. In short, ecological design works best where people have fun working together and are energized by a powerful vision.

Change in organizations is difficult in large part because it threatens entrenched interests and established ways of doing things. The typical institutional response to innovation, like that of an organism to an invading agent, is to isolate and encyst it to keep it from infecting the entire body—a form of ostracism. The effort to calibrate organizational outputs with biophysical realities requires the courage and openness to question institutional purposes relative to larger problems as well as the directions of society. For example, there is not much sense in trying to eliminate cancer-causing or endocrine-disrupting chemicals from building materials while teaching students the kind of promiscuous chemistry that created ozone holes and toxic waste dumps, and put some several hundred organochlorine chemicals in their bodies. There is little logic in offering classes on the geophysics of climatic change, or ethics for that matter, in inefficient buildings that contribute to those problems. It makes no sense to talk about paying the full costs of what we do while the economics department is mired deep in the bowels of a paradigm that celebrates growth, greed, and consumption on a finite planet. The fact is that a fair portion of the curriculum offered in institutions of higher education does not fit a planet with a biosphere, nor will it equip its graduates very well to navigate through the bottleneck years ahead. Some of what they will learn, indeed, is inimical to their future. And it makes no sense to offer four years of the higher learning while operating institutions in ways that undermine the world graduates will inherit. Designing for whole systems requires the willingness to confront the hypocrisies, discrepancies, and destructiveness of the modern world, and change established routines and assumptions accordingly. Colleges and universities ought themselves to be models of ecological design. But the barriers are many.

In part, ecological design is the effort to harmonize the near term with the long term. But most college accounting procedures focus on the short term and the initial costs of projects. Design requires utilizing institutional assets in more creative ways and setting more astute systemwide priorities. Yet for many who pride themselves on being realists, fiduciary responsibility is applicable to a few years at most and costs imposed elsewhere are ignored. Operational decisions that directly or indirectly cause the liquidation of natural capital are not included in the accounting. An ecologically sound and morally robust perspective, on the other hand, requires that such costs be accounted for. It will make little sense to our grandchildren that we balanced our institutional books while we helped to unbalance the carbon or nitrogen cycle, or invested in companies that widely dispersed persistent organic pollutants. The challenge before colleges and universities is to comprehend and master the implications of the fact that the entire web of life is in jeopardy, and as a result, all that we hold dear is in danger. In turn, that challenge, in turn, poses a series of other one that go to the core of higher education.

### Redefining Knowledge

Becoming a learning organization requires a reassessment of our chief stock-in-trade by relating the effects of ideas, research, and knowledge relative to our long-term ecological prospects. We assume that our products— course units, books, articles, and so forth—are indisputably good and that more is better. Alas, reality is more complicated. When Thomas Midgley Jr. invented chlorofluorocarbons, knowledge increased, but so did ignorance because no one knew their effects on the chemistry of the stratosphere. In other words, it is possible to increase knowledge in ways that also expand the interface with the unknown, which is to say ignorance. Knowledge is and has always been a source of liberation *and* danger. Further, the Enlightenment-era faith in the transparency of cause and effect is mocked by a world of great and indecipherable human-generated complexity. There is probably no way, for example, to reliably ascertain cause and effect in a world in which a hundred thousand chemicals used in industry mix randomly in the biosphere and our own bodies. The sheer volume and velocity of human-generated change overlaying that of "natural" processes defies comprehension, to say nothing about our ability to control it all. Much of the reductionist knowledge implicit, perhaps complicit, in this process was generated in colleges and universities without thought for the consequences, let alone alternatives better suited to the longevity of the human enterprise. Were colleges and universities to become learning organizations they would first have to rethink the substance and process of learning relative to larger standards of human and ecological health. Is it possible that some kinds of knowledge, taught without reference to the larger context, can have the effect of undermining human health and ecological resilience? I do not know whether there is trivial or even dangerous knowledge, but I do believe that there are trivial, misleading, and perhaps dangerous ways to research and teach virtually anything by treating it in isolation from its larger ecological, cultural, and moral context. Colleges and universities in a learning mode would ask not whether our students have high SAT and GRE scores but whether they are safe for a planet with a biosphere. If not, what knowledge and personal experience do they need in order to help make a world that is ecologically sustainable, compassionate, and prosperous over the long haul?

One answer is that they need to know how to solve problems that cross the conventional lines of disciplines. In Senge's words (2000, 276), they need "experience in producing more effective action," not more disconnected facts. This view changes the role of the teacher and the goal of education. To promote learning, as distinct from teaching, Senge argues that the professor "needs to become a designer of learning processes in which she or he participates along with the student . . . relinquishing the presumption of being the expert" (284). From institutions organized around "an overintellectualized view of knowledge divorce[d] from effective action and real-life contexts" (289), the academy becomes a broker between theory and practice, thinking and acting.

**Institutional Dynamics**

The transition to becoming a learning organization changes the dynamics within the institution. All organizations exist in a continual tension between the maintenance of order, at one end, and creativity, at the other.

The tension is unavoidable, but managed properly, it is a sign of health. Learning organizations of all kinds, however, encourage innovation and risk taking on a scale small enough to be manageable yet large enough to instruct about possibilities. Good commercial organizations have their "Skunk Works" or test beds where new ideas are created and tried out (Everett Rogers 1995, 139). On the other hand, colleges and universities, where creativity is said to be much admired, are often hostile to innovation beyond the tinkering kind. This is often this is because formal authority and power are rigidly hierarchical, and as Senge puts it (2000, 294–295), serve as "a poor vehicle to cause imagination, commitment, passion, patience, and perseverance—the hallmarks of radical innovation that threaten the status quo." In order to become learning organizations, there must be the core honesty "to articulate the numerous ways and means that [the institution] uses to squash innovation and force conformity" (Birkeland 2002, 11). And the ways are many: aloofness, unanswered memos, lost correspondence, the arts of reprisal, damning with faint praise, excessive secrecy, the closed door, pomposity and self-importance, strategic delay, the lack of informal contact, and the power of superior resentment. I suspect that these, again, are mostly the manifestations of the fear of failure. But whatever the source, they chill the inclination to creativity, and impede learning and accurate feedback about the internal operations of the institution as well as its external impacts. Colleges and universities as learning organizations would celebrate and reward initiative and risk taking, and when mistakes occur, would practice what Senge (2000, 300) calls "real forgiveness" that includes "reconciliation, mending the relationships that may have been hurt by the mistake." Learning can occur within an organization only when human relations are elevated by forgiveness as well as the practice of gratitude, enthusiasm, and openness.

## Structure

Colleges and universities as learning organizations would amend their academic structure enough to overcome the kind of closure associated with highly impermeable discipline-centric departments. The big conversations about the human future necessarily occur across the lines of conventionally organized thought. But cross-disciplinary conversations are still rare because they are not much encouraged, and difficult because we now speak in a cacophony of arcane, specialized languages and too seldom in a common tongue. Scholars, teachers, and students must organize something akin to a jailbreak from the constraints of artificial structure, and obscure jargon to talk clearly and plainly about what really ails us individually and collectively. We have good examples of plain talk across disciplinary boundaries in journals such as *Ecological Economics* and *Conservation Biology* as well as fruitful collaboration such as that between Carl McDaniel, a biologist, and John Gowdy, an economist (McDaniel and Gowdy 1999). Learning organizations would find ways to bring together the academic equivalent of "flexible production teams" in business organizations that would cross academic divisions while focusing on solving real problems.

### Time and Discounting

Learning organizations are oriented to time differently. At the individual level, faculty and staff ought to spend the best hours of the day doing the most important things, which seldom include filling out reports, responding to an endless stream of e-mails, or shuffling paper. Learning organizations minimize trivia and maximize the opportunities for important things, including lateral thinking. Further, most organizations operate by the fiscal year and have short-term expectations about payback for investments as well as expenditures, thereby discounting the future. Learning organizations would extend the time horizon for financial accounting and investments relative to energy, water, materials, buildings, and land management. Organizational time is measured in, say, one to three years, but learning organizations stretch the horizon out to a decade or longer without losing sight of a more distant horizon measured as ecological time.

### Managing Conflicts

Learning requires an institutional environment in which conflicts are dealt with openly and fairly to encourage people to grow out of pettiness, vindictiveness, and the fear of failure. "Building relationships characterized by openness," Senge observes (2000, 284), "may be one of the most high-leverage actions to build organizations characterized by openness." In

Senge's view, an underlying openness is a spirit of agape, or "a commitment to serve one another and willingness to be vulnerable in the context of that service" (285). And the immunities afforded by tenure can on occasion be abused in remarkably destructive ways. The arbitrary exercise of power or the abuse of tenure can corrupt institutions like an infection in a body. There can be no real learning at the organizational level where personal growth and healthy human relations are thwarted. Learning organizations create dependable ways to air differences, resolve conflicts, and encourage people to grow to higher levels of maturity and fulfillment.

## Resource Flows and Campus Ecology

The operation of educational institutions in ways that undermine the future of the students we purport to educate cannot be justified. As learning organizations, colleges and universities would monitor their environmental impacts and amend their operational guidelines in order to eliminate pollution, carbon dioxide emissions, and toxic chemicals, and support the emergence of sustainable local economies. Construction and building renovation would conform to the highest standards possible. Other standards for the purchase of materials, food, and energy, as well as landscaping and investment are being tested by the Campus Ecology Program of the National Wildlife Federation. The aim is to develop rating systems similar to that of *U.S. News and World Report* to appraise the environmental performance of colleges and universities. The implementation of these standards will require changes in plant management and operations, including systems to provide prompt and accurate feedback about all environmental impacts relating to energy use, materials flows, water consumption, landscape management, and waste cycling. Reducing energy consumption and beginning the transition to solar energy, for example, requires metering energy use so that everyone on the campus has quick feedback on what they consume along with consistent incentives to conserve. Further, upgrading buildings to high-performance standards is rather like going from typewriters to notebook computers. One needs periodic maintenance; the other needs regular software upgrades and hardware changes. One stands alone; the other is networked to a global information system. In other words, the management of high-performance buildings requires a higher level of professional skill, and the capability to manage and upgrade complex systems in a technologically dynamic environment.

## Boundaries

All organizations set boundaries that define them as systems. Typically, colleges and universities have been inward-looking organizations consisting of students, faculty, administrators, trustees, staff, donors, and various professional organizations. What happens a quarter of an inch outside the campus has seldom been a matter of concern, but no organization can exist for long as an island in a sea of urban or rural poverty. Institutional learning means redefining organizational boundaries to include the local community and the world beyond. The recent growth of the service-learning movement on college campuses is evidence that boundaries are being extended, as is the concern for the economic and social health of surrounding neighborhoods. Further learning will extend the boundaries to include those affected in other places and times by institutional purchasing, investments, and operations.

## Catalysts

Who will drive the learning process? "It is easy," in Senge's words (2000, 293), "to look at the depth and breadth of these issues and conclude that only university presidents and boards have the power to bring about the types of changes needed." But, continues Senge, "this would be exactly the wrong conclusion." The limits to executive, top-down leadership are many, and not least is the separation of presidents from the day-to-day realities of the institutions. Imaginative and intellectually dynamic deans could play a catalytic role by drawing faculty together across departmental and divisional lines. Senge, however, believes that learning in academic organizations will be driven lower in the hierarchy by clusters of faculty and departmental chairs, and increasingly by students "who move about the system as a whole the most and with the most ease" (296). Ideally, learning would occur as a composite process involving the entire institution. But this requires that presidents and deans also help to remove impediments to learning that are often little more than habit, ego, and turf defense.

Learning organizations, in short, relate what they do with the way the world works as a physical system by applying the art and science of ecological design. In the post-fossil-fuel world, we will have to reshape how we provision ourselves with food, energy, materials, water, livelihood, health care, shelter, transportation, and community. This is what Thomas Berry (1999) calls the "Great Work" of our time. Events beginning with those of September 11, 2001, give added urgency to rethinking how to achieve resilience and security by design—for everyone. And colleges and universities can lead in this process by becoming visible and dynamic models of ecological design, transitioning from organizations that advance learning to ones capable themselves of learning.

More specifically, what might be learned about the process of planning and design in the creation of the Adam Joseph Lewis Center? I do not know what the administration or trustees learned, but close to the project eight lessons stand out:

## 1. Thoroughly Integrate the Design Process
In the making of the Lewis Center, the design team was not as well integrated as it should have been. An ambitious building program and visionary design were therefore not sufficiently calibrated with the engineering. Part of the difficulty lay in the fact that in the mid-1990s, the talent necessary to design a high-performance building was not available locally. As a result, we assembled a team that included a dozen or more people scattered throughout the United States, thereby making coordination difficult and costly. More important, the mechanical engineers did not entirely share the architects' design vision. The resulting lack of integration of engineering with the overall design goals proved to be the weakest part of the building design.

## 2. Maintain Creative "Flow"
After participating in one of the early design charettes, one faculty veteran described the event as the most exciting he could recall in his time at Oberlin. The energy of the first months diminished by the end of 1997,

however, largely because of the unnecessarily slow pace of decision making by the college. What should have taken a year or so to design was extended for thirty months, impairing the creative flow of the design process and the morale of those involved.

### 3. Develop a Larger Learning Process
This project originated on the periphery of institutional consciousness. No formal or informal feedback loops bridged this project with other building projects, or to institutional operations or trustees. The project had no strong advocate within the administration, which may explain why no effort was made to develop a shared vision, what Senge labels "common mental models" among the trustees, senior staff, facilities management, and faculty. The administration initiated no review of the project after its commissioning with all the participants to determine what worked well and what did not.[4] Thus, different and somewhat antagonistic views of the project and the design process existed among the college administration, faculty, and design group that worked on the building. It is fair to say that the Lewis Center did not at that time reflect a deeper institutional commitment to sustainability, energy efficiency, solar power, ecological restoration, and biological diversity, which were all central to both the building program and the Environmental Studies Program. On the contrary, the project has been regarded as an isolated experiment, not as the beginning of a larger change. Several years after commissioning the building, a member of the design team observed that "our story truly isn't their story." Perhaps in time this will change.

### 4. Account for the Life-Cycle Costs *and* Collateral Benefits of Buildings
The cost of a building, as described in chapter 7, is often confused with the initial price of the thing, leaving out the life-cycle and environmental costs. For example, building decisions often favor the low bid or the cheapest technology even though they commit the institution to higher costs in the long run. As a result, institutions often get cheap buildings that come in "on budget," but are expensive to operate and maintain, not to mention envi-

---

4. I organized a retrospective on the project with the design team on August 13–14, 2002.

ronmentally destructive. A full assessment would include the life-cycle costs of operation, maintenance, and its environmental impacts. Further, costs stand in relation to benefits. In this case, the collateral—and mostly unaccounted for—benefits to Oberlin College include a substantial amount of national publicity, increased student yield, increased donor interest in the college, and a facility that enlivens the curriculum in environmental studies and attracts a rising level of student interest. And the future stream of savings from efficiency is an asset that can be used to leverage smarter decisions in the near term—yet another derivative of doing the right things in a smart way.

### 5. Plan for and Celebrate Success

The difference between success and failure is often only the stubborn refusal to fail in the face of daunting odds—more a matter of will than of intellect. Success begins by envisioning success and planning for it. In a team setting, momentum toward a successful conclusion is built and maintained by competent professionalism along with a psychology of encouragement, appreciation, and generosity. And the difference between a good outcome and a great one is built into the personal dynamics that let a vision grow to its full stature or stop it short.

### 6. The Building Program Equals the Fund-raising Strategy

As a rule, about half of the money for college and university buildings must be borrowed. If this experience is a useful guide, the ideas embedded in the building program are as important as the need for the building itself. Lacking exciting ideas, it is hard to create enthusiasm about the project among potential donors, or anyone else for that matter. Buildings are means, not ends, but a means to what? The Lewis Center was conceived as an experiment in education relative to solar technology, ecological engineering, products of service, ecological landscaping, sustainable forestry, and the art and science of ecological design. We intended to better equip our students to solve twenty-first-century problems. This will require significant changes in how we think about buildings and their larger upstream and downstream effects over the long haul. This is both daunting and exciting, but if we intend to stay around awhile longer it is absolutely

**Table 9.1**
Design Processes Compared

|  | Conventional | Ecological |
|---|---|---|
| Scope: | Limited | Broad |
| Process: (front-loaded) | Serial | Integrated |
| Focus: | Components | System |
| Risk: | Averse | Acceptable |
| Incentives: (efficiency) | Fragmented | Performance |
| Costs: | Short term | Life cycle |

necessary to rethink the "built" environment as a keystone of a sustainable world. Good ideas, in other words, tend to attract money.

### 7. Watch Your Flanks and Rear, and Protect the Vision

All of us working on the project, the president included, were variously applauded, criticized, and sometimes held up to ridicule. For those intending to take a path less traveled, it is some comfort to remember that ideas often proceed from opposition to ridicule and finally to acceptance as merely obvious.

Misinterpretations of the project were also common. An e-mail sent by an earnest young Japanese woman, for example, excitedly asked for a tour of the "Oberlin poop building," the one, as she put it with great admiration, "powered by human feces." For its part, the press sometimes got the story wrong. The *Chronicle of Higher Education* (June 21, 2002), for example, described the building as reflecting the larger financial problems of the college in the bear market of 2002 and as failing to meet expectations about energy use and wastewater systems. Wrong on all three counts, the reporter later admitted on the phone that he'd added this to lend some controversy to an otherwise dull article.

### 8. Commonsense Rules of Good Management and Human Relations

- Invite dialogue and encourage novelty
- Encourage dissenting views, and assign flatterers to do manual labor

- Admit mistakes
- Get out of your office and meet people where they work
- Read widely
- Make energy and materials efficiency a visible priority
- Reward effort, initiative, and risk taking
- Express gratitude, keeping in mind that words like "thank you" count for a great deal
- Encourage an atmosphere of celebration
- Lead, let others manage, and know the difference

# 10

# The Political Economy of Buildings in the Postpetroleum World

Even as the economy scales new technological heights, the energy that powers it is condemning it to death. . . . [I]n the final analysis, it is a choice between sunlight and ash.

—Hermann Scheer

Show me the typical derelict highway leading into any U.S. city replete with the usual array of fast-food joints, and I will show you a larger system that necessarily includes depleted soils, poorly paid migrant laborers, soil erosion, feed lots, factory farms, industrial slaughterhouses, offshore dead zones, groundwater depletion, chemical contamination, and an amazingly rotund and sickly population becoming even more so. Show me a shopping mall and its surrounding asphalt parking lots, and I will show you a larger system that includes sweatshops, poverty, human depravity, pollution, ruined landscapes, oil wars, foul air, and a degree of commercially driven human silliness that mocks the belief that we are anything truly like an intelligent species. It is called political economy, which is the acknowledgment that everything is eventually connected to political realities, the conduct of the public business, and ultimately a much larger economy that goes by various names—nature, ecology, or the biosphere. But by any name, the reality is the same; we humans are one with the birds, fish, bugs, animals, microbes, trees, rocks, and seas—all passengers, as Adlai Stevenson once put it, "on a little space ship, dependent on its vulnerable reserves of air and soil." And our tendency to separate, isolate, and fragment always runs afoul of the fact that the pieces are "hitched to everything else in the universe."

Political scientist Harold Lasswell once warned of the consequences of an "architecture of opulence—of sleek and commanding office buildings, apartment houses, and other structures," including the possibilities for "long-run political destabilization." Such architecture, as Anne Whiston Spirn notes (1998, 258), "operates on a worldwide scale to reassure the rich, the strong, and the self-confident and to provoke and radicalize the poor and the weak." After the destruction of the World Trade Center on September 11, 2001, we know more acutely how the disaffected can be radicalized and how dangerous a force that can be. But the fact is that every building is part of a larger fabric of resource extraction, energy use, environmental impacts, and human relationships, which is to say, a political economy. Michael M'Gonigle defines political economy as "the study of society's way of organizing both economic production and political processes that affect it and are affected by it . . . the 'system dynamics' of a society's processes of economic and political self-maintenance" (quoted in Orr 2002, 205). Political economy has to do with the way society provisions itself with food, energy, materials, and water from farms, wells, mines, forests, and the hydrosphere and returns its wastes back to nature; society's energy sources and related technologies; the corresponding distribution of wealth, power, public policy, and societal risk; and how these, in turn, affect governance and longer-term prospects. In other words, buildings, societal infrastructure, highways, materials, and energy use are all manifestations of economic and political decisions along with their consequences for global ecology.

Students of political economy from Karl Marx to the present, however, have mostly avoided any discussion of the ecological consequences of human productivity (Scheer 2002, 4). But the stability of regional and global ecologies is being undermined by the overwhelming domination of industrial systems and the supposed necessity of controlling the resources required for perpetual growth. This is an old story. For example, historian Karl Wittfogel (1957) once traced the origins of what he termed "Oriental despotism" to the manner in which ancient Middle Eastern kingships organized irrigation systems, requiring large amounts of labor, and hence taxation, military power, and centralized political authority. We could now add to that story the longer-term effects of the destruction of soils and deforestation to an equation that also includes overpopulation, famine, the loss of genetic diversity, political instability, and resource wars requiring even further centralization of authority to the point of collapse.

While the details differ, every civilization has a political-economic strategy for capturing sunlight in one form or another and the resources necessary to its survival. Richard Heinberg identifies five strategies used by expanding societies (2003, 19–29):

1. Takeover by moving into new habitats
2. Improve technology and the efficiency of energy capture
3. Specialize to improve efficiencies
4. Enlarge scope by trade and globalization
5. Draw down stocks of nonrenewable energy sources

Our political economy, unsurprisingly, is organized around the capture and combustion of fossil fuels, and principally around strategies 4 and 5: globalization and drawdown. Its physical manifestation includes oil wells, coal mines, pipelines, supertankers, railroads, refineries, distribution networks, and gasoline stations as well as the economic, political, legal, and military apparatus necessary to profit, persuade, perjure, and protect. It is also manifest in the mind-set of mobility, consumption, sprawl, and a growing psychological distance from the places in which we live. As a strategy, it will work only in the short run, and is fraught with increasing risk and a growing potential for international conflict and eventual collapse. The reason is not hard to find: rising demand for a finite resource. Our inability to move beyond petroleum is partly explicable by the economic power and political muscle of corporations engaged in selling fossil fuels—a two trillion dollars per year worldwide business underwritten by millions of dollars contributed to political campaigns and billions more in public subsidies. It is a political economy organized around the centralization of corporate power under the curious notion, dating from 1886, that corporations ought to be protected as "persons" by the U.S. Bill of Rights (Hartmann 2002, 95–135). Whatever was intended, the political economy of fossil fuels has proven to be a prescription for great political, economic, and ecological mischief. But many believe that the end is in sight.

In 1957, petroleum geologist M. King Hubbert famously predicted that the peak of U.S. oil extraction in the lower forty-eight would occur in the year 1970. Applying the same methodology to world oil extraction, his former colleague Colin Campbell, among others, predicts a peak sometime within a few years to a decade (Campbell 1988). Others, including geologists at the U.S. Geological Survey, are somewhat more optimistic, even in the face of evidence that oil reserves have been significantly overestimated by major suppliers such as Shell Oil, and that Saudi oil fields are showing signs of depressurizing, indicative of declining extraction (Klare 2004b). But the difference between optimists and pessimists regarding the future of oil extraction is a matter of only one to three decades, not much time relative to that necessary to make a graceful transition to a new energy base. Nor is there significant difference about the effects of rising demand for oil from developing countries such as China. The upshot is that as we approach the peak of world oil extraction, rising demand will lead to increasing prices and serious global conflict. At the same time, the mounting scientific evidence about the imminence and possible severity of climate change ahead gives every reason to move as rapidly as possible from the combustion of fossil fuels, beginning with coal and oil, toward both advanced energy efficiency and renewable sources of supply.

With hindsight, the fossil-fuel era will appear as a spike lasting about a century. The story of how it will end is presently being written. Forecasts of economic growth say that the global economy will expand severalfold in the century ahead, and with it the physical infrastructure of buildings, houses, factories, and roads. But the fossil energy required for the extraction, processing, manufacture, and transport of materials necessary for construction, and that required to maintain it, will be increasingly expensive. And the possibility of severe disruption due to rapid climate change is no longer the distant science-fictional scenario it was once thought to be. Atmospheric scientist David Keeling recently speculated that the first hard evidence of runaway climate change may now exist in the recent, inexplicable increase of atmospheric carbon dioxide per year not attributable to the combustion of fossil fuels. Even without that dire possibility, we are approaching the end of a brief era in which we could burn cheaply priced fossil fuels while ignoring the ecological consequences.

Subsequent generations, if able to reflect amid the emergencies bequeathed to them, will find our bovine obtuseness on issues of energy and climate destabilization curious, perhaps warranting the moral censure rather like that we attach to slave owners. Much of the public discourse about the terrorist attacks on the World Trade Center failed to connect the motive behind that event with the fact that our automotive energy efficiency is no better than it was in 1980, making our involvement in the politics of an unstable region a matter of necessity, not choice. During the presidential campaigns of 2000 and 2004, hardly a word was spoken about issues of energy, climate change, or environmental quality, which will all compound and eventually overwhelm every other issue now on the public agenda. But we, the people and our political representatives, fell short of our full duties as citizens to engage the large concerns of the time with alacrity, intelligence, and conviction, victims, perhaps, of what Erik Davis has called a "consensus trance" (quoted in Kunstler 2005, 26).

The way forward is clear, however. If we wish to avoid the worst, we must now aim by every means possible to phase out reliance on fossil energy by adopting better technology to exploit the considerable opportunities for energy efficiency, by phasing in renewable sources of energy, and by redesigning a postpetroleum society that meets human needs with elegant design, not brute force. It would be overly pessimistic to think that we're not up to it, on the one hand, and foolish to believe that the transition will be easy, on the other. Humans do seem to have a knack for getting it right, as Winston Churchill once noted, but only after exhausting all other possibilities. The question in our time is who will lead—before we have exhausted all good choices. Not putting too fine a point on it, the political leaders of the United States have been cowards on the big issues of our day that are directly or indirectly related to our use of coal and oil along with their effects on climate and health. In that vacuum, it is time for others with greater courage and foresight to lead, and none have more reason or obligation to act than those obliged to educate and equip the young for life without cheap oil but with a lot more intelligence.

The world of the twenty-first century will require large changes in the way we think about the energy and material requirements of buildings. The leader in establishing environmental standards for buildings has been the U.S. Green Building Council (<www.usgbc.org>), which developed the benchmark standards for the design and construction of high-performance buildings. The degree of "greenness" is rated platinum (highest), gold, silver (heavy metals!), and certified (lowest) depending on the number of points accorded by specific criteria. But the architecture of buildings is a small part of a much larger problem that has to do with the mind-set and ecological competence engendered by the built environment. Accordingly, the members of the design group hoped that the Lewis Center might make a small yet compelling statement about the possibilities for a different political economy, situated at the crossroads of education and architecture. In the waning years of the fossil-fuel era, educators have no more urgent task than to equip young people with the skills and aptitudes they will need in order to meet the challenges of the transition to a political-economic system that uses current sunshine. Daunting at the global level, that vision is far more comprehensible and manageable on the scale of a building, community, and college. But where do we begin?

First, the design process is an opportunity to teach leadership and the skills of imaginative problem-solving on a local scale. The age of fossil fuels, beginning with the giant trusts of the late nineteenth century, fostered highly centralized politics dominated by corporate behemoths. One result was to make people more passive, dependent, subservient, and incompetent. The solar era ahead will require us to be smarter about energy use and more competent, learning to provide a substantial fraction of our energy by improved efficiency, local ingenuity, distributed technologies, better design, and cooperation. The process of engaging students in the design of the built environment and infrastructure is one way we can help them acquire the skills of leadership, creativity, and communication they will need in the years ahead. In that effort, we, their teachers, must first be engaged in the shaping of our own buildings and campuses, and with the effort to fit them to the local ecology. The lesson of exclusion is that we are not permitted to participate in the creation of the world in which we live. Outside the campus, roads, suburbs, malls, power plants, and office towers come into existence with little or no public involvement. At either scale, we learn to be passive and disengaged in the making of the built environment and in its effects on the larger environment. Driving home on a traffic-choked freeway past endless miles of necrotic urban development, we may on occasion reflect about the curious disconnectedness of our lives and our political impotence. We've been well taught not to connect what we see all about us with the quality of our lives, or to become aware of the relationships between our health and that of the land slowly dying all around us.

We aimed to make the design of the Lewis Center as inclusive as possible and seize the opportunity to learn together. My students live in a world that is coming undone. We aspired to see how things might be put back together in the microcosm of a 13,700-square-foot building. The thirteen design charettes helped participants see larger patterns as well as the connections between the building and the health of the larger world beyond, and to participate in the making of a better world that incorporated our best values.

Second, research and education in the petrochemical era were based on the faith that we had solved the energy problem once and for all, or would soon do so. The years ahead will require a different agenda directed to meeting the basic challenges of shelter, food, health care, community design, security, environmental quality, and economic renewal without benefit of cheap fossil energy. Colleges and universities have an opportunity to lead in this transition, beginning with the design and construction of academic buildings. By doing so, the campus becomes the focus of study along with the related techniques of analysis, ecological competence, and technological skill adapted to a specific place. Each building is a unique ecosystem within the larger ecosystems of landscape and region with particular soils, landforms, hydrology, and energy flows. Buildings take in energy, materials, and water, and release heat, waste, and pollution. In a fossil-fuel-powered world every effort has been made to make such things invisible, hiding furnaces and hot water heaters in basements, and wires and pipes behind walls. Similarly, the infrastructure that connected buildings to power plants, sewage treatment facilities, wells, mines, and forests has been mostly out of sight, and hence out of mind. Most of us in the fossil-fuel age are thus unaware of the underlying political and ecological realities of our lives. Ecologically designed buildings and institutions afford a chance to make such relationships explicit, thereby becoming part of the educational process and research agenda organized around the study of local resource flows, energy use, and environmental opportunities.

Third, we will face mounting problems with water quality and quantity in the years ahead, in which the hydrologic cycle will be more vigorous and unpredictable due to climate destabilization. But water and wastewater are still out of sight and mind, again because they are out of sight in pipes concealed in walls and buried in the ground. In the post-fossil-fuel world, we will need a generation that understands how to purify water using the science of ecological engineering, how to recharge groundwater, and how to restore rivers and streams. We aimed, accordingly, to make water retention, efficient use, and purification central in the Lewis Center as a means to promote water intelligence and create a generation of what John Todd calls "water stewards." Wastewater is treated on-site in the Living Machine. Research focused on the management and performance of the Living Machine has proven to be one of the features most popular with the students. Outside the building, water is a central feature of the landscape. Storm water is retained in an underground tank, and used to recharge the wetland and pond on the east side of the building. The pond is a major attraction for passersby. In my design class of 2004, the students were charged with the task of honoring the life and thought of John Lyle by highlighting those design aspects of central importance in his work, including water, local materials, sunlight, and conversation. The result, as discussed earlier, was a small amphitheater designed in the shape of the Fibonacci curve with a flow form as a central feature. A small stream of water will course through curving flow forms celebrating water purification and oxygenation while providing white sound in the background. The power will be provided by a small photovoltaic array operating only when the building is exporting power to the grid.

The largest challenge ahead for the rising generation is that of removing five billion tons of carbon from our energy budget by making the transition from fossil energy to efficiency and sunlight. Stated in those terms, the task is overwhelming. We aimed, however, to reduce the problem to the manageable and comprehensible scale of a single building powered as much as possible by sunlight. In its sixth year, powered by two photovoltaic arrays, the Lewis Center generated more power than it required over the course of a year, exporting the surplus back to the grid. A charging station in the adjacent parking lot powers electric vehicles by sunlight. The idea has taken hold beyond the Lewis Center. In 2004, the college agreed to purchase green power from the municipal utility that provides 60 percent of its electricity. And the trustees adopted an environmental policy for the campus that had been painstakingly drafted over two years by a committee of faculty, administrators, and students, and includes the idea that Oberlin ought to become "carbon neutral" (see appendix).

Fifth, a typical building has thousands of materials imported from all over the world. For the most part these are selected by price, performance, and aesthetics, not environmental cost, embodied energy, or life-cycle performance. The U.S. Green Building Council and small organizations such as BuildingGreen, Inc., in Brattleboro, Vermont, have improved the information available about the true costs of materials. The longer-term goal is to make buildings part of a smarter political economy in which the chain of custody from mine, well, forest, and manufacturer is tracked, judged, and authenticated by rigorous and impartially applied environmental standards. The Certified Forest Products Council, for example, set criteria for certified wood that requires sustainable forest management practices. ISO 14000 (International Organization for Standardization) includes similar measures for industry and business that permit buyers to know the environmental costs of materials and their life-cycle impacts.

The most commonly cited example, as discussed earlier, of the latter is that of Interface, Inc., a maker of carpet tiles that are leased to customers and returned eventually to be remade into new product when worn-out. Ray Anderson, the CEO and founder of Interface, is creating a new materials economy, one that creates no waste and is powered by solar energy (<www.interfacesustainability.com>). The company has eliminated 54 percent of its carbon emissions in the past decade while increasing sales. For the present generation of students, this represents career opportunities to build profitable companies based on closed materials cycles that result in no waste and no carbon emissions. For a new generation of entrepreneurs, it represents both challenges and opportunities to create a political economy organized around the proposition that the logic of capitalism ought also to apply to "human" capital as well as the "natural capital" of soils, forests, water, and biological diversity.

Sixth, landscapes are also part of the fossil-fueled political economy. In the United States, 27.6 million acres are maintained as lawn requires as much herbicides, insecticides, and fungicides—than is used in all of Indian farming (Bormann, Balmori, and Geballe 2001, 51). Similarly the U.S. food system requires, by one estimate, sixteen calories to produce one calorie of grain and seventy calories for one calorie of meat (Kunstler 2005, 241). On average, food is transported nearly fifteen hundred miles from where it is grown or produced to where it is eaten. Consumers in north-central Ohio, for example, spend more than six billion dollars on food each year, but only about two hundred million dollars of that is grown within the region.

Our intention was to spark the ecological imagination of a generation who will have to rediscover how to feed themselves to a much greater extent by local gardens and farms. In order to equip the students for a radically different food system, we asked them to help design and manage the landscape around the Lewis Center, which includes a restored wetland, a pond, an orchard, and raised-bed gardens. A mile and a half away, a local community supported farm and ecological restoration project is located on seventy acres leased from the college. The project, begun by a former student who worked on the Lewis Center, is the start of a local foods system that includes a farmers' market and a network of local producers growing mostly organic fruits, vegetables, and small grains.

Seventh, the industrial order imposes costs that are dispersed over the larger society, or are passed on to the disenfranchised or to future generations. The rising generation will need an honest economics that accurately values the natural capital of soils, forests, ecological resilience, biological diversity, and climate stability. The Lewis Center, accordingly, was intended to make the costs as transparent as possible—part of a larger conversation about economics and ecology.

Eighth, buildings in the industrial age were often designed to be disposable, useful for a short time until the wrecker's ball. From now on, buildings will need to last longer and be more adaptable than those of the past. This means that their purposes will evolve over time with the changing needs of the owners and the community. The idea, too, that buildings, like churches, would be used only for a few hours a week, will soon prove to be too expensive. Multiple uses and evolving purposes will become the norm. Similarly, building performance, once presumed to be static, will have to improve as more efficient and cost-effective technologies become available. In the political economy of the twenty-first century, in other words, buildings should be designed to last, serve multiple uses, and evolve to higher levels of performance.

Ninth, the measures of building performance will change to include energy efficiency, occupancy use, the percentage of solar capture, the indoor air quality, the outgoing water quality, and interactions between the building and the surrounding environment. The design of systems in the

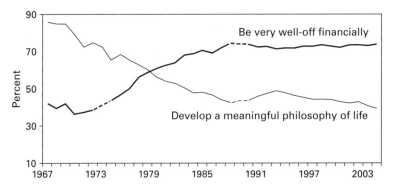

**Figure 10.1**
Contrasting values of College Students (*Source:* Sax 2004)

Lewis Center to monitor, analyze, and display performance data is the subject both of classes and ongoing research projects. The Web site for the building is designed and maintained, in large part, by students working with faculty and staff. One result has been the creation of a small company specializing in gathering, analyzing, and displaying data on building performance. Its goal is to develop the art and science of data display in high-performance buildings to improve performance with quick and accurate feedback as well as to educate people about interactions between the building and the environment. One experiment, conducted as an honor's project, showed that over a two-week energy competition in Oberlin dormitories, students with feedback on their energy use saved nearly twice as much energy as those without such information (Shunturov 2005).

Finally, political economy is not just about materials, energy, landscapes, and buildings but about the kind of people we intend to become. The ambitions of the current generation of college students are said to be predominantly toward making money. University of California at Los Angeles researcher Linda Sax (2004) has tracked the value orientations of students since 1967, and the trends are not entirely encouraging (see figure 10.1). A large majority aim now to be well-off financially while fewer aspire to develop a "meaningful philosophy of life." Such evidence, I suspect, says much more about us than it does about our students, and what it says is that we have generally failed to put the opportunities and challenges of an improved human future before them in a realistic and compelling way (as well as provide adequate financial support for their education). The total impact of television, advertising, and education gives them too little reason to enlarge their view of their future and their role in making a larger human vision. But there are better possibilities for those perceptive and alert enough to see them, and thus to become the pioneers of a new age in which humanity has sobered down to live and prosper within the means of sunlight, soils, and ecology.

# IV

## Pedagogy

# 11

## The Origins of the Ideas

Once in his life a man . . . ought to give himself up to a particular landscape in his experience, to look at it from as many angles as he can, to wonder about it, to dwell upon it. He ought to imagine that he touches it with his hands at every season and listen to the sounds that are made upon it. He ought to imagine the creatures there and all the faintest motions of the wind. He ought to recollect the glare of noon and all the colors of the dawn and dusk.

—Scott Momaday

Much that traveled under the name of liberal education did not in fact liberate, because it was not in fact a removal of ignorance but an indoctrination with new forms of ignorance; or because the ignorance it removed was trivial, and the knowledge substituted was not of how to use critical intelligence but of how to use a collection of information, more or less inaccurate, for social climbing.

—Wayne Booth

I have lived in nine places in my life, but I dream about only one: a small valley in the southern Ozarks carved out over the last million years or so by a clear stream that the local people know as Meadowcreek. I lived in the Meadowcreek Valley for eleven years, and in some ways I still do and probably always will. As places go, it had a lot going against it. Meadowcreek was remote from some of the essential amenities of the good life. The nearest bank was twenty-five miles away. The nearest shopping mall was one hundred miles to the south. The nearest town, Fox, was three miles distant by treacherous dirt roads. Fox, Arkansas, has never made anyone's annual listing of the most desirable places to live. It has no Starbucks or places of fine dining. The general store on County Highway 263 stocked mostly white bread, soft drinks, canned goods, cigarettes, and some hardware items. It functioned as the town hall, where the conversation is slow but nonstop until a stranger wanders in to ask directions. The post office across the road was the only other establishment of note. There you could get your mail, opinions about the weather, and a sympathetic hearing about what hurts. Within a quarter mile of the post office were four churches, all of the kind that connect Christianity with sin, tears, redemption in the blood, and glory spelled with a capital G, punctuated by hallelujahs. JD's garage was down the road a bit along with most of the mechanical detritus he'd accumulated over a half century of repairing all manner of things. He would take nothing more than two dollars for a tire change. The vacant building across an unpaved street has housed any number of dreams. Donny Branscomb tried to make a go of a café there, but people in Fox don't eat out much, and selling coffee and cigarettes didn't pay his bills. His next line of work was driving a tour bus for a company in Little Rock.

The surrounding Ozark hills have little of the grandeur of the Rockies, or of the Appalachian mountains for that matter, although they are scenic enough. Summers can be brutally hot and muggy. If the heat and humidity don't kill you, the ticks and saber-toothed chiggers might. The Ozark region looks something like a parallelogram stretching along an axis from east-central Missouri southwest into Oklahoma. What are called mountains in the Ozarks are not particularly mountainous; the highest elevations seldom exceed two thousand feet. For all of their rural charm, the Ozarks remain an economic backwater roughly equidistant between St. Louis and Little Rock, and Memphis and Tulsa. To the south, I-40 runs east and west. To the northwest, I-44 runs between Joplin, Missouri, and Saint Louis. There is hardly a straight stretch of highway anywhere in between. If you manage to get in, it's not easy to get out. Stay long enough and you may not want to.

The word Ozarks came from the French *Aux-Arcs*, which means "to the Arkansas post" (Rafferty 1980, 4). The French named it, but geology and water shaped it. Between the Precambrian and Pennsylvanian ages, most of the Ozarks were covered by an ancient sea. Sixty-five million years ago the first of a series of uplifts occurred, raising the Ozarks above the surrounding country. The resulting plateau is the highest ground between the Appalachians and the Rockies. The rugged landscape of the Ozarks, however, is the ongoing project of water working its will on land above an ancient seabed. The Ozarks are known for limestone caves, clear springs, and spectacular bluffs overlooking pristine, slightly bluish streams below.

The first human occupants of the region reportedly were Osage Indians. They were evicted in the early nineteenth century by land-hungry Scotch-Irish settlers spilling across Tennessee and Kentucky from the Appalachians. These self-reliant settlers came armed with axes, biblical self-assurance fortified by homemade whiskey, and strong beliefs in the rights of property. Nevertheless, this was not, as the Osage and later the Cherokee may have noted, an equal opportunity belief. After the native people, the first thing to go were the virgin forests, which were cut over in less than fifty years. Prime Ozark white oak went to Memphis and Saint Louis to make furniture, railroad ties, and barrel staves. Having sold their forests for a pittance, Ozark settlers turned to agriculture in earnest, but without much success. Their ideas about farming originated mostly in England, where by comparison, the soils were deep, the topography was rolling, and the rainfall tended to be gentle. In the Ozarks, though, thin rocky soils, steep hillsides, and summer drought punctuated by violent downpours typical of the southern midcontinent conspired against prosperity. Instead, the Ozark economy formed around subsistence farming with cattle, hogs, chickens, marginal timbering, and lots of doing without. All of this is to say that the nineteenth-century settlers came with habits and expectations that did not fit well with the ecology and topography of the region. It is an old story.

If geology and water shaped the Ozark landscape, its mindscape was formed in the union of isolation with hardscrabble poverty. The difference between aspiration and situation was made up by evangelical religion, alcohol, resignation, folk music, and a love of the land. But the national stereotype of the Ozark personality created by Al Capp in his Dogpatch cartoons bears scant resemblance to the human reality. Ozark people, like rural people virtually everywhere, have learned to make do with what they have, which for the most part isn't much. On the whole, they do so without much self-consciousness of being victims of economic oppression or poverty. They'd much prefer being left alone to being helped. They are independent, self-reliant, often suspicious of outsiders, resistant to new ideas, and clannish, but not more parochial in their way than, say, cosmopolitan New Yorkers are in theirs. And if you have a choice of where to have your car break down at 2:00 a.m. some dark, rainy night, you'd be smart to arrange it in the Ozarks, where the word neighbor is still regarded as a verb.

Ecologically and culturally the Ozark region is a meeting ground. The oak, hickory, and ash forests are similar to those of the southern Appalachians, but I often found cactus on south-facing ridgetops, survivors of a hotter and drier age. Similarly, the humble armadillo, a native of the southwest, is migrating northward to take up residence in the Ozarks. Not a few have become embedded in the highway system. Culturally, too, the Ozarks are a mix between the mountain culture of the Appalachians and the cowboy culture of the Southwest. There were as many cowboy hats as baseball caps on the hat rack in the Rainbow Café in Mountain View. The rodeo, such as it is, came to town each fall, but seldom traveled much further east. There were a scattering of mailboxes with such and such "Ranch" posted on what otherwise looked a lot like a hill farm plus a few worn-out cows.

Split personality and all, few regions of the United States arouse such devotion and loyalty in their residents. Ozark people oftentimes think of themselves as part of that region first, before listing other and lesser loyalties to state, church, and nation. Many high school graduates stay put despite the lack of local opportunities for "upward mobility." Those who do leave rarely go far away and they tend to return when they've saved enough money. There is a rich literature about the life and natural history of the region. The contrast between a region that seems to give so little yet arouse such a strong sense of place is striking. I grew up in western Pennsylvania, which by comparison is a lush land of milk and honey with rolling hills, fertile soils, and a temperate climate. Yet most of the people I knew while growing up had little sense of regional identity and only a superficial knowledge of the place. To this day, I know of no significant book about the natural history of the region despite its apparent economic and ecological advantages. And once gone from Pennsylvania, few return.

Meadowcreek runs through the southwestern corner of Stone County in the Boston Mountains of the southern Ozarks toward the middle fork of the Little Red River. Stone County is 110 miles due north of Little Rock. On government maps, the county ranks as the fifth-poorest one in the forty-ninth-wealthiest state of the union. State bean counters were often moved to give thanks to God for creating Mississippi, which is a thin statistical film between Arkansas and the bottom of the barrel.

The Meadowcreek Valley is three miles west of Fox, three miles southeast by jeep trail and deep faith from Flag, and about five miles north of the ghost town of Arlberg. Coming from any direction, however, you have to want to get there to get there. Few arrived by accident. It was a test of determination, nerves, tires, tie-rods, and brakes. Some found the precipitous descent into the valley on a rough, narrow, unpaved road with a sheer drop of two hundred feet on one side something of a spiritual experience. I recall the driver of a cement mixer who was delivering a load of concrete and forgot to gear down at the top of the hill. Halfway down he'd exhausted the reservoir of air for his air brakes, but in that omission found an urgent need for Jesus. At the bottom, one could infer from his incoherent stammer and the color of his face that he had undergone a high-speed conversion. He swore he'd never do it again.

The valley is three miles long, running north-south, by one mile to a mile and a half wide. To the north, the valley forks into Bear Pen Hollow and another unnamed hollow leading to Flag. To the south, the valley opens into a U-shaped gorge through which the middle fork of the Little Red River flows on its way to the White River. On each side, the valley floor rises up to flat benches and then rises more steeply to the ridgetops above. Rock outcroppings at the same elevation all around make the valley look like a giant bathtub with a crusty ring. From floor to ridgetop the elevation averages six hundred feet.

From the bluff known as "Pinnacle Point" at the southwest corner of the valley, you can see the length of the Meadowcreek Valley to the north and the gorge cut by the middle fork to the south. Below, on the east side of the valley, is what remains of the Bond family homestead, an Arkansas "dogtrot" house with two rooms on either side of an enclosed walkway. Most people in Stone County were reportedly born, courted, married, or shot there. It now sits abandoned and derelict. Southwest of Pinnacle Point is Bee Bluff with a sheer rock face on the south side that looks as if it had been cut with a knife. On the bench immediately below the eastern face of the bluff is a wooded cemetery containing a catalog of rural tragedy and hardship.

Angel sent from God 1-12-1901
Returned to her Savior 4-7-1903

At one time the valley reportedly had some forty homesteads and the largest school in the county. Little remains other than the stones around an occasional well or door threshold, and the daffodils that bloom each spring where cabins once stood. When we moved to Meadowcreek in 1979, the only human residents were a Baptist preacher and his sad-faced, heavily burdened wife, who rented a rundown house at the north end, and a couple the locals called hippies, who lived in what was left of an old homestead two miles to the south under the shadow of Pinnacle Point. Most of the valley was owned by a local doctor who used it for grazing cattle. Otherwise the land was becoming forest again. Fencerows were overgrown with cedar and greenbrier. Lichen-covered rock walls were falling down. Deer, raccoon, and stray hunting dogs had the run of the place.

I first saw the valley on a somber, cold, and blustery February day. The region had been through some of the worst freeze-thaw weather that anyone could remember. Creeks were swollen by heavy rains and the roads were nearly impassable, even with four-wheel drive. We hiked and drove around the valley until well after dark, comforted somehow that we had seen it at its worst. Later, we discovered how relative that word can be. On our way out, in the darkness of evening, the road bottomed out and we were stuck in mud that nearly covered the wheels. We had passed a house a quarter mile or so back, and slogged through the dark and the mud to ask for help. Before we could knock on the door, a voice inside boomed out, "I figured you'd be acoming back. I'll get the tractor." His name was Lonnie Lee, a bull of a man in his prime, and as famous for his hospitality as for his temper. A logger and woodsman by profession, but a musician and storyteller at heart, Lonnie had us on our way, or so we thought. Another mile and we heard the sound of metal on stone, and discovered that we had lost a tire in the mud and were traveling on three tires and one bare wheel. Things are like that in the Ozarks. Easy becomes hard. Fast goes slow. Certainties are less certain. Tires fall off. A spare change and we were on our way again. We moved into the valley the following June.

We came as interlopers to a place to which we had neither attachments nor roots. What we had were ideas, energy, a bit of cash, and a belief that we might do great and good things in that place. Our intent was to create an educational center without the disciplinary blinders, shortsightedness, and bureaucracy of conventional educational institutions. We found this place quite by serendipity; it was a good choice for reasons that we could not have known in advance and a poor choice for obvious reasons we refused to see. Of course, we became the first students, and the place itself became both our tutor and the curriculum.

Like most Americans, I had not thought much about the importance of place. I had lived in seven other locations by 1979, and could not tell you much about them that you could not discover for yourself with a map and a day's tour. I fancied myself an environmentalist, but I would have flunked the most basic test of bioregional knowledge about the seven previous places where I'd lived. In this regard I was typical. On average, Americans are increasingly ignorant about where they live as well as how they are provisioned with food, energy, water, material, and the services of nature. The reasons are not hard to find. We live like nomads, moving eight to ten times in a lifetime. Restlessness is part of the national psyche. America was discovered by tribes who walked east across the Bering Strait when it was above water, and later by Europeans who sailed from the opposite direction looking for India. The descendants of the latter included Daniel Boone, swarms of pioneers, armies of salespeople, herds of tourists, consultants by the thousands, and tribes of migrants in their fossil-fueled SUVs and mobile homes. Our cultural heroes have usually been one variation or another on the theme of lonely stranger who wanders into town, does some awesome and mostly violent thing, departs, and is never heard from again. The settlers who clean up the mess and get the kids back to school do not make such salable or salacious movie subjects. I know of no film about, say, Henry David Thoreau, who said he did most of his traveling at home. What is the cause of our restlessness and our fascination with restlessness?

Perhaps it is hardwired into us; after all, many of our ancestral tribes migrated with the seasons and the food supply. That's true enough, but our mobility is driven by neither calories nor the calendar. It's a deeper kind of itch for opportunity, the chance to get rich, and the lure of excitement that infects bored people. With us, in other words, it's a mind thing, not a physical or even spiritual necessity. And movement can become addictive. A friend of mine drives an eighteen-wheeler for a living. He's tried to settle into a nine-to-five job at home, but cannot do it for long to save himself or his family. A couple of weeks at home and he comes unglued and must get back on the road to preserve his sanity in an insane system. He just has it a bit worse than the rest of us.

We've made it easy to get up and go. First on post roads carved into the wilderness, and then in succession, canals, railroads, interstate highways, and airports: the great U.S. motion sickness. We talk about colonizing space, and I suppose we may try that too. More likely, however, our restlessness will be met by purveyors of virtual reality who will sell us the simulated version of any fantasy or destination we—or they—can dream up. Want to go to the moon? Step into a virtual reality simulator and off you go—reality, or their version of it, for a price.

This gets closer to the heart of the problem. Whatever our hardwiring, motion in service to fantasy is now the core of the national economy. Imagine for a moment what would happen if Americans one day decided to stay put. Car companies would go even more broke along with all of the other companies that sell us roads, tires, gasoline, insurance, lodging, and hamburgers. The national economy would collapse and I think "they" know that very well, which explains why a sizable part of the national advertising budget is spent to keep us restless and on the go. Whatever wanderlust exists in the human soul has been amplified into a positive feedback system that goes like this: more roads and airports → more oil wells, oil spills, oil refineries, oil wars, military spending, mines, malls, Disney Worlds, sprawl, ugliness, pollution, and noise → fewer neighbors, neighborhoods, livable communities, distinctive places, and solitude → more people trying to escape → more roads and airports—a cycle of futility, destruction, and violence.

Of course, the lack of a sense of place is not just a function of rootlessness. It also has to do with the way we are fed, clothed, supplied, and fueled. Modern technology has unhitched us from our places. We are no longer competent to do much for ourselves. Most of us are effortlessly provisioned from distant agribusiness, feedlots, wells, mines, and factories that we know virtually nothing about. We consign our wastes to other, equally unknown places. All of this is said to be economically efficient, but for whom, how, and how long is never explained because, I think, it cannot be both explained and justified.

Our relation to our places has been further weakened by the U.S. tendency to commercialize land so that places come to be regarded solely as real estate. For many people, however, land is abstract because they neither own any nor have easy access to it. The experience of place as an enduring relationship with a landscape and all of its life-forms is increasingly unlikely for the 80 percent of Americans who live in urban areas along with the growing number on the downhill side of the middle class.

The weakening sense of place and the competence necessary to live well in a particular place is now epidemic in our culture. It is, I think, at the heart of what is called the ecological crisis. All of the numbers foreshadowing one disaster or another, all of the sigmoid trend lines surging upward and others in free fall, represent the sum total of our collective disconnectedness to the places in which we live and earn our livelihood. The reasons are straightforward.

The growing distance between consumers and producers creates innumerable possibilities for political and ecological mischief. An economy grown to a global scale not only invites irresponsibility, it cannot work otherwise and remain profitable for the few who run it. The global economy entices consumers to consume more than they need. To do so, they must be largely ignorant about the ecological and human consequences of their consumption, including the effects of it on themselves. The global economy created the kind of dependence that breeds what Thomas Jefferson called "venality," which inevitably corrupts political life as thoroughly as it debases citizens. A global economy can only exist at a scale beyond the possibility of democratic control, and perhaps beyond control of any kind. It is nonetheless defended because of its supposed efficiency. But no estimate of its true efficiency can be made unless all of its costs could be known and compared with those of alternative ways to do the same or better things. Finally, by destroying all other economies and cultural possibilities, the global economy places the human future in extreme jeopardy. By homogenizing the human enterprise in the name of "development" or "progress," we are, in effect, betting it all on one roll of the dice.

In late fall 1983, we moved into a passive-solar house that we built on the site of what had once been a steam-powered sawmill. Little of the mill remained but the rock pad where the boiler and steam engine once sat along with rusted pipes, wrenches, ax heads, and bolts, all overgrown with greenbrier, cedar, and sweet gum. The place had become so overgrown that it was an eyesore to the few who traveled the dirt road that ran along the east edge of the site at the foot of a steep hill. The house was nestled in the arm of a steep hill to the east and a low boulder-strewn wooded hill to the north. Looking to the west through a patch of second-growth trees, across what local people called the "sand field," past Meadowcreek, the west ridge rose six hundred feet to rock bluffs and chimney rocks at the top. To the south, the house looked down the three miles of the Meadowcreek Valley to the gorge of the Middle Fork and the bluffs beyond. At night, the only visible evidence of human occupation was a light at a Methodist church camp seven miles distant.

I began to clear the site in my spare time in late fall 1982—mostly because it offended my idea of what an edge ought to look like. Farm boundaries, fencerows, and the edges of fields, I'd learned, should be neat and manicured. René Descartes would have liked it that way. And this was a conviction for which I was then prepared to shed blood. Those familiar with greenbrier may know how much blood can be shed in the clearing of roughly an acre of land overrun with it. As the brush, vines, briers, and small trees gave way, traces of the old sawmill became apparent. The owners of the mill had dug out a basin, long since overgrown, that collected water from a natural seep at the back of the site. This water was used to cool the boiler, which sat on a rock pad fifteen feet long by five feet wide, and had become anchored at one end by a giant sycamore tree. Heat had made the upper layers of rock brittle so that they could be broken apart by hand. Still, most of the rock was useful for building retaining walls around the house.

Remnants of rusty hand-forged tools and metalware lay all about: head blocks from the sawmill, old buggy-wheel rims, pipes, and other things I could not identify. My collection, carefully cleaned and covered with rust-resistant paint, was eventually nailed up to the side of my woodshed. The collection testified to human ingenuity and perseverance in the face of necessity. For example, some nameless person had taken two pieces of strap metal, hot welded them together, and beveled one edge to make a workable chisel. We discovered dozens of wrenches, perhaps made by the same person with similar homespun resourcefulness. I showed one piece of rusty pipe split at the seams to an itinerant philosopher with a keen sense of place and a compassionate heart. He uttered a low sigh and said he hoped that the child who had forgotten to drain the boiler some frosty night long ago was not rebuked too harshly. So did I.

While I cleared the site, the place was working on me in its own fashion. I would often stop work to gaze down the valley or look up at the bluffs to the west. I wondered who had owned the mill. What were they like? What kind of life did they have in this place? Why did they leave? Several hundred yards to the south at the end of the sand field, where Meadowcreek had once run diagonally across the valley floor, was the site of an ancient Osage Indian village recently excavated by local archaeologists. What were these Indians' lives like here? Were they, in some sense, still here? The place had voices, I tell you.

It also had sounds. Across the sand field, Meadowcreek, on its way to the Gulf of Mexico via the Middle Fork, White River, and Mississippi, tumbles over and around boulders the size of cars. The first heavy rains in the late fall would raise the water level and the sound of rushing water would again fill the valley. In the late evening, owls in the woods across the field would begin their nightly conversations. I'd occasionally join in until they discovered that I had nothing sensible to say, at which point they would descend into a sullen silence so as not to encourage me further. In the spring and early summer, the chuck-will's-widows and tree frogs would hold their evening serenades. Once a month or so, a pack of coyotes would interrupt their raids on the local chicken houses to hold a symposium in the valley. Unlike owls who converse patiently throughout the night, coyotes handle their business quickly, seldom taking longer than thirty minutes, and then it's back to work. By late fall the wind, which blows hot straight up the valley all summer long, shifts and comes cold down the valley out of the Bear Pen. Pieces of ancient seabed raised to bluff height would sometimes be heard breaking loose and crashing to the forest floor below. Except for an occasional pickup, however, few human-made sounds intruded on the symphony of wind and rushing water. And although humans in the past century had taken a terrible toll on the valley, the wounds were healing One could imagine this as a wilderness in the remaking.

I do not recall when the thought of building a house in this place first came to us, but the logic of the location was clear. The site was sheltered from the north wind yet open to the summer sun and winds to the south. It was shaded from the hot summer sun by woods on the west side, and the daytime heat was tempered by cooler air descending in the night. Built in the valley, the house was still high enough to be above the floodplain. And the view down Meadowcreek Valley framed by high ridges on either side was an endless and ever-changing delight. This logic was nevertheless just a rationalization for holding a deeper conversation with a particular place and its nameless guardian spirits. We had to build there.

Once I invited a well-known cosmopolitan writer from San Francisco to give a talk at Meadowcreek to our students and staff on the theme of the importance of place. Her talk was sophisticated, smart, and full of allusions to great writers and big ideas. But she was honest enough to admit that she had no sense of place, only words and thoughts about it. By her own admission, place was simply an alluring abstraction. In the back of the room, listening intently, were several Ozark women whose daily lives were lived to the rhythms and demands of place. They competently lived the reality, privations, and joys that the visiting writer for the most part could only talk about. Yet, they could no more intellectualize about place and its significance than they could repeal the law of gravity or make their husbands give up tobacco. Afterward, I asked several of them what they thought about the talk, to which they responded that they did not understand a word of it. "One who knows does not say and one who says does not know"—Lao Tzu.

Attachment to place grows by stealth, and mere words and thoughts give way to something deeper. In time, the boundary of the person and the place can become almost indistinguishable. There are people who die quickly when uprooted from their ancestral homes. I have come to believe that driving people from the places in which they are rooted is about the most cruel punishment that one human can inflict on another. But I do not think that one can plan to become attached or centered in a place. It takes time, patience, and perhaps poverty, but most certainly a great deal of necessity. It cannot happen during a vacation, although a kind of infatuation with a place can occur in that length of time. It will not happen without something akin perhaps to a marriage vow, a commitment to a particular location for better or for worse. Can it happen in a city? Not likely, at least not likely in the cities that we've built. My urban friends will protest that they too have a sense of place. By my reckoning, however, what they have is a sense of habitat shaped by familiarity. The sense of place is the affinity for what nature—not humans—has done in a particular location and the competence to live accordingly.

I doubt that we can ever come to love the planet as some claim to do, but I know that we can learn to love particular places, and that will require a great deal of competence and forbearance. I believe that the love of place and the acceptance of the discipline of place, far from being a quaint relic of a bygone age, will prove to be essential to anything like a fair, decent, and durable civilization.

The world is now engaged in the early stages of what will be a long and contentious debate about the human prospect in a future without cheap oil and on the brink of nasty climate surprises. On one side are those who see problems but not dilemmas and certainly no cause for alarm. A bit of technology here, a policy change there, add a dash of luck, and we will arrive at the magic kingdom of what they call sustainability. In other words, we don't have to prove ourselves worthy, just clever. On the other side are those who believe that we must first "become native" to our places before all of these other things can be added unto us—a more arduous route with the aroma of brimstone and repentance to it. Advocates of the former often prefer to eat organically grown vegetables and vacation far from the ecological effects of their vocation. Advocates of the latter sometimes motor about in four-wheel drive trucks, use chain saws, and communicate by e-mail. Meanwhile, the bottleneck ahead comes closer.

Elaine and I left the Meadowcreek Valley in June 1990 after eleven challenging, difficult, and rewarding years. We'd arrived in 1979 from one of the centers of wealth and power in U.S. society: Chapel Hill, North Carolina. Fox, Arkansas, is by every measure at the periphery, and the world of power and wealth looks quite different from the outside looking in. I'd arrived full of the self-assurance of thinking myself well educated, knowledgeable, and armed with a compelling point of view. Eleven years later, I knew how phony that assurance can be. We set out to create an educational experiment, a cross between places like Black Mountain College, Deep Springs College, and a few others at the boundary of U.S. education and imagination. I thought my own education and background in and around the academy would be adequate to the challenge. From the age of five onward, I had been in or around higher education as the son of a college president, a student, and a faculty member. I soon discovered how irrelevant much of that experience was. In all of that time I recall few serious conversations about the purposes and nature of education, and none at all about the adequacy of formal education relative to our role as members in the community of life. It was assumed that mastery of a subject matter was sufficient in order to teach others, and that those very subjects are properly conceived and important.

In the 1970s, I had grown disillusioned by the rigid separation of disciplines in the academy along with its complacency and indifference to big questions about the human future. I was disillusioned, too, about what I perceived to be the separation of head, hands, and heart in the learned world. Education, it was assumed, began at the neck and worked up, but dealt with only half of what remained. The other half—that part of mind where feeling, humor, poetry, and integration reside—was considered lacking in rigor by people who were often, I thought, unable to distinguish between rigor and rigor mortis. The resulting wars among head, hands, and heart as well as between the world of theory and practical experience were fought, but without much awareness, in every classroom, school, and college in the land, and in the minds and lives of every student. Problems we often diagnose as ones of bad behavior and low motivation among those to be educated more likely reflect the miscalibration between schooling and our full humanity trying to break free; they are made more difficult by bad parenting along with too much television, affluence, sugar, caffeine, and drugs. On the political science faculty at the University of North Carolina I found only two colleagues out of thirty-six sympathetic to such woolly ideas: one who worked as a poet in his spare time, and the other a man who'd spent his academic life thinking about connections and systems. Mostly, it was not considered appropriate to discuss the directions or adequacy of knowledge and research, and certainly not as these applied, or perhaps even contributed, to problems of human tenure on Earth. Basketball and basking comfortably in self-satisfaction were the main sports.

The idea behind the Meadowcreek experiment was that we would draw a line around the 1,500 acres we'd bought and make everything that happened inside curriculum: how we farmed the 250 acres of farmland, how we built, how we managed the 1,200 acres of forest, how we applied the ecological knowledge necessary to manage the place, and how we supplied ourselves with energy. We intended this valley to be a laboratory to study some of the problems of sustainable living and livelihood. Our curriculum coalesced around sustainable agriculture, forestry, applied ecology, rural economic development, and renewable energy technology delivered through internships with college graduates, January terms, conferences, seminars, and scholar-in-residence programs. Broadly, if it had to do with the subject of sustainability, it was fair game for us. Over a decade or so the number of conference guests, students, and visitors rose to several thousand per year, and the list of attendees, visiting faculty, and conference participants included a roster of the most prominent thinkers and activists in the country, including Wendell Berry, Wes Jackson, Amory and Hunter Lovins, Donella Meadows, and John and Nancy Todd.

The place itself became part of the curriculum in ways we did not anticipate. The land, as Thoreau noted, had its own expectations lurking below all of our confident talk about education and our clumsy efforts to render place into pedagogy. Places have a mind of their own that we aren't privy to. The curriculum of that place came to include particular events, such as a five-hundred-year flood, the hottest and driest summer on record, and the coldest winter ever recorded, along with the mysterious events we sterilize and pigeonhole with academic words like ecology, forestry, botany, soil science, and animal behavior.

One moonlit night I decided to head south down the valley toward the Middle Fork, about an hour-long walk. On my return through the tree breaks, the moon rising above the east ridge, I became aware that I was being followed. The safety of home was a long way off. Heart racing, I quickened my pace through a tree break dividing one field from another, went another twenty paces or so, and then turned around. Following close behind me was a lone coyote perhaps crossed with a bit of red wolf—a formidably large animal. I had no weapon and wasn't nearly fast enough to outrun it. But when I stopped, it stopped and then did not budge. We were eye to eye in the awkward, wordless boundary between species. The coyote's intentions were unknown to me, and I suppose mine were to him. Not knowing what else to do, I spoke a few words, assuming we ought to talk this out and that language might be an advantage of sorts. The coyote cocked its head to one side, ears perked up. The animal would occasionally look away and then look back with what I interpreted hopefully as a quizzical but slightly interested look on its face. I was encouraged and greatly relieved. After a few minutes of monolog and perked ears, I decided to sit down; the coyote reciprocated. I took this as a good sign and continued to talk softly, and even tried to sing a bit, and from time to time our eyes met and I heard the coyote make something like a low yip, yip that sounded friendly enough—an interspecies communication of sorts. By now the moon was nearly overhead and we were fully visible to each other. After what may have been five or ten minutes, I stood up and the coyote stood as well. I took one slow step forward; the animal responded by splaying out its feet, ready to bolt. Another step and the coyote bounded off, turned and looked back, and then disappeared into the night. I stood and watched him fade into the trees along the creek and then walked home blessed in some nameless way.

I had ventured into the coyote's world of night foraging and mating, and I think it was simply curious about this lone, misplaced human. I had no weapon and no machine, which made me more approachable, and I believe we did communicate in a fashion. Extending it a bit further, the coyote was both curious and courteous. And those who do not believe that animals think have never ventured alone and vulnerable into a conversation with one on its terms and in its native habitat. We still regard nature as a mere commodity and animals as abstractions, much as Descartes did. For the rising generation, the experience of nature, in any form, is rare, and it is increasingly alien to the enclosed curriculum of the academy where the matters of greatest consequence have to do with grade point averages, course units, careers, routines, tenure, and U.S. News and World Report's annual ranking. And I find this to be a serious loss to our ability to think and our humanity.

I had a PhD, but had not been educated to think much about education, the Latin root of which means to draw forth. Who is qualified, and by what standards, to midwife the birth of personhood in another, spark another's mind into the state of awareness, or properly appraise the results? What does it mean to be educated, and by what standard is that mysterious process appraised? In some circles, great stock is placed in the mastery of routine knowledge, or what Brazilian educator Paulo Freiere describes as the banking model of education. Others, deemed more progressive, emphasize the process of learning, which mostly means the cultivation of a kind of disciplined curiosity. Both, however, conceive education in philosopher Mary Midgley's word, "anthropolatry," the worship of human accomplishments, history, and mastery over nature. As anthropolatry, the study of nature is mostly intended to fathom how the world works so as to permit a more complete human mastery and a finer level of manipulation extending down into genes and atoms (Midgley 1996a). My experience at Meadowcreek opened the door to the different possibility that education somehow ought to be more of a dialogue requiring the capacity to listen in silence to wind, water, animals, the sky, nighttime sounds, and what a Native American once described as earthsong—the sort of things dismissed by anthropolators as romantic nonsense.

Confronted by the mysteries of a place I did not know and slightly bookish by nature, I turned to all of those writers on education that I had avoided in my earlier years as a college teacher, including John Dewey, Albert Schweitzer, Maria Montessori, J. Glenn Gray, and Alfred North Whitehead. There is, I discovered, a useful criticism of the foundations of contemporary education in their writings that emphasizes the importance of place, individual creativity, our implicatedness in the world, reverence, and the stultifying effects of "secondhand learning," as Whitehead (1967, 51) once put it. From a variety of sources, we know that the things most deeply embedded in us are formed by the combination of experience and doing with the practice of reflection and articulation. And we know, too, that what Rachel Carson (1984) called "the sense of wonder" requires childhood experience in nature and constant practice as well as early validation by adults. The cultivation of the sense of wonder, however, takes us to the edge, where language loses its power to describe and where analysis, the taking apart of things, goes limp before the mystery of creation, where the only appropriate response is prayerful silence.

# 12

## The Green Campus Movement

Universities have a major role in the education, research, policy formation, and information exchange necessary to make [sustainability] possible. Thus, university leaders must initiate and support [the] mobilization of internal and external resources so that their institutions respond to this urgent threat.
—Talloires Declaration, 1990

In June 1987, we hosted the senior staff from Hendrix College in Conway, Arkansas, for a weekend retreat at Meadowcreek. The food served in the kitchen of our conference center was mostly from our own farm, a fact that moved President Joe Hatcher to casually ask why students at Hendrix could not be fed from local farms. Beginning with that offhand question, a project subsequently emerged to examine the food system at Hendrix College. The study was patterned on one done by the Rocky Mountain Institute the year before in which the researchers compared the energy and water requirements of organic and conventional systems of raising cattle. The idea was to use the study of the Hendrix food system to educate students about the larger issues of food and agriculture and to encourage the college to shift its food purchases to support local farmers. I took the proposal to Edith Muma and Steve Viederman of the New York–based Jessie Smith Noyes Foundation, which had funded work in sustainable agriculture. At their recommendation, foundation trustees voted to make a grant of fifty-three thousand dollars to pay for the study. Sam Passmore from our staff served as the project director, working with the Hendrix College dean of students.

Sam divided the students into two teams, the first of which was asked to learn all that they could about local agriculture within a forty-mile radius of the town of Conway. That team studied soils, the numbers of farmers, cropping patterns, and farm economics as well as the potential to grow other crops with changes in farm practices along with some capital investment in greenhouses and equipment. They interviewed farmers, farm implement dealers, county extension agents, and government officials, and quickly discovered that the college was buying nothing within that forty-mile radius and that only 6 percent of its food supply originated in Arkansas, a mostly agricultural state. Further, the college was importing nearly half of its fruits and vegetables from Mexico, highly tainted with pesticides banned in the United States, and thereby undermining the intent behind a recently established college "wellness policy." They also uncovered a sizable potential to build a regional food system with numerous advantages for farmers, institutions, and eaters alike.

The second group of students studied food service invoices to determine the specific farms and feedlots that supplied the cafeteria. Later in the summer, Sam and members of the team traveled though the Southwest out to California, developing a video documentary that included interviews with farmers, migrant laborers in California, and food brokers in Los Angeles, and a visual record of feedlots and corporate farms. It was apparent that whatever the price of the food served on campus, the cost in human and ecological terms was much larger when measured in soil erosion, the loss of biological diversity, water pollution, the depletion of groundwater, and the damage to the health of farmers and farmworkers. The food system, they discovered, is full of absurdities. For example, rice farms and cattle ranches existed within a few miles of the campus, but the college imported its rice from Louisiana and its beef from a Texas feedlot that produced more sewage than the city of Philadelphia. Oddly, some of the steers in that feedlot were born in Arkansas. Students learned firsthand that the food system of agricultural commodities, agribusiness, feedlots, farm suppliers, and processing and distribution centers had grown as a result of cheap oil, a confusing array of corporate subsidies originating in the industrial mindset that ruled throughout agribusiness and schools of agriculture. In other words, the college was participating in a slow-motion disaster that undermined its students' health along with that of farmers, farmworkers (who have the highest leukemia rates of any occupational group in the United States), and the land. Underlying this system is a belief that agriculture is a subject properly confined to land-grant universities. In fact, food, nutrition, soils, and farming first ought to be part of a liberal education, a subject that involves health, ethics, science, the social sciences, and particular places, and only then as a technical problem of agronomy. The priorities of the system, the students learned, are upside down.

Sam and the students subsequently edited dozens of hours of film into a twenty-minute documentary on the Hendrix food system that was shown to the students, faculty, and staff at the college. With an agronomist on the Meadowcreek staff, the students put the two studies together into a proposal to the college to increase local food purchases from 6 to 50 percent or more, encourage farmers to eliminate toxic chemicals, and develop local food-processing systems. The study showed that the college could improve the quality of the food served in its dining hall, support the local farm economy, reduce the ecological damage from industrial farming, and use its food system to further educate students on the connections among food, health, and agriculture.

The public response to the project was considerable. Governor Bill Clinton cited the study in his sesquicentennial address to the state. The state legislature and the Arkansas chamber of commerce publicly commended the college, mostly because it reduced the flow of money going to other states, particularly Texas. The college subsequently agreed to implement the proposal under the direction of the dean of students. In order to facilitate the project's implementation, Meadowcreek and Hendrix College sought and received support from the Winthrop Rockefeller Foundation in Little Rock to fund a broker between farmers and the college as well as to develop a wider market. Subsequently, the college did dramatically increase its local food purchases as a result, but with a change in the presidency and other college personnel, commitment eventually faded. Meadowcreek sponsored similar studies in 1988 and 1989 at St. Olaf, Carleton, and Oberlin colleges with broadly similar results. And the idea was replicated on several dozen other campuses across the country, including Swarthmore College. At Oberlin, local food buying took root and flourishes to this day in the co-op dining halls and the campus dining service.

A number of other efforts took place about the same time. In 1989, April Smith (1993), a student in the Planning Program at the University of

California at Los Angeles, wrote a master's thesis on the environmental impacts of the university on the Los Angeles area and later published a useful book on how to audit campus environmental impacts. In the early 1990s, the National Wildlife Federation hired Julian Keniry to organize efforts on college and university campuses through a newly established Campus Ecology Program. At Tufts University, Dean Anthony Cortese organized the first major university response through the Ecological Literacy Institute on campus, bringing in faculty from every discipline to rebuild the curriculum course by course. Due to Cortese's leadership and that of President Jean Mayer, Tufts sponsored a conference of college and university presidents at Talloires, France in 1990, resulting in a declaration of institutional responsibility and commitment to protect the environment and equip students for careers in environmental stewardship. Subsequently signed by hundreds of presidents, that statement articulated a vision of higher education more radical than many of the signatories realized.

After moving to Oberlin in 1990 from Meadowcreek, I initiated a course called "The Campus and the Biosphere," based on an article I'd written for the *Harvard Educational Review* in 1990 (Orr 1992). The intention behind the class was to extend the logic of the Hendrix food study to include food, energy, water, materials, and waste handling, assembling information and support for what eventually became a comprehensive college environmental policy. Within a few years, that class had been replicated at dozens of other colleges as students, faculty, and staff began to systematically study resource use and environmental impacts on their own campuses. In the early 1990s, Walter Simpson initiated a highly successful program to improve energy efficiency at the State University of New York at Buffalo that has saved cumulatively a hundred million dollars, or about nine million dollars each year. All told, what had begun in the late 1980s with a few tentative and isolated efforts to study campus food systems and environmental impacts had by the middle of the next decade flourished into a broad-based movement abetted significantly by biannual conferences at Ball State University organized by Bob Koester, organizations like Second Nature—headed by Tony Cortese—the National Wildlife Federation Campus Ecology Program, University Leaders for a Sustainable Future, and the coalescence of a remarkable group of educators and organizers. This group included, in addition to Cortese, Keniry,

Koester, and Simpson, Peggy Barlett at Emory University, Don Brown in Pennsylvania State government, Wynn Calder and Rick Clugston at the Center for Respect of Life and Environment, Geoffrey Chase at San Diego State University, Carnegie Mellon University president Jared Cohen, Peter Corcoran at Florida Gulf Coast University, climate scientist Bill Moomaw and Sarah Creighton at Tufts University, Nan Jenks-Jay at Middlebury College, Eric Pallant and Michael Maniates at Allegheny College, Rocky Rohwedder at Sonoma State, Berea College president Larry Shinn, Environmental Center at the University of Colorado director (and later, mayor of Boulder) Will Toor, and Don Wheeler at Ramapo College.

With growing evidence of serious climate instability ahead, a number of scholars, activists, nonprofit organizations, and national environmental organizations began to focus on climate, and what might be done to reduce inefficient energy use on campuses and promote the use of solar energy. A conviction grew that we in higher education had to act because of the overwhelming importance of the issue and the leadership vacuum in Washington. Don Brown organized a group of Pennsylvania colleges and universities to promote the purchase of green energy. An Oberlin alumnus, Don Wheeler at Ramapo State College, similarly brought together several dozen New Jersey colleges and universities with the same intent. The Clean Air, Cool Planet initiative organized by Bill Moomaw brought New England institutions into a coalition to implement the Kyoto standard. Students at the University of North Carolina and the University of Colorado, among others, voted to raise student fees to purchase green power and improve campus energy efficiencies. At Oberlin the trustees adopted a policy which included the idea of becoming carbon neutral. By 2005, dozens of colleges and universities were taking significant steps toward energy efficiency and the adoption of renewable energy (Apollo Alliance and Energy Action 2005).

In less than two decades the campus environmental movement had grown from small and isolated projects into a broad-based movement of students, professors, activists, and nonprofit organizations aiming to reduce campus environmental impacts. Connecting the various organizations and projects were four widely accepted principles, beginning with the idea that institutions that aspire to induct young people into responsible adulthood ought themselves to act responsibly relative to energy, resources, and land. It is wrong, in other words, to operate institutions in ways that undermine the ecological foundations of the world our graduates will inherit.

Second, the roughly fifteen million college students as well as million and a half faculty, along with the several hundred billion dollars of annual purchasing power and a like amount of investment funds, give institutions of higher education great leverage on the future. We in higher education are not powerless: we are visible and respected; we have access to the leaders of today through alumni and to those of tomorrow, the students in our classes. In short, we have the power to implement a vision of a future better than that in prospect.

It makes little sense, however, to reduce campus environmental impacts, and leave the curriculum and educational programs untouched. The deeper and more challenging goal is not simply to green campus operations but to improve the "still-unlovely" human mind. The third principle follows: ecological disorder reflects a prior disorder of mind and is therefore a matter of great importance for those organizations that purport to improve minds. In other words, the goal of education is first and foremost to equip minds for life on a planet with a biosphere. But how is that to be done?

The fourth principle, then, is aimed at practical change using the campus and its system of inputs, outputs, buildings, and landscapes as a laboratory for the study of the major challenges subsumed in the word sustainability. Every college and university campus is a microcosm of the larger society, including inputs of food, energy, materials, and water, and outputs of waste in varying forms large enough to be a significant economic and political force yet small enough to be usefully studied. And every college and university is part of a regional ecology and economy forming an even larger network of resource flows and practical possibilities for change.

For students, the use of the campus as a laboratory reduces problems of bewildering complexity and scale to manageable and solvable dimensions. It connects them to practical issues. It is difficult to say how we might best deal with global climate change, for example, but not nearly so difficult to improve energy efficiency in a single building or dormitory. Engaging students in solving practical problems requires that they think across disciplinary boundaries, become proficient at moving ideas into operational reality, engage the politics of institutional change that include staff, administrators, and faculty, and learn the art of constructive change. Most important, in helping to solve real problems they learn how to connect knowledge, action, and practical vision.

Today's students will live their lives as humankind nears and passes the peak of global oil extraction—the beginning of the end of an age. Theirs will be a progressively more constrained world in which the long-distance transport of food, water, and materials will become more expensive and difficult. We need to equip them for the transition to the solar age that will change food and agricultural systems, housing and land use, and our means of livelihood and entire economies. For the rising generation, in short, the future will pose a series of unprecedented global challenges. Our students will have to sharply reduce the emission of greenhouse gases, make a rapid transition to solar energy, stabilize population, stop the loss of species diversity, improve the efficiency of materials use by orders of magnitude, eliminate toxic pollution, grow their food and fiber sustainably, build sustainable cities, reform political institutions to work within the limits of natural systems, and improve basic fairness within and between generations. No generation has ever faced a more daunting agenda, and none has ever had to do so much in such a short span of time. But we are still educating them, for the most part, as if the future will be an extension of the past hundred years.

In fall 1990, I returned to the academy from my eleven years in Arkansas to teach in the Environmental Studies Program at Oberlin College. Oberlin has a proud history as the first U.S. college to accept African Americans in the 1830s and the first to admit women as full students. From that beginning the college established a national reputation as a progressive institution at the forefront of social change in civil rights, women's liberation, peace activism, and gay rights. The words "Learning and Labor" still adorn the college seal, but the idea that these are related in any important way is mostly regarded as a quaint relic of a bygone era, if still thriving at a few other places including Berea College in Kentucky, founded by Oberlin students in the late 1800s for children from impoverished mountain communities.

The Environmental Studies Program at Oberlin was initiated by an extraordinary group of students who organized a January term in 1979 on the subject of the human future. That venture led to the formation of the program in collaboration with a core group of faculty in history, English, biology, government, and philosophy. Like most academic enterprises founded as programs, not departments, in the 1970s and 1980s, the Environmental Studies Program at Oberlin was still a kind of curricular outlier to what was considered to be the more important business of the college, having to do with conventional disciplines administered within the typical departmental structure. The initial assumptions behind such programs acknowledged the significance of environmental issues, but not necessarily any more inclusive logic inherent in the possibility that human maladjustment in its earthly habitat might require more thoroughgoing change in education. Environmentalism, in other words, was one of many critical issues, but not widely regarded as more important than any other and certainly not a cause for any deeper transformation. Pluralism, the belief that the academy is a kind of marketplace in which all viewpoints are equally valid and equally deserving of time and attention, is the prevailing philosophy. That permits us to teach, say, economics as a story of infinite human expansion, world without end, but also courses in ecology having to do with the limits of nature. And what do we make of students who earn A's in both? In the cognitive dissonance and cacophony of perspectives, do we confuse them, thereby impairing their ability to develop a worldview that calibrates the needs and desires of humankind with the realities of the biosphere? Pluralism is certainly a valuable antidote to one kind of absolutism or another, yet it does not always help our students develop a coherent and ecologically solvent worldview.

After eleven years at the periphery wrestling with busted fences, recalcitrant cows, and the relationship between place and pedagogy on the back forty, the transition back into the academy was harder than I'd anticipated. Type A by nature and shaped by over a decade of hustling and the practical labors of farming, forestry, and building, I struggled with the slower pace of college life and the tedium of long meetings often with short purposes. Mostly, however, I discovered how much those eleven years had changed my views of the process and substance of education. I had come to believe that:

• Humankind, a precocious upstart ape, has a long way to go and a short time to get there, as country philosopher Jerry Reed once put it. Our situation is rather like the passengers in the old joke who hear the pilot say that there is good and bad news. The good news is that the flight is running ahead of schedule. The bad news is that they're lost.

• As a species, we are promising in many ways—as we assume in moments of self-congratulation—but no one can say for certain exactly what that promise might be. Opinions divide between those who think us like a cosmic dandelion destined to send our seed out to fill every nook and cranny of the universe, and those who would prefer a more modest and spiritually deeper course. I believe these to be mutually exclusive paths. But celebration of humankind, Midgley's anthropolatry, is deeply, perhaps fatally, embedded in both.

• The world is one and indivisible, and that every attempt to reduce it to its components, however useful in the short term, distorts reality and misleads us into thinking ourselves to be smarter than we really are. Discovering "the pattern that connects" is hard for us, particularly when it includes competing values, the distant future, and the rights of other species. Beyond reductionism, other modes of knowing, characteristic of other cultures and times, have little or no standing within the prevailing beliefs about what constitutes rigorous thinking. Across its various departments and programs, the academy is largely a monoculture.

• Our serious problems are first and foremost ones of heart and empathy, and only secondarily those of intellect. In other words, mere smartness is much overrated and is not, as widely believed, entirely synonymous with intelligence (Midgley 1990). But good-heartedness is a kind of long-term intelligence.

• Education ought to help each of us overcome the centripetal tug of greed, illusion, and ill will, but that this is a lifelong process that only begins with formal schooling.

• That part of education initiated in classrooms ought to equip us, as J. Glenn Gray once said (1984), to understand our implicatedness in life— that no person can be an island or should want to be.

• The idea that the truth will set us free is just a slogan. Truth (spelled with a capital T), I suspect, is furtive, seldom showing itself in air-conditioned rooms, as Wendell Berry remarked. When it does choose to show itself, it is likely to be daunting, confusing, conflicting, ironic, and perhaps even terrifying, but not necessarily liberating as we understand that word. It is more likely to be hard, demanding, and elusive. The path of least resistance is to seek smaller truths and live comfortably in the denial of larger ones. The proper role of education is to jar us out of that somnambulant state, and prepare us to be worthy of the encounter with Truth if and when we are so graced. This is a lifelong and deeply personal quest, and yes, this is to admit the utility of pluralism of a sort.

- What is advertised as the "explosion of knowledge" is largely fraudulent. What has exploded, as Jacques Barzun once noted (1993, 222), is mostly "(1) repetition in swollen fragments of what was known more compactly and elegantly before; (2) repetition, conscious or not, of new knowledge found by others; (3) repetition of oneself in diverse forms; and (4) original worthlessness." Certainly our technological prowess, hence our capacity to muck around in lots of things and lots of ways, has exploded, but that should not be confused with knowledge, a more complicated thing, or wisdom, which is still more mysterious.

We presume to improve the ability to think, mostly in one disciplinary silo or another, but the harder and more important task is to encourage the ability to think about thinking. For example, if skepticism is the essence of science, then the only scientific approach to science is to be skeptical of its assumptions, methods, and even its results.

- Thinking is overrated relative to experience, particularly to the experience of nature. But the experience of nature refines, clarifies, and instructs thinking so that there is no clear line between the two. It follows that the growing evidence of "nature deficit disorder" ought to be a matter of concern to those who presume to improve thinking and the capacity to know what we ought to think about (Louv 2005).

- One of the best things we can do for the young, aside from getting them outdoors, is to introduce them to the world of large ideas, the Great Conversation. The worst thing we can do is to make them technicians of one sort or another in preparation for successful careers in an economy that mines coal, oil, soil, forests, oceans, people, and the future.

- Thomas Merton (1985, 11) was on to something when he advised students, "Be anything you like, be madmen, drunks, and bastards of every shape and form, but at all costs avoid one thing: success." We've had enough success and it's just about ruined us.

And I believe, too, that the world is rich in possibilities. I do not think that we are fated to poison ourselves or cause the heat death of the Earth. I think that we can rise above division, hard-heartedness, greed, illusion, and ill will. And we are capable, in short, of becoming citizens in the larger community of life and that doing so would ennoble humankind.

That's my story, and I'm sticking to it!

My colleagues, a smart, dedicated, and mostly tolerant lot, would be greatly amused by any such quaint profession of belief. Much of the reason for this is that the academy typically offers little encouragement to extend beyond the borders of one's own graduate training and expertise. To the contrary, there are often penalties for doing so, sometimes subtle and sometimes not so subtle, that can whittle us down to the dimension of the organization. Our stock in trade is not so much worldviews, paradigms, and operational philosophies as it is course units, credit hours, and research that keeps smart people gainfully employed. Colleges and universities have become businesses whose managers often fashion themselves as corporate executives, with students as their customers.

In that setting, it is not thought to be useful for career advancement to orient one's expertise on any larger topography. Doing so would require expending considerable effort to know things beyond one's graduate training, including the principles of other disciplines. For the most part, we college professors are content to offer ourselves as experts in one small piece of our respective fields. As Jacques Barzun observed (1975, 11), it is "a tacit denial of intellect [resting] on the superstition that understanding is identical with professional skill." From this Tower of Babel of competing disciplines, subdisciplines, and research projects, one does not talk much about the coherence of our worldviews relative to natural systems, or even about the human prospect in a world of terrorism, nuclear weapons, and climate change. What does seem to get our attention, alas, has to do with parking permits, retirement benefits, promotions, salary raises, and the enhancement of our particular fiefdoms. The larger structure of incentives and rules offers few rewards for asking large questions, including those having to do with the purposes and effects of the system. Chaucer's scholar, who would trade his cloak for a book, or Socrates, an unpublished rabble-rouser, for that matter, would have little prospect of being tenured in today's university.

During the planning charettes at Oberlin College in fall 1995, a larger vision emerged that changed the project from being just a building to one that would become central to the educational experience of later generations of students. From the start, the building was intended to evolve toward higher levels of performance with better technologies and management skill. In other words, the building began to emerge as a kind of pedagogy and ongoing research project.

Sometimes we believed that we were plowing new ground. In fact, much of the planning merely extended and updated questions that were asked long before. Thomas Jefferson's academical village was designed as a statement about pedagogy, the relation between students and faculty, and a symbolic representation of the role of knowledge in a democratic society. One hundred and seventy years later, we traversed much of the same ground, armed with a bit more history and a lot more science. But we were also asking many of the same questions having to do with relationship of education, pedagogy, architecture, and disciplinary perspectives to the Great Conversation, and the human prospect. From the beginning, the building and surrounding landscape were conceived not just as a location in which classes occurred but as an evolving laboratory for the study of most of the significant problems of sustainability having to do with growing food, restoring degraded ecologies, purifying wastewater, and harnessing the energy of sunlight. The building and landscape were intended not, in other words, to be neutral relative to the larger mission of learning and research but rather to be a melding of place, architecture, and subject matter.

We intended the Lewis Center to be a storied place beginning with that of its natural history as a place on glacial till deposited ten thousand years ago. We intended the building and landscape to provoke students' own stories of their part in the design process. The benches and raised garden beds made from carved stone retrieved from the college boneyard tell the story of the labor and creativity of particular students. The orchard, gardens, and vineyard were an ongoing narrative of faculty and student engagement with the landscape. Building data and their display tell yet another story of how building systems actually function in what is sometimes called "real time." The making of storied places, we believed, would encourage a higher level of mindfulness and creativity as well as form lifelong habits of creative engagement with particular buildings and places.

The Lewis Center was meant to promote ecological competence in our students and visitors. Gardens, orchards, the Living Machine, data gathering and analysis, and solar technology were intended as ways to join operational systems with the development of practical solutions. We intended this to be a site in which minds and hands would be joined to do practical and useful things. The effect we wanted for our students was to develop the habit of rolling up their sleeves and getting down to work to solve real problems.

The Lewis Center, in short, was intended as a means, not an end in itself; a process, not a result. Most important, it was supposed to be a means to deepen the thinking of students and faculty alike about the human role in nature, including practical alternatives. It was intended as a means to equip students with the practical and analytic skills necessary for careers in the many aspects of ecological design, and to give them justifiable hope that our problems are indeed solvable. It was intended as a means to begin a practical conversation about the substance and process of education in the context of a model of ecological design.

# 13

## The Rest of the Story

It ain't over till it's over.
—Yogi Berra

We sat in the midst of my office, cluttered with papers, books, and the paraphernalia of academic life, professor and student. Sadhu Johnston was one of the best students I'd known; he was smart, energetic, and ambitious. On his own he'd organized, among other things, an electronic billboard on campus to minimize paper used for events flyers and announcements. But facing graduation he had no specific plans or prospects. Several weeks before we met, I'd been asked by the president of the George Gund Foundation to organize a speakers series in downtown Cleveland to transfer what we'd learned about ecological design from the Lewis Center to the wider northeast Ohio community. For lack of time I had to decline. But as Sadhu and I talked, it dawned on me that he had the energy, wit, and entrepreneurial personality to make that project successful. When I raised the prospect with him, he was eager to take it on. We met with the foundation staff and officers, who were sufficiently impressed to provide office space for Sadhu and open doors in Cleveland.

For two years thereafter, Sadhu brought in the leaders in the field of ecological design, many of whom had been involved in the design of the Lewis Center design. For most sessions, held in the auditorium of the Cleveland Public Library, it was standing room only. Representatives of the mayor's office and the philanthropic community mingled with developers, architects, engineers, representatives of the business community, and environmentalists. From that beginning, Sadhu and others organized the Cleveland Green Building Coalition as an offshoot of the U.S. Green

Building Council. Among its early projects, the group purchased an abandoned bank building in a transitional neighborhood on the west side of the city. Four and a half million dollars later the building, rehabilitated to standards, reopened with a bank as the anchor tenant on the ground floor and four floors of office space for nonprofit organizations above. It became the hub of ecological design and environmental activity in and around the city, including the offices of Eco-City Cleveland, one of the best urban environmental groups in the United States. Having accomplished a great deal in a short time, Sadhu was lured to Chicago to work in the office of Mayor Richard M. Daley. But the Green Building Coalition continued under new leadership, and more important, the ideas of ecological design had taken hold in dozens of projects around the region.

It was registration week in fall 1999, and seven students had asked me to sponsor a private reading in the spring semester. Each was interested in the large issues of sustainability, but more specifically in how these might be applied to the town of Oberlin. We organized the reading around the relationship between downtown renewal and the need to improve the housing of students renting rooms throughout the town. I agreed to invite several architects and urban designers to Oberlin to raise the vision of what small towns could become. As we read, walked the town, and discussed possibilities, the idea emerged that students' needs for housing and the need for downtown renewal might be joined, and that the future of the college depended a great deal on the economic health of the downtown economy. The college was committed to improving student housing, but rather than build new dorms it could put those funds in a low-interest loan fund for downtown building owners. Those interested in improving their property, adding rental rooms above the stores at street level, and expanding businesses would be eligible for loans along with design assistance to meet environmental standards. The results would be to improve student housing, raise property values for building owners, create a twenty-four-hour presence in the downtown and thus increase security, revitalize downtown businesses, and develop a small-town ambience with rooftop gardens, great restaurants, prosperous businesses, rebuilt infrastructure, and economic resilience. When the semester ended, the students submitted a report to the college that attracted a trustee's interest and financial support, which they used to create a nonprofit organization aiming to galvanize interest in downtown renewal. In the end, however, it wasn't to be quite as they had hoped.

A year later Josh Rosen, Naomi Sabel, and Ben Ezinga showed up in my office to talk about a similar idea on a smaller scale. They were juniors, majoring in politics, environmental studies, and economics. They had the same impulse and drive to work on revitalizing the Oberlin downtown and a practical turn of mind. We talked over the same issues of small-town revitalization and what three young people aged twenty might do. Sometime during the conversation I mentioned that the building that once housed the Buick dealership in town was probably for sale and could be the location for a business of some sort. Beyond that meager idea, I really had no clue what three smart, idealistic, and energetic students might do to improve the downtown economy. I went off to London to teach for a semester, and returned the following summer to discover that the three had formed a partnership and were making plans to buy not just one building but most of a city block. They intended to design and build a three-story building with six businesses at street level and two floors of mixed-income housing above. And they were serious about it. Their personal commitment and determination secured funding from the city council and leading citizens around the town. On about any day they could be found talking and conspiring around a table in the Black River Café, slowly weaving the threads of the project together. As their ideas jelled, the estimated cost of the building went from a few million to over seventeen million but they were undaunted.

At one point, Naomi called to ask for an appointment to talk about raising additional funds. The conversation went like this. "Before we start, I have some good news," she said. "Oh, really, what is it?" I responded. "My uncle just got out of prison," said Naomi. "Well that is good news," I replied somewhat warily. "What did he do to land in prison?" I inquired. "He killed a man," she replied. "Huh . . . why did he do that?" I asked even more cautiously. "He worked as a contract killer for the Mafia," she casually responded. Remembering that this was supposed to be a fund-raising conversation, I pulled out my wallet with a degree of alacrity seldom seen, offering its entire contents and whatever other spare cash I could find. Naomi, a formidable woman, is chutzpah on speed.

By whatever means, Josh, Ben, and Naomi raised the money, brought in the expertise, and moved the project ahead. Nothing stopped them for long. The groundbreaking is scheduled for the fall of 2006, with completion by late the following year. The longer-term result will be to anchor the economy of the east side of the downtown and improve the property values nearby, thereby encouraging renovation, generating jobs and investment, drawing residents into the downtown, and reducing crime. The project provides a case study in small-town renewal, financing, and ecological design, and an example of courage, leadership, and boldness for generations of students.

In fall 1999, I wrote a short article for the *Chronicle of Higher Education* saying that the argument for delaying the transition to energy efficiency and renewable energy was roughly similar to that made for slavery during the gag-rule era in the late 1830s (Orr 2002, 143–151). That similarity was of more than incidental importance to Oberlin College, which has long prided itself on being the first U.S. college to admit African Americans and women. I maintained that future generations will regard our procrastination on climate destabilization like we regard the moral shortcomings of slaveholders, and our reasoning will be thought no more robust or convincing than theirs for owning other human beings. The most obvious difference between slavery and the effects of climate change is that the former could be changed by war or manumission, but the latter are permanent, global, and perhaps self-reinforcing. A second difference is that climate change will affect everyone on the planet, not just the minority in servitude.

In January 2000, I requested permission to raise funds for a study of the costs and benefits of various strategies for the college to reach climate neutrality. But when the idea was presented to the senior staff, the atmosphere was icy to indifferent. Of the dozen or so people assembled, only two spoke in favor of the effort; the others were noncommittal, baffled I think by the idea that colleges could do something about a global problem, beyond throwing words at it. While radical in one sense, the study I proposed was comparable, say, to efforts decades before to develop a coherent approach to the revolution in information technology. This was intended as a scouting expedition of the terrain ahead where rapid technological changes in efficiency and distributed energy systems intersected the possible cataclysm of climate destabilization looming ahead. With less than full exuberance, five months later the administration approved the effort to raise the necessary funds.

The study was quickly funded, and the Rocky Mountain Institute in Snowmass, Colorado, was hired to do the research and write the report. I hired a staff person to serve as the liaison between the college and the institute and keep the project moving smoothly. But again, this was not specifically a college initiative, and without a strong vocal champion in the administration, college personnel were sometimes reluctant to provide information to the Rocky Mountain Institute researchers. The draft report was submitted to the president's office for comment in December 2001, and the final report was delivered in January 2002. The report identified three scenarios by which the college could achieve a state of "climate neutrality." The scenarios were arranged by cost and feasibility, ranging from the purchase of offsets somewhere else equivalent to our own carbon emissions to radically improving efficiency and using on-site solar energy. However conceived, planning to balance the carbon books of any organization, even over a period of several decades, is a considerable challenge. Still, we intended to begin a conversation toward that end, yet one with implications for campus operations, finances, and curriculum.

When the final report appeared, though, fear won out. The "2020 Report," as it became known, was immediately embargoed by the president. Her reluctance apparently had to do with the erroneous belief that the adoption of the report would commit the college to ruinous expenditures. In fact, no such thing was being proposed. We had intended to begin a conversation around three broad strategies by which the college might move toward climate neutrality. We'd invested nearly a quarter of a million dollars and lots of energy to provide the groundwork for an institution-wide discussion only to have it thrown out without explanation.

Confronting what appeared to be implacable resistance, there are only so many things to do, one of which is to study the situation. In fall 2002, accordingly, I focused my environmental policy class on the subject of climate change and specifically on responses to the threat of climate change, at the federal level at one end of the spectrum and the college at the other. Rather than fight the administration about the issue, we would study their behavior as if we were anthropologists in a strange land. The class was organized to research student, faculty, staff, administration, and trustee knowledge about climate change and their resulting opinions. We wanted to know what people knew about the subject and what they thought the college should do about it, if anything. I also brought the principal investigator of the 2020 Report to campus to meet with the class and the Environmental Policy Advisory Committee, which I chaired. As the semester progressed, students as well as helpful faculty developed elaborate and highly professional survey instruments, and then began to interview members of the college community. By the end of the semester, they had assembled a detailed study showing a strong campuswide consensus for a proactive energy and climate policy. The project was publicized in the campus newspaper, and copies were given to the trustees before their December meeting.

Other students formed a group called Climate Justice that aimed to galvanize the college into action. Letters and e-mails poured into the president's office. A group of alumni concerned about climate change, led by Carl McDaniel, a biologist from Rensselaer Polytechnic Institute, formed an outside group to assist the college in meeting its higher mission. The upshot of all the e-mailing, study, and organizing was that the issue of establishing a college policy on climate was put on the agenda for discussion at a subsequent trustee meeting in March 2003. The president asked Bill Moomaw, a member of the UN Intergovernmental Panel on Climate Change, to present the scientific evidence, and she wanted me to present the 2020 Report. The discussion was friendly and constructive.

This effort dovetailed with another. For nearly a decade, students in my campus and the biosphere classes had studied campus resource flows and environmental problems and had developed a series of reports for the college administration. In fall 2001, the president appointed a committee to make recommendations for a College environmental policy. The president's Environmental Policy Advisory Committee met regularly for two years beginning in fall 2001, and reported its recommendations to the president in summer 2003. The committee proposed a policy covering the areas of building standards, grounds management, purchasing, transportation, and energy as well as ways to integrate operations with curriculum and research. Significantly, the document proposed the goal of climate neutrality without specifying a timetable. The committee—consisting of the vice president for finance, the director of facilities management, and a mixture of faculty and students—met over lunch almost every week during the academic year. What began as a fairly contentious issue became a highly amicable and constructive one. The committee's recommendations, modified by the administration, went to the trustees in March 2004. The actual proposal they adopted had been watered down considerably to a single statement of intent with the body of our report serving as background and guidelines for campus policy. It is not clear to me that all of the trustees understood the full implications of the report or the reasons behind it, but in any case they approved the motion unanimously (see appendix).

The prototype for the building monitoring system was one designed and built by my brother Wil at the conference center at Meadowcreek in the late 1980s. But John Petersen, a systems ecologist, took the idea to another level, developing and installing 150 sensors throughout the building and adjacent landscape, and designing a sophisticated data-gathering, analysis, and display system described above. The system has become a part of a network of high-performance buildings and a growing database for anyone in the world studying building performance. In May 2004, John and two students, Michael Murray and Vladislav Shunturov, incorporated as Lucid Designs, Inc. The idea that buildings might be designed as high-performance systems with rapid feedback and become part of a larger educational fabric had gone commercial taking another step forward.

The Clark farm, on the east side of Oberlin, had been conventionally farmed for as long as anyone could remember. The college owned the land, renting it out to a local farmer who grew corn and soybeans with lots of help from his friends in the chemical business. In 1998, the college turned over the property management to a group of faculty and others with interests in organic agriculture. As with most land in northern Ohio, the Clark farm was once part of the wetland that stretched along the south shore of Lake Erie from the west side of Cleveland to Toledo and beyond. Agriculture was possible only as long as the land could be drained, but the drainage system on the Clark farm was failing. The group formed to manage the property decided to let nature have a lot of it back. With the drainage tiles blocked, a sizable wetland once again formed in the center of the property, inviting birds and other animals long absent.

Brad Masi, a 1993 college alumus who I'd brought back to work on the Lewis Center in 1995, took over the task of making the Clark farm into a laboratory for small-scale agriculture, ecological restoration, and woodlot management, and a hub for rethinking the loss of farms and the prospects for the regional food system. Americans mostly assume that we've solved the problem of food once and for all. Our supermarket shelves are reliably stocked with a dazzling array of foods from all over the world. But behind the apparent abundance, another story is emerging, one written in statistics about soil loss, groundwater depletion, chemical contamination, antibiotic resistance, rural poverty, the loss of farms and farmers, and the rising costs of oil. On the horizon, the prospect of climate change along with the resulting heat waves and decline in rainfall mid-continent will have consequences for agriculture that we cannot imagine. We haven't solved the food problem at all. To the contrary, we've set ourselves up for a catastrophe—unless, that is, we begin to take steps now to preserve farmland and the knowledge of how to farm, and rebuild local farm economies.

Brad undertook the complex and long-term task of organizing the effort on what was renamed the George Jones Farm, after a revered Oberlin College biologist. The goals included the establishment of a twenty-acre truck farm for local markets, the restoration of wetlands on part of the farmland, the maintenance of a small woodlot, and education for a younger generation increasingly cut off from the realities of food and agriculture. On the side, Brad worked on the larger issues of regional food systems and farmland preservation. As of this writing the Jones farm includes a straw-bale office building, two greenhouses, equipment storage areas, four separate experiments in wetland restoration, two acres of vegetables for local markets, and a lot of volunteer labor. The prospect of a prosperous community-supported farm and farm education center looms ahead.

The original plans for the Lewis Center included a straw-bale greenhouse and mechanical shop separated from the main building. As the development went forward, however, our vision grew to accommodate a more expansive landscape plan and the laboratory needs of a systems ecologist in the program. The house adjacent to the Lewis Center was owned by the college and used as a rental property. It had a past, but no particularly distinguished history. Faced with the choice of new construction or doing adaptive reuse, the college chose the latter, mostly to preserve the character of historical housing along Elm Street. In fall 2005, the program occupied renovated facilities that serve as a greenhouse, laboratory, and additional classroom space.

The final part of the story to this point was the addition of a second photovoltaic array, above the parking lot. Designed by Stephen Strong, founder of Solar Design Associates, the array generates about a hundred kilowatts, making the Lewis Center the first academic building to generate more energy on-site than it uses over the course of a year. As with the design of the Lewis Center, students were engaged in the design of both the laboratory space and the photovoltaic array.

The acre and a quarter comprising the Adam Joseph Lewis Center—a restored wetland, gardens, orchards, water storage, two photovoltaic arrays, and a restored building—is a laboratory for the study of some of the problems of sustainability at a scale small enough to be comprehensible but still large enough to be significant. It is a place designed to engender hopefulness as well as the ecological and design competence to act faithfully on that hope.

No story is ever finished. Rather, each of our little stories morphs into others very different and often ironic, or they join like eddies in a larger flow of events that later appear with enough distance as currents in the big river of history. The story of the Lewis Center is a rivulet in the larger stream of events at a small liberal arts college, and a tributary of the story of U.S. higher education. It is also a small part of a revolution in the way we design and build—an alternative history, by no means certain to survive or even deflect the course of events very much. But the efforts described here and those of tens of thousands around the world constitute the stirrings of an alternative historical trend that perhaps one day will be depicted as that time in which we chose to step back from the brink of nuclear wars, terrorism, violence, gross inequity, and ecological malfeasance. The result would be no nirvana, but could be a more durable, fair, and decent order.

If that happier scenario comes to be, it will appear, I think, as a kind of eco-logical enlightenment formed around the art and science of ecological design, similar in some ways to the eighteenth-century Enlightenment premised on the faith that humans could rise above superstition, arbitrary authority, and violence. The resulting change would have transformed fields as seemingly different as agriculture, manufacturing, waste cycling, technology, shelter, and human settlements. Its hallmarks, previously de-scribed, are elegance, efficiency, and a superior economy informed by ecol-ogy, generosity, and fairness. We have reason to hope, as well, for a deeper reconciliation of our wants and needs with what Earth can willingly pro-vide. Perhaps one day we will come to see that "to live, we must daily break the body and shed the blood of Creation. When we do this knowingly, lovingly, skillfully, reverently, it is a sacrament. When we do it ignorantly, greedily, clumsily, destructively, it is a desecration. In such desecration we condemn ourselves to spiritual and moral loneliness, and others to want" (W. Berry 1981, 281).

# Appendix A

## Oberlin College Environmental Policy

This document was prepared by members of the president's Environmental Policy Advisory Committee (EPAC) during the course of academic years 2001–2 and 2002–3. The EPAC members are listed at the end of the document.

The Environmental Policy Statement for Oberlin College is presented first. The short statement outlines the general principles that should govern all activities on campus. It should be included in the college mission statement and/or displayed on the Oberlin College Web site. More specific recommendations regarding different activities on campus are given in subsequent sections. The section on energy production and use, which has implications for all campus activities, is presented first. The next four sections outline policies for grounds (landscaping), buildings, transportation, and material use. The final section outlines the steps deemed necessary to successfully implement the proposed policy.

### Table of Contents

**Environmental Policy Statement for Oberlin College**

As an institution of higher learning, Oberlin College has a special obligation to ensure that the ways we educate our students, manage our internal affairs, and interact with the broader community serve as an example that others might follow. In keeping with our history of courageous and morally sensitive leadership on issues of race, gender, and labor, Oberlin College embraces an ethic of environmental stewardship. We are committed to developing a more sustainable relationship between humans and the rest of the natural world through teaching and research, through design and implementation of institutional policies, and through management of energy flows and material cycles. We recognize that it is not enough merely to decrease the rate at which we deplete and degrade local and global resources. We therefore strive to be proactive and systematic. The College will play a leading role in developing a community that operates on renewable resources and works to restore and enhance the ecological functions on which future generations depend. Environmental stewardship is both a goal that guides daily life and a core priority that informs all aspects of decision-making at Oberlin College.

## I    Energy Production and Use

### General Policy Statement

Energy transformation and use results in a variety of environmental pollutants, having impacts locally, regionally, and globally. Fossil fuels, particularly coal, are the greatest source of energy-related pollution. The principal impacts associated with using fossil fuels are the release of $CO_2$ and other pollutants into the atmosphere. The scientific consensus is that the buildup of $CO_2$ in the atmosphere has already led to undesirable changes in the global climate, including an increase in average land surface temperature and an increasing frequency of storms, floods, and extreme weather events. Without action, the magnitude of climate change is expected to increase. Stabilization of climate is contingent on achieving a state in which $CO_2$ released through human activities is balanced by $CO_2$ removed through biological processes.

Alternative energy sources are receiving increased attention by academic institutions. Within the framework of fossil fuels, the burning of natural gas ($CH_4$) produces the least amount of $CO_2$ per unit of energy. Oil ($CH_2$) is next, and coal (CH) produces the most $CO_2$. The carbon in the fuel becomes $CO_2$; the hydrogen becomes $H_2O$. Another form of gaseous energy, which was once a major component of widely used consumer gas, is hydrogen gas ($H_2$). Many experts expect that hydrogen gas ($H_2$) will become the major stored and distributed source of convertible energy in the not-too-distant future. Sources of "green" energy include solar, hydroelectric, geothermal, and wind. Wind and solar energy are the best candidates for the northeastern Ohio region. Rapid developments are occurring in these technologies, which could ease the cost of decreasing the dependence on fossil fuels.

As an institution of higher education, Oberlin has a special obligation to be proactive and responsible in energy management. Oberlin will pursue a long-term goal of reducing energy use and achieving "carbon neutrality" in which the release of $CO_2$ and other greenhouse gases through all activities associated with the College is minimized and balanced by activities that remove carbon from the atmosphere. Carbon neutrality is an essential goal for achieving climate stability, but one that may take many years to achieve.

Responsible energy management should take account of environmental costs as well as operational costs. The environmental impact must be evaluated, and the attendant costs considered in decisions regarding campus energy use. The College recognizes that, in some cases, a monetary premium is required to achieve the desired environmental benefits. In the broadest sense, Oberlin College seeks to: implement aggressive conservation strategies that reduce energy use; increase efficiency of electricity and heat production and consumption; shift towards less polluting sources of energy. Oberlin recognizes that technology, energy costs, and knowledge are dynamic, and that a regular reassessment of options and goals is therefore essential to energy management. Many energy conservation measures can be adopted in the short term, but changes in the infrastructure (buildings, heating plant, consumption of electricity) will require long-range planning and large capital investments.

Specific energy conservation practices for various College activities are spelled out within the following sections pertaining to policies specific to grounds, buildings, transportation, and materials stated in the following sections. What follows is a general description of the current status, approaches, and policy recommendations for reducing energy use.

### Status of Facilities and Energy Use

Oberlin College is nearly 100 percent reliant on fossil fuels for energy, and most of this energy is derived by burning coal. The College owns and operates a coal-fired heating plant (with supplemental use of natural gas at transitional times of the year) to generate the bulk of the campus's heating requirements. Natural gas provides space and water heating at local sites. A small amount of electricity is produced through cogeneration. However, the bulk of campus electricity is purchased from Oberlin Municipal Light and Power [OMLP]. OMLP obtains most of its electricity (83 percent) from coal-fired power plants.[1] The college owns or rents a number of vehicles which are almost 100 percent reliant on fossil fuels.

### Reducing Energy Consumption

Since Facilities Resource Management assumed operation of the campus in July of 1998, fossil fuel use has decreased by 15%. There is, however, room for substantial further improvements. A twofold approach to reducing energy consumption consists of 1) improving the thermal efficiency of buildings and operating efficiency of equipment, and 2) instituting creative policies and educational initiatives that encourage students, faculty, and staff to conserve energy. Buildings and activities within buildings currently account for greater than 90% of campus energy consumption. Effort should therefore focus on building renovation and on selecting appliances that minimize the use of energy (see EPAC statement on facilities in Section III). Innovative incentives should be created to encourage students, faculty, and staff to purchase and manage personal electronic equipment to minimize energy use.

1. The local OMLP plant is gas-fired but is only run occasionally to offset high costs of peak loads. OMLP has a stake in a hydroelectric project in West Virginia

## Increasing Efficiency and Decreasing Environmental Costs of Production and Distribution

Minimizing pollution associated with energy production should be accomplished with a twofold approach that focuses on increasing efficiency of energy production and generation, and on shifting to less polluting forms of energy production. Coal is the most polluting of fossil fuels, generating toxic particulates locally,[2] acid deposition regionally, and contributing disproportionately to global climate change relative to other fossil fuels. Recognizing this fact, Oberlin College seeks to reduce its dependence on coal for both heating and electricity.

## Education

The strong link between energy use and environmental quality provides an ideal practical opportunity to engage and educate Oberlin students, staff, and community in efforts to reduce energy use and shift to renewable sources. The College should

- Incorporate energy conservation education as a component of freshman orientation.
- Provide students with a conduit for making suggestions for enhancing campus energy efficiency that are then acted on by the College.
- Engage students in the process of designing policies and educational campaigns to increase energy efficiency.
- Provide students with information about specific environmental improvements made by the College.

## Specific Recommendations

- An individual within facilities planning should be given primary responsibility and time to oversee training and comprehensive and continuous monitoring and assessment of both energy performance and policy efficacy. The monitoring should establish a baseline and include regular measurements of energy use with the Rocky Mountain Institute spreadsheets

---

and is actively exploring participation in wind generation in Northern Ohio. OMLP purchases methane-generated electricity from the BFI landfill site.

2. An electrostatic precipitator, recently refitted, reduces particulate emissions to a low level but does not remove most sulfur oxides.

and report serving as a point of departure.[3] This individual should report to the administration, and be advised by a designated group of staff, faculty, and students with expertise in energy issues including environmental impact. An annual report should assess progress and opportunities for further improvement in energy performance. Updates on improvements in efficiency of energy use should be made available through various campus media.

• Given the disproportionate pollution associated with burning coal, Oberlin's coal-fired steam plant should be replaced as soon as it becomes economically feasible to do so. A comprehensive study should be commissioned to assess the best available technology for replacing Oberlin College's coal-fired plant with a high-efficiency cogeneration facility that is capable of supplying a greater fraction of campus electricity as well as heating and cooling needs.

• Oberlin should seek to engage in collaborative efforts with other colleges that share our goal of reducing dependence on fossil fuels.

• The College should engage with Oberlin Municipal Light and Power to coordinate decisions regarding electrical energy production, and to encourage a shift from coal-fired power to other less polluting or renewable energy sources such as natural gas, solar, and wind. The College should investigate opportunities for purchasing a significant fraction of energy from renewables.

## II    Grounds

### General Policy Statement

Urban landscapes address aesthetic sensitivities and more mundane issues like storm water and traffic management; they also articulate the values of people and institutions, and so are instructive. Educational institutions like Oberlin College should strive to illustrate how these disparate purposes and functions can be integrated in ways that assure that built landscapes are practical, healthful for body and soul, and levy no unnecessary burdens on our planet. In essence, such spaces should foster a sense of

3. Committee members studied the 2020 Report done by the Rocky Mountain Institute and used the content of this report as background for their deliberations.

place and realization that nature welcomes our presence everywhere if we manage it wisely.

Because built landscapes take many forms and must provide many services, opportunities to use them to demonstrate responsible use of natural resources vary. Nevertheless, even the most intensively managed sites—those that require substantial inputs of pesticides, nutrients, and human labor—can be managed to emulate nature more faithfully than conventional practices allow. Many circumstances determine whether a given landscape can be more or less consistent with the principles of sustainability. Determining which practices to apply to specific sites requires that we consider priorities and compromise appropriately.

Oberlin College maintains about 650 acres of land, approximately 200 of which are intensely managed. Spaces such as athletic fields and beds of bulbs and annuals present substantial challenges to sustainable practices. However, most of the campus and all of the 450 acres that receive less regular maintenance can be managed to promote biodiversity, sequester large amounts of carbon, and reduce the likelihood of introductions of invasive plants into adjacent natural habitats. In effect, all landscapes can be maintained in ways that minimize or eliminate dependence on nonrenewable energy sources and environmentally harmful chemicals.

Oberlin College's landscape, no less than its classrooms, laboratories, and other teaching facilities, is part of the educational apparatus of the institution. Hence, the campus grounds should be managed in ways that accord with the College's efforts to provide its students the tools they need to become responsible world citizens.

Institution of the practices and principles listed below will help us align the message that we indirectly voice through our landscape with the call for responsibility that we so pointedly celebrate through our formal curriculum.

### *Further Reduce Dependence on Chemicals in Accordance with the Principles of Integrated Pest Management [IPM]*

• Expand reliance on cultural practices (e.g., soil aeration, high cutting length) that improve the health of turf short of applying fertilizers and pesticides.

• Landscape with pest-resistant horticultural material and native flora whenever possible.

• Substitute compost for chemical fertilizers and purchased mulch, and employ additional organic methods whenever practical.

• Reduce the use of pesticides (fungicides, herbicides, and insecticides) to applications consistent with the principles of IPM.

• Substitute sand or less toxic salts for sodium chloride to control ice and help reduce corrosion on equipment, where feasible.

*Utilize Equipment and Strategies That Reduce Reliance on Fossil Fuels*

• Replace existing equipment with machinery powered by other means than gasoline and diesel fuel.

• Increase the extent of low-input plantings to replace turf.

*Develop Electronic Databases and Maps That Help Manage the Campus Landscape in an Environmentally Sustainable and Efficient Fashion*

• Employ Computer assisted technology (CAD) to promote ecologically sound practices for maintaining existing plantings and planning new ones.

• Use this database to expand efforts to create native landscapes/ communities and remove exotics, where practical.

• Use this database to partition the campus into zones distinguished by acceptable levels of chemical and energy use and choice of plant materials.

*Involve the Oberlin Community in Grounds Installations and Management, Whenever Practical*

• Expand the "dig-ins" to allow greater opportunity to involve all Oberlin community members in the campus landscape and inform them about the principles of ecological sustainability.

• Label plants and plant communities in high-visibility areas.

• Expand the student summer-internship program.

• Create a course on grounds management.

• Establish a campus landscape advisory group that includes faculty to serve as a resource for the Grounds Department and the College Administration.

*Remain Apprised of Developments That Allow Improvements on the Techniques and Principles Listed Above*

*Ensure That All Plans Submitted for New and Renovated Landscapes Conform to the Principles and Practices Articulated Above*
A campus body, perhaps most appropriately the Architectural Review Committee, should examine all plans to that purpose. That evaluating body should assure that it has timely input from persons familiar with grounds technology, perhaps obtained by consulting with members of the landscape advisory committee.

## III   Facilities Construction, Modernization, and Maintenance

*General Policy Statement*
Facilities construction, modernization, and maintenance must be considered in any campus-wide environmental plan. Consequently, Oberlin College will strive to program, construct, and operate buildings in ways that maximize resource-use efficiency, utilize energy generated from renewable sources, manage storm water effectively, and generally minimize adverse impacts on humans and the natural environment.

*Standards for Building Construction and Modernization*
The College will pursue the goals articulated in the preceding paragraph by adopting certain environmental design standards and practices. Although design standards specific to Oberlin College are possible, such standards would require frequent modification to keep pace with changing technology and shifting local circumstances. Accordingly, Oberlin College's standards for building design and construction and the modernization of existing facilities will be those developed by the U.S. Green Building Council [USGBC] and set forth in the LEED (Leadership in Energy and Environmental Design guidelines; details available at <http://www.usgbc.org/LEED/index.asp>).

The LEED standard is the most comprehensive standard available for the design and construction of high-performance buildings. Moreover, these standards are scheduled for updating by the USGBC to accommodate advances in the building and materials industries, and energy technology. Additionally, the LEED standard will be expanded and resolved to eventually apply to specific kinds of structures.

The LEED standard will be used flexibly for the construction of new buildings and the modernization of existing ones. College expectations regarding LEED standards will be included in each Request for Proposals, along with milestone dates for periodic review of compliance. Responses from architects will include the LEED checklist and a range of possible scores and associated economic costs. Appropriate College staff will be LEED trained and certified to provide the necessary in-house expertise to evaluate this input.

The College will strive to maximize the LEED ratings (silver, gold, platinum) achieved for all of its facilities projects. Adherence to high goals should apply even when financial constraints are severe because such practice accords with the institution's academic mission and will increase the economy of its physical operations. A consistent high goal may also increase appeal to potential contributors.

### The Design Process

Design errors typically occur early in the design process, and principally because architects, engineers, and clients fail to treat the components of buildings as parts of a unified system. Without appropriate integration, the resulting structures often perform below expectations, and the cost of correction may be high. Therefore, design teams charged to integrate building components will conduct the program and design phases for all Oberlin building projects. These teams will include building and landscape architects, engineers, day lighting and materials experts, energy consultants, staff charged with operation and maintenance, and representative faculty and student users. Experience amply demonstrates that improved building performance can justify the increased costs of "front-loading," i.e., can justify the practice of paying more for green compared to more conventional construction, to achieve lower operating costs.

### Monitoring/Information

The College will systematically monitor, review, and improve end-use efficiencies for the consumption of electrical and thermal (heating and cooling) energy and water across campus. To this end, individual buildings will be equipped with sensors that monitor electricity and water consumption and HVAC. Additionally, motion sensors will be installed in offices and dormitories to adjust HVAC and electric usages to actual needs.

## Oversight

The Architectural Review Committee and appropriate Committees of the Oberlin College Board of Trustees will review compliance with LEED standards for new construction and major renovations. These bodies should be expanded to include members with expertise in resource-use technology and LEED standards. The General Faculty Planning Committee will receive regular reports on actions taken by the Facilities Office to improve energy-use and water-use efficiencies. A budget line will be established to use the savings that accrue from these efforts to fund additional improvements in facilities performance.

## Materials and Maintenance

The College will seek to identify and, where possible, eliminate materials of known toxicity used in construction, maintenance, and operations, and minimize the use of any other products that may threaten health. The College will institute procedures to accomplish these goals according to recommendations from a Materials Safety Group that will consist of appropriate facilities staff, faculty, and students.

## Materials Reuse/Recycling

The College will seek arrangements that allow it to inventory and store for eventual reuse, items such as furniture and reusable building materials salvaged from renovations or left unused during new construction. Planning for new building projects will include a mandatory review of all salvage on hand in order to reduce purchases of new materials. Salvaged materials with value, but no foreseeable utility on campus, will be sold or donated to other users.

The College will seek opportunities to secure an adequately sized and managed storage facility for salvaged materials.

*Education*

Buildings are part of the College's educational apparatus; they instruct about energy and material use and about land and landscapes. High-performance buildings can raise awareness about possibilities for reducing environmental impacts, harnessing solar energy, supporting local industries, and promoting biological diversity. For these reasons, data derived from the systems installed to monitor building performance will be displayed to promote awareness of the built environment and its connections with nature. In effect, Oberlin College buildings, to the extent feasible, will serve as laboratories and demonstrations to inform faculty, students, and staff about challenges related to climate change and the current energy economy, and how to deal with them responsibly.

Because high-performance buildings compared to more conventional ones require greater technological sophistication to understand and operate, we recommend that the individuals who maintain and use them be trained in the appropriate theory and operations.

## IV   Transportation

*General Policy Statement*

In order to live up to Oberlin College's commitment to environmental stewardship, the general area of transportation must be considered. Over the years, Oberlin students, faculty, and staff have become increasingly reliant on the use of cars for their day-to-day activities, and for their transportation to and from the campus. This increasing use of cars has negatively altered the quality of life on campus and in town through the attendant growth of centrally-located parking lots and increased traffic. More importantly, however, it has contributed to a collective pattern of environmental disregard. The overall goal of the College's transportation policy should therefore be to encourage a new ethic of environmental responsibility. This goal can be achieved through policies that aim to reduce the use of cars, increase the efficiency of the vehicles that continue to be used, and encourage alternative modes of transportation, such as bicycles. The strong link between transportation use and environmental quality also provides an ideal opportunity to engage and educate Oberlin students, faculty, and staff in efforts to reduce car use and shift to more efficient means of transportation.

To meet the goal stated above, the College should adopt policies that result in limiting on-campus transportation as much as possible to pedestrians; bicycles; and transportation for emergency vehicles, visitors, persons with disabilities, and deliveries and maintenance. There are several types of transportation relevant to reducing the use of automobiles, including on-campus activity, transportation between the campus and the city of Oberlin, transportation between the campus and surrounding areas in Northeast Ohio (e.g., the airport, Cleveland), and travel from campus to more remote locations (e.g., students traveling home for holidays). In addition, there are several classes of transportation users to consider, including students living on campus, students living off campus, faculty and staff traveling to and from the workplace, College employees using College vehicles on the job, and students using College vehicles for field trips, athletic events, and performances. Successful attempts to alter current patterns of transportation use need to recognize the set of concerns unique to each type of transportation and each type of transportation user. Further, the College should be a leader in the community with regard to purchasing and/or renting fuel-efficient or alternative-fuel vehicles. This leadership should pertain to the College's own fleet of vehicles and should involve incentive structures to alter the purchasing habits of students, faculty, and staff. More specific guidelines for meeting these objectives are listed below.

### Parking and Enforcement

- In order to reduce nonessential car use, the College's approach to parking must be reconsidered. Some policy changes will require consultation with the City Council and/or changing the zoning designations of new structures.
- No new central lots should be built. The college should explore alternative parking plans. For example, the College should consider building convenient remote lots, with permeable surfaces, on college land to accommodate travel to and from campus, but to limit car use on campus and around town. Building lots such as these could then create opportunities for reducing the size of existing central lots.

• Overall, the total number of parking spaces on College property should not increase.

• Performances constitute an important part of both the College curriculum and the cultural life of the City. The College's parking policy must ensure that sufficient spaces exist to accommodate performance attendees. Non-Oberlin residents should not be discouraged from attending performances due to parking concerns.

• The College needs to develop successful ways to monitor car use by students, faculty, and staff.

• Existing parking regulations need to be enforced rigorously.

• Any car that is parked on College property routinely should have to be registered with Campus Security. Student registration is of particular concern in this area. Possible methods of improving registration records include:

• Asking students living in campus housing to sign a statement at the start of every academic year indicating whether they have brought a car to Oberlin.

• Requiring students living off campus to register their cars if they routinely park their cars on college property.

• Other regular users of Oberlin facilities, such as people with recreation passes for the fitness center, should receive parking passes and be required to register their cars.

• "Failure to register" penalties should be issued when appropriate and enforced.

### Encouraging the Use of Efficient Vehicles and Alternative Modes of Transportation

• The College should adopt a policy whereby all new vehicles rented or purchased by the College are fuel-efficient, hybrids, or run by alternative sources of energy. This policy should include rental agreements for vehicles that are rented for long-term use.

• Multiple opportunities exist to encourage car-use changes among students. These opportunities include:

• Developing programs to encourage students with cars to bring fuel-efficient or alternative-fuel cars. This program might involve color-coded parking stickers, which would send a powerful symbolic message about College values.

• Adopting policies that facilitate students' abilities to meet their travel needs without personal cars. For example:

• The current policy whereby students can rent cars through the College could be expanded to permit easy and inexpensive rentals for non-college functions.

• Programs that provide extra transportation opportunities around breaks could be developed, including a bus rental program to provide transportation to and from major destinations such as Boston, Chicago, New York City, and Washington, DC.

• Policies such as these could diminish the number of personal cars that are used for occasional trips away from Oberlin. Cars sitting in lots for long periods of time are not a problem. However, once cars are brought to campus, the likelihood that they will be used regularly for short trips around town increases.

• Opportunities also exist to alter the car-use habits of faculty and staff. These include:

• Developing a program that encourages faculty and staff to purchase fuel-efficient or alternative-fuel cars.

• Developing an incentive system that facilitates and encourages carpooling.

• Ensuring a safe and convenient environment for bicycle users will facilitate and encourage bicycle use. To this end, the College could:

• Build covered bicycle storage areas in convenient locations across campus.

• Consider adding bicycle lanes on roads.

• Develop an incentive system to encourage faculty to commute by bicycle.

### Measurement

• Rigorous and systematic measurement of transportation use should take place.

• The College currently lacks reliable information on the number of students with cars, and on the frequency with which students, faculty, and staff use their cars to get around town and/or around campus.

• An initial study of current transportation use should be conducted.

• Measurement of transportation use should address all of the types of transportation and transportation users listed in earlier parts of this statement.

• Measurement should be conducted at regular intervals, and results should be made available to the public.

### *Consultation with the City of Oberlin*

• In order to design and implement successful and environmentally responsible transportation policies, the College will need to consult regularly with relevant parties in the city of Oberlin, including the City Council and the Police Department.

• One immediate area of collaboration and partnership could involve the creation of bicycle lanes and/or road signs reminding drivers to share the road with bicyclists. Bicycle lanes and signs allow for safer bicycle transportation and send a powerful symbolic message about the environmental ethos of the community.

### *Education*

• The College should incorporate education about transportation policies as a component of freshman orientation. For example, orientation could include trips that teach students how to use LCT.

• Information about the LCT (Lorain County Transit) program, the ability to rent cars through the college, etc., should be made easily available to new and returning students.

• The College should engage students in the process of designing policies and educational campaigns to minimize day-to-day car use.

• The College should provide students with information.

### V   Purchasing, Reuse, and Disposal

### *General Policy Statement*

Oberlin College purchases many products that it consumes or uses, and in the second instance, eventually exports or discards. The College's decision to conduct business in an environmentally responsible fashion mandates that all of these activities be pursued in ways consistent with policy outlined in this document. Moreover, the College recognizes that the purchase and disposal of materials are inseparable and linked with material use on campus, and it seeks solutions that simultaneously address all aspects of resource use.

Sustainability is achieved in part by eliminating the concept of waste, which means that material by-products from one process become useful inputs for other processes (i.e., material loops are closed). The three-Rs of resource-use efficiency—reduce, reuse, and recycle—are paramount to College policy. In fact, Oberlin College seeks to exceed existing regional, national, and international goals regarding the safe use of materials and material-use efficiency. Nothing less would be defensible for a leading institution of higher learning.

### General Policy Objectives

- Minimize consumption by using materials as efficiently as possible and for as long as possible, i.e., maximize the useful life of materials.
- Select materials that minimize environmental costs and maximize environmental benefits on campus and beyond. This means favoring materials that are recycled or reusable, sustainably harvested, and nontoxic and biodegradable, and energy efficient in the sense of a low-demand appliance.
- Effect objectives one and two by using "life-cycle analysis" and "full-cost accounting." Life-cycle analysis is accomplished by considering the origin and fate of a material or service. Employing full-cost accounting to reveal the environmental costs of its extraction, manufacture, and disposal that may not be fully reflected in its market price.
- Favor local products to minimize fossil fuel use and spoilage in transport, maximize nutritional value, and support the local economy. For example, favor locally produced foods to minimize fossil fuel use for transportation, to help sustain farmland and economy, and to provide a means for recycling food waste for future food production.
- Develop and, if possible, collaborate with others to develop infrastructure that facilitates all of the goals itemized above. Central to this effort is the establishment of a local facility to inventory and manage reusable materials.

- Educate students, faculty, staff, and the vendors from whom we purchase materials and services about strategies that promote resource-use efficiency.
- Seek arrangements with the city of Oberlin and other nearby institutions that help promote the goals articulated above.
- Monitor purchasing, disposal, and recycling activities.
- Continuously update policy to insure that the objectives articulated in the College's environmental policy on purchasing, reuse, and disposal are accomplished.
- Make it easy for all members of the Oberlin community to comply with College policy on purchases, reuse, and disposal (e.g., inform them about where to dispose of items such as spent batteries and obsolete equipment).

### Relationships with Vendors

The College favors vendors with demonstrated expertise and commitment to high resource-use efficiency. This policy increases the likelihood that the College will be able to achieve the goals outlined in this document by increasing its opportunity to:

- Communicate environmental procurement strategy to vendors. Specifically, the College will convey in writing its goals for resource reduction, and will encourage vendors to help us achieve these goals. This document will emphasize the institution's adherence to "total product life-cycle analysis," leading to closed-loop scenarios in product development, design, packaging, shipping, and the return of products for recycling, reuse, and remanufacturing.
- Minimize packaging and use only recyclable packaging.
- Assure that vendors notify buying staff of all of the environmentally sensitive products or services that they provide and plan to provide.
- Favor "Products of Service" when available. This arrangement allows the consumer to purchase the service of a product while the manufacturer retains material ownership of that product. It creates an economic incentive for the manufacturer to create durable products that can easily be remanufactured.
- Favor energy-efficient products.

• When possible, purchase reusable or reused products.
• Favor materials with high recycled content if comparable in quality to products composed of virgin materials.
• The College will minimize the generation of materials destined for land-fills or incineration. It will seek relationships with waste vendors that help it achieve this goal by developing cooperative mechanisms to audit, monitor, and reduce waste streams.

## Material Inputs

### City Water
• Minimize water use by promptly repairing leaks and installing water-saving devices such as low-volume showerheads.
• Seek out and demonstrate in selected buildings emerging water-saving technology such as gray-water systems. Encourage a culture of water conservation. For instance, post signs in the gym and dorms with tips on saving water.
• Campus landscape strategies that can reduce demand are described in the Grounds section of this document.

### Rainwater
Develop policy that takes maximum advantage of this resource, for example, the practice of storing and using rainwater to irrigate landscape vegetation (also see the Buildings and Grounds sections of this document for references to storm-water management).

### Consumable Office Supplies
Favor materials with a high recycled content.

### Student Durables
Establish arrangements (e.g., annual public sales, donations to non-profits) that responsibly take advantage of the large varied collections of durables (e.g., furniture, consumer electronics) regularly abandoned by students at the end of the school year. Salvageable bicycles should be donated to the Oberlin Bicycle Coop to encourage environmentally sensitive transportation.

*Office Equipment*
Favor energy-efficient appliances. Select printers and copiers capable of making double-sided copies and set double-sided copying as the default mode. Select equipment capable of handling paper with a high recycled content.

*Durable Goods*
- Purchase appliances that use water and energy efficiently (e.g., washers, driers, refrigerators).
- Favor wood products from forests certified as sustainably managed.

*Food and Food Service*
- Favor local products.
- Where possible, favor farms that follow sustainable land-use practices.
- Minimize the use of disposable containers and utensils by food service.

**Material Outputs**

*Wastewater*
Wastewater production can best be minimized through conservation measures that reduce fresh water use. Installations, such as gray-water systems, are mentioned in the section on inputs.

*Storm-Water Overflow*
Description of the challenges related to storm-water management are provided in the Buildings and Grounds sections of this document.

*Organic Wastes (Food Waste, Yard Waste)*
The College will encourage the development of a composting facility, either on or off campus, and will institute policy that mandates the composting of all food waste from College dining halls. It will investigate the possibilities for collective efforts with the city of Oberlin and other local institutions.

*Other Wastes (Glass, Plastic, Etc.)*
The College will recycle as much of these materials as possible.

*Locally "Downcyclable" Wastes*
The College will strive to maximize the useful life of all of the products it uses, for example, the additional use of single-sided printing paper as scratch paper.

*Computers*
State-of-the-art computer equipment is necessary for a variety of educational and administrative tasks, and as a result, equipment is often replaced well before its useful life is over. The College will strive to reuse older computers for less demanding applications on campus, and will attempt to sell or donate computer equipment when it is no longer useful to the College.

*Hazardous Wastes (Biohazards, Toxic Chemicals, Batteries)*
The College will seek to identify vendors who can recycle hazardous wastes from products that it cannot avoid purchasing such as unused paints and spent solvents. All hazardous material will be managed to minimize adverse effects on human health and the environment.

*Solids for Landfill*
Oberlin will treat wastes destined for landfills in ways that minimize the potential for negative effects following burial.

*Facility for Managing Reusables*
The college will seek ways to collect, store, and manage reusable materials (e.g., furniture, construction materials) on campus.

*Education*
Oberlin College's environmental policy will succeed only to the extent that students, faculty, staff, and the larger community with which it interacts adopt a culture of environmental stewardship. Education that fosters this culture will be accomplished through continuous campus-wide education on material use, specifically via:

• Freshman orientation materials and organized discussions specifically designed to promote and demonstrate the institution's goal of "closing the loop" in material cycles.

• Training programs tailored to match the particular responsibilities and expertise of staff that explain both policy objectives and specific practices relevant to their member's duties. For instance, administrative assistants in each department will receive instruction on purchasing and resource conservation practices relevant to office management, while custodial staff will receive instruction on material use.

• Signage throughout the institution that explains the objectives as well as the policy. Such signage should be updated to provide the College community with feedback on the achievement of goals. Recycling barrels, for example, might display statistics on the percentage of solid waste the institution has recently recycled.

• Policy that encourages faculty members to maximize material-use efficiency in the classroom.

• Policy that encourages collaborative research and perhaps courses involving faculty, students, staff, and vendors on new ways in which the institution might increase resource-use efficiency. For instance, managers of existing internal funding programs, such as the Mellon Assistantship Program, would be encouraged to solicit and fund scholarships on this topic.

• Assistance to the larger community, including local schools and civic organizations, in developing and implementing policies that promote resource-use efficiency.

• Creation of a transparent and public system for accounting and monitoring policy implementation so that students and other community members can more easily engage in and assess the process.

## VI   Implementation

*Preamble*

Good policies are most likely to succeed when executed by dedicated individuals well versed in the principles that underlie those policies. In order to implement the policies contained in this document, the College must therefore educate the individuals responsible for its operations and actively encourage the culture necessary to achieve compliance by the entire campus community. To this end, the Environmental Policy Advisory Committee (EPAC) recommends that the College adopt the following measures.

## *Commit to Campus-Wide Environmental Education*

Oberlin College exists to foster knowledge, tolerance, and respect among its students so that they might contribute to progressive and equitable societal development. Environmentally literate students, faculty, staff, administrators, alumni, and trustees are crucial to this goal. What follows are the educational initiatives necessary to promote effective environmental stewardship.

- New students will be informed about environmental imperatives and related College responsibilities and policies during preenrollment orientation. Appropriate literature will be produced to support this event.
- New members of the faculty and staff will receive similar orientation.
- Faculty and staff from time to time will attend training sessions on compliance with College environmental policy.
- Pamphlets, signs, and surveys will be used to raise awareness and promote positive behavior regarding College environmental policy.
- Real-time computer displays and/or biannual postings about water use and energy use and production will be maintained, where feasible. This information will also be posted on the College Web site.

These educational policies will do much to alter the behavior of Oberlin College community members in relation to the natural environment, and will increase the effectiveness of other institutional initiatives.

## *Assemble an Annual Report of Key Indicators and Conduct Retrospectives*

Progress cannot be measured without baselines. The EPAC therefore recommends that a suite of key indicators be assembled annually and posted on the Oberlin College Web site. College performance in all of these categories should be compared against appropriate benchmarks and verified by outside authorities. Indicators that belong in such a report include:

- *Energy*  Energy use broken down by type (electricity, heat) for every building amenable to break out, related carbon dioxide and other GHG emissions.
- *Grounds*  Fertilizers, pesticides, and fuels used; percentage of campus square footage maintained without pesticides and artificial fertilizers.
- *Transportation*  Miles per gallon of the College's vehicle fleet, both vehicles owned and rented by the college.

- *Materials Use*   Amount of glass, paper, aluminum, etc., recycled as a percentage of those materials consumed; percentage of all paper purchased that has recycled content; total water use; total volume of waste sent to landfills.

Every two years following adoption of its environmental policy, the College will take stock of its progress and identify any shortfalls, and announce how it intends to rectify them.

### Designate a Staff Position for Environmental Policy Implementation

A person with appropriate expertise will oversee the day-to-day implementation of environmental policy, and seek arrangements with other colleges and universities, environmental organizations, and the city of Oberlin that can help achieve goals as described below. A technical advisory group consisting of on- and off-campus ad hoc consultants and staff will be assembled to provide this person assistance.

### Network with Peer Institutions and Environmental Advisory Groups

Organizations and institutions dedicated to environmental sustainability and conservation are valuable sources of information and advice, and Oberlin College policymakers should take greater advantage of this resource. Moreover, colleges and universities with similar buying practices can form purchasing consortia for green power, recycled paper, etc., as well as "sharing consortia" to facilitate the reuse of office equipment, building materials, etc. Consequently, the EPAC recommends that:

- The College join a nationally or internationally recognized voluntary action program such as the World Wildlife Fund's Climate Savers program.
- The College collaborate with other educational institutions to help effect its environmental policies.
- The College bring expert individuals and advisory groups to campus for consultation with the EPAC and the environmental oversight staff member as needed.

### Set Priorities: The Continuing Role of the EPAC

Policy priorities, guidelines, and adjustments should continue to be set by representatives of the administration, faculty, student body, facilities operations department, and the city of Oberlin and possibly others. The EPAC, therefore, will be a permanent standing committee and charged to:

- Suggest ways to improve policy and practice, and solicit proposals from the campus community for the same purposes.
- Provide input for the annual environmental report, reviewing that report and presenting the information contained in that report to the greater College community and peer institutions.
- Ensure that the implementation recommendations laid out in this document and in future documents are approved and adopted by the necessary agents.
- Compose the biannual evaluative "report card" mentioned above on the success of campus environmental policy.

EPAC Members

| Name | | Since |
| --- | --- | --- |
| Baumann, Fran | Oberlin community representative | 2002 |
| Benzing, David | Faculty, biology | 2001 |
| Craig, Norm | Faculty, chemistry, emeritus | 2001 |
| Evans, Andrew | Administration, finance | 2001 |
| Filardi, Sal | Facilities planing and construction | 2001 |
| French, Rebecca | Student, junior | 2002 |
| Gaudin, Sylvestre | Faculty, economics | 2001 |
| Gerber, Carl | Alumnus, former EPA | 2001 |
| Jahns, Claire | Student, senior | 2001 |
| Morgenstern, Richard | Alumnus, resources for the future | 2001 |
| Orr, David* | Faculty, Environmental Studies | 2001 |
| Petersen, John | Faculty, Environmental Studies | 2001 |
| Schildkraut, Debbie | Faculty, politics | 2001 |
| Skinner, Bill** | Faculty, geology, emeritus | 2001 |
| Turner, Caroline | Students, senior | 2002 |

\* Chair, fall 2001, fall 2002, and spring 2003
\** Chair, spring 2003

# References

Abram, David. 1996. *The Spell of the Sensuous*. New York: Pantheon.

Ackerman, Diane. 1991. *A Natural History of the Senses*. New York: Vintage.

Adam Joseph Lewis Center, Project Goals and Principles, Oberlin College, April 19, 1996.

Adamson, Davis, Lisa Matthiessen, and Peter Morris. n.d. Costing Green: A Comprehensive Cost Database and Budgeting Methodology.

Alexander, Christopher. 2001–2004. *The Nature of Order*. 4 vols. Berkeley: Center for Environmental Structure.

Alexander, Christopher, Sara Ishikawa, and Murray Silverstein. 1977. *A Pattern Language*. Oxford: Oxford University Press.

Anderson, Ray. 1998. *Mid-Course Correction*. Atlanta, GA: Peregrinzilla Press.

Apollo Alliance and Energy Action. 2005. *New Energy for Campuses*.

Bartlett, John. 1968. *Familiar Quotations*. 14th ed. Boston: Little, Brown.

Bartlett, Peggy, and Geoffrey Chase, eds. 2004. *Sustainability on Campus*. Cambridge, MA: MIT Press.

Barzun, Jacques. 1975. *The House of Intellect*. Chicago: University of Chicago Press.

Barzun, Jacques. 1993. *The American University*. Chicago: University of Chicago Press.

Beard, Mary. 2003. *The Parthenon*. Cambridge: Harvard University Press.

Beatley, Tim. 2004. *Native to Nowhere*. Washington, DC: Island Press.

Benyus, Janine. 1998. *Biomimicry*. New York: HarperCollins.

Berlin, Isaiah. 1953. *The Hedgehog and the Fox*. New York: Oxford Univ. Press.

Berry, Thomas. 1988. *The Dream of the Earth*. San Francisco: Sierra Club Books.

Berry, Thomas. 1999. *The Great Work*. New York: Bell Tower.

Berry, Wendell. 1981. *The Gift of Good Land*. San Francisco: North Point Press.

Berry, Wendell. 1987. *Home Economics*. San Francisco: North Point Press.

Birkeland, Janis. 2002. *Design for Sustainability.* London: Earthscan.

Blodgett, Geoffrey. 1985. *Oberlin Architecture.* Oberlin, OH: Oberlin College.

Blodgett, Geoffrey. 2001a. *Cass Gilbert: The Early Years.* Minneapolis: Minnesota Historical Society Press.

Blodgett, Geoffrey. 2001b. Oberlin the Grand Collaboration. In *Cass Gilbert, Life and Work,* ed. Barbara Christen and Steve Flanders, 206–219. New York: W. W. Norton.

Bok, Derek. 2003. *Universities in the Marketplace.* Princeton, NJ: Princeton University Press.

Booth, Wayne. 1991. *The Vocation of a Teacher.* Chicago: University of Chicago Press.

Bormann, Herbert, Diana Balmori, and Gordon Geballe. 2001. *Redesigning the American Lawn.* New Haven, CT: Yale University Press.

Bortoft, Henri. 1996. *The Wholeness of Nature.* Hudson, NY: Lindisfarne Press.

Brand, Stewart. 1995. *How Buildings Learn.* New York: Penguin.

Burchell, Robert, Anthony Downs, Sahan Mukherji, and Barbara McCann. 2005. *Sprawl Costs: Economic Impacts of Unchecked Development.* Washington, DC: Island Press.

Burtt, E. A. 1954. *The Metaphysical Foundations of Modern Science.* New York: Doubleday.

Calaprice, Alice, ed. 2005. *The New Quotable Gustein.* Princeton, NJ: Princeton University Press.

Campbell, Colin. 1988. *The Coming Oil Crisis.* Essex, UK: Multi-Science Publishing.

Capra, Fritjof. 1996. *The Web of Life.* New York: Anchor Books.

Capra, Fritjof. 2002. *The Hidden Connections.* New York: HarperCollins.

Carson, Rachel. 1984. *The Sense of Wonder.* New York: Harper Perennial.

Catton, William. 1980. *Overshoot.* Urbana: University of Illinois Press.

Chippindale, Christopher. 2004. *Stonehenge Complete.* 3rd ed. London: Thames and Hudson.

Council on Environmental Quality. 1974. *The Costs of Sprawl.* Washington, DC: U.S. Government Printing Office.

Cox, Harvey. 1999. The Market as God. *Atlantic Monthly* (March): 18–23.

Creighton, Sarah. 1998. *Greening of the Ivory Tower.* Cambridge, MA: MIT Press.

Daily, Gretchen, ed. 1997. *Nature's Services: Societal Dependence on Natural Ecosystems.* Washington, DC: Island Press.

Daly, Herman. 1996. *Beyond Growth.* Boston: Beacon Press.

Daly, Herman, and John Cobb. 1989. *For the Common Good.* Boston: Beacon Press.

Day, Christopher. 2002. *Spirit and Place.* Oxford: Architectural Press.

Deffeyes, Kenneth. 2001. *Hubbert's Peak*. Princeton, NJ: Princeton University Press.

Deffeyes, Kenneth. 2005. The Truth beneath the Surface. *New York Times*, March 25, A19.

Dewey, John. 1981. *The Philosophy of John Dewey*, ed. John McDermott. Chicago: University of Chicago Press.

Diamond, Jared. *Collapse: How Societies Choose to Fail or Succeed*. New York: Viking.

Dubos, Rene. 1972. *A God Within*. New York: Scribners.

Eliot, T. S. [1936] 1971. *The Complete Poems and Plays*. New York: Harcourt, Brace and World.

Fernández-Galiano, Luis. 2000. *Fire and Memory*. Cambridge, MA: MIT Press.

Fisher, Thomas. 2001. Revisiting the Discipline of Architecture. In *The Discipline of Architecture*, ed. Andrzej Piotrowski and Julia Robinson, 1–9. Minneapolis: University of Minnesota Press.

Fletcher, Robert S. 1943. *A History of Oberlin College*. 2 vols. Oberlin, OH: Oberlin College.

Fox, Warwick, ed. 2000. *Ethics and the Built Environment*. London: Routledge.

Franke, Richard, and Barbara Chasin. 1991. *Kerala: Radical Reform as Development in an Indian State*. San Francisco: Institute for Food and Development Policy.

Freyfogle, Eric. 2003. *The Land We Share*. Washington, DC: Island Press.

Frumkin, Howard, Frank Lawrence, and Richard Jackson. 2004. *Urban Sprawl and Public Health*. Washington, DC: Island Press.

Gates, Jeff. 1998. *The Ownership Solution*. Reading, MA: Addison-Wesley.

Gates, Jeff. 2000. *Democracy at Risk*. Cambridge, MA: Perseus.

Gates, Jeff. 2002. Globalization's Challenge: Attuning the Global to the Local. *Reflections* 3, no. 4 (Summer): 28–37.

Gates, Jeff. 2003. We the Unreasonable. *Tikkun* 18, no. 4 (July–August): 47–52.

Geiser, Kenneth. 2001. *Materials Matter*. Cambridge, MA: MIT Press.

Gelbspan, Ross. 2004. *Boiling Point*. New York: Basic Books.

Gleick, James. 1987. *Chaos: Making a New Science*. New York: Viking Penguin.

Goethe, Johann Wolfgang von. 1952. *Goethe's Botanical Writings*. Trans. Bertha Mueller. Honolulu: University of Hawaii Press.

Goodwin, Brian. 1994. *How the Leopard Changed Its Spots: The Evolution of Complexity*. New York: Simon and Schuster.

Graff, Gerald. 2003. *Clueless in Academe*. New Haven, CT: Yale University Press.

Gray, J. Glenn. 1984. *Rethinking American Education*. Middletown, CT: Wesleyan University Press.

Greider, William. 2003. *The Soul of Capitalism*. New York: Simon and Schuster.

Grillo, Paul. 1975. *Form, Function, and Design*. New York: Dover.

Grudin, Robert. 1990. *The Grace of Great Things*. New York: Ticknor and Fields.

Grudin, Robert. 1992. *Book*. New York: Random House.

Hall, Peter, and Colin Ward. 1998. *Sociable Cities: The Legacy of Ebenezer Howard*. New York: John Wiley.

Hardman, Keith. 1987. *Charles Grandison Finney: 1792–1875*. Syracuse, NY: Syracuse University Press.

Hartmann, Thom. 2002. *Unequal Protection*. Emmaus, PA: Rodale Press.

Hawken, Paul, Amory Lovins, and L. Hunter Lovins. 1999. *Natural Capitalism*. Boston: Little, Brown and Company.

Heinberg, Richard. 2003. *The Party's Over*. Gabriola Island, BC: New Society Publishers.

Heinberg, Richard. 2004. *Power Down*. Gabriola Island, BC: New Society Publishers.

Heinz Center. 2002. *The State of the Nation's Ecosystems*. New York: Cambridge University Press.

Higgs, Eric. 2003. *Nature by Design*. Cambridge, MA: MIT Press.

Homer-Dixon, Thomas. 2000. *The Ingenuity Gap*. New York: Knopf.

Hurwit, Jeffrey. 2004. *The Acropolis in the Age of Pericles*. New York: Cambridge University Press.

Hyde, Lewis. 1983. *The Gift*. New York: Vintage Press.

Interface, Inc. 2004. *2004 Annual Report*. Atlanta, GA: Interface, Inc.

Jackson, Kenneth. 1985. *Crabgrass Frontier: The Suburbanization of the United States*. New York: Oxford University Press.

Jackson, Wes. 1980. *New Roots for Agriculture*. Lincoln: University of Nebraska Press.

James, Robert Rhodes, ed. 1998. *Churchill Speaks, 1897–1963*. New York: Barnes and Noble.

Jenkyns, Richard. 2004. *Westminster Abbey*. Cambridge: Harvard University Press.

Jensen, Jens. [1939] 1990. *Siftings*. Baltimore, MD: Johns Hopkins University Press.

Johnson, Bart, and Kristina Hills, eds. 2001. *Ecology and Design: Frameworks for Learning*. Washington, DC: Island Press.

Kaplan, Rachel, and Stephen Kaplan. 1989. *The Experience of Nature*. New York: Cambridge University Press.

Kaplan, Rachel, and Stephen Kaplan. 1998. *With People in Mind*. Washington, DC: Island Press.

Kaptchuk, Ted. 2000. *The Web That Has No Weaver*. New York: McGraw-Hill.

Kats, Gregory. 2003. The Costs and Financial Benefits of Green Buildings. California Sustainable Building Task Force.

Keller, Elizabeth Fox. 1983. *A Feeling for the Organism.* New York: W. H. Freeman.

Kellert, Stephen. 1996. *The Value of Life.* Washington, DC: Island Press.

Kellert, Stephen. 2005. *Building for Life.* Washington, DC: Island Press.

Keniry, Julian. 1995. *Ecodemia.* Washington, DC: National Wildlife Federation.

Kibbert, Charles, ed. 1999. *Reshaping the Built Environment.* Washington, DC: Island Press.

Kibbert, Charles, Jan Sendzimir, and G. Bradley Guy, eds. 2002. *Construction Ecology: Nature as the Basis for Green Buildings.* London: Spon Press.

Klare, Michael. 2004a. *Blood and Oil.* New York: Metropolitan Books.

Klare, Michael. 2004b. Crude Awakening. *Nation,* November 8, 35–41.

Kohak, Erazim. 1984. *The Embers and the Stars.* Chicago: University of Chicago Press.

Kovel, Joel. 2002. *The Enemy of Nature.* London: Zed Books.

Kraybill, Donald. 1989. *The Riddle of Amish Culture.* Baltimore, MD: Johns Hopkins University Press.

Kunstler, James Howard. 2005. *The Long Emergency.* New York: Atlantic Monthly Press.

Kurtz, John. *John Frederick Oberlin.* Boulder: Westview Press, 1976.

Lawrence, D. H. 1971. *The Complete Poems of D. H. Lawrence.* Miranda Sola Piuto and Warner Roberts, ed. New York: Viking Press.

Le Corbusier. [1929] 1987. *The City of To-Morrow and Its Planning.* New York: Dover.

Le Corbusier. [1931] 1986. *Towards a New Architecture.* New York: Dover.

Leopold, Aldo. [1949] 1987. *A Sand County Almanac.* New York: Oxford University Press.

Leopold, Aldo. 1955/1972. *Round River.* New York: Oxford University Press.

Levy, Matthys, and Mario Salvadori. 1992. *Why Buildings Fall Down.* New York: W. W. Norton.

Lewis, C. S. 1947. *The Abolition of Man.* New York: Macmillan.

Logsden, Gene. 2000. *At Nature's Pace.* White River Junction, VT: Chelsea Green.

Louv, Richard. 2005. *Last Child in the Woods.* Chapel Hill, NC: Algonquin Books.

Lovejoy, Arthur O. [1936] 1974. *The Great Chain of Being.* Cambridge, MA: Harvard University Press.

Lovins, Amory. 2002. *Small Is Profitable.* Snowmass, CO: Rocky Mountain Institute.

Lovins, Amory, and Hunter Lovins. 1982. *Brittle Power.* Andover, MA: Brick House.

Loy, David. 2002. *A Buddhist History of the West.* Albany: State University of New York.

Lux, Kenneth. 1990. *Adam Smith's Mistake.* Boston: Shambhala.

Lyle, John. 1994. *Regenerative Design for Sustainable Development.* New York: John Wiley.

Malin, Nadav. 2000. Building Commissioning. *Environmental Building News* 9, no. 2 (February).

Malin, Nadav. 2004. Integrated Design. *Environmental Building News* 13, no. 11 (November).

Malin, Nadav, and Jessica Boehland. 2002. Oberlin College's Lewis Center. *Environmental Building News* 11, nos. 7–8 (July–August).

Malin, Nadav, and Jessica Boehland. 2003a. Spotlight on LEED. *Environmental Building News* 12, no. 12 (December).

Malin, Nadav, and Jessica Boehland. 2003b. Post-Occupancy Evaluation. *Environmental Building News* 12, no. 9 (September).

Malin, Nadav, and Alex Wilson. 2003. Forest Certification Growing Fast. *Environmental Building News* 12, no. 4 (April).

Martin, Calvin. *The Way of the Human Being.* New Haven, CT: Yale University Press.

McDaniel, Carl, and John Gowdy. 1999. *Paradise for Sale.* Berkeley: University of California Press.

McDonough, William, and Michael Braungart. 2002. *Cradle to Cradle.* Washington, DC: North Point Press.

McHarg, Ian. 1969. *Design with Nature.* Garden City, NY: Doubleday.

McHarg, Ian. 1996. *A Quest for Life.* New York: John Wiley.

McHarg, Ian, and Frederick Steiner, eds. 1998. *To Heal the Earth.* Washington, DC: Island Press.

McKibben, Bill. 1995. *Hope Human and Wild.* Boston: Little, Brown and Company.

Meier, Christian. 2000. *Athens: A Portrait of the City in Its Golden Age.* London: Pimlico.

Melman, Seymour. 2001. *After Capitalism.* New York: Knopf.

Merchant, Carolyn. 1982. *The Death of Nature.* New York: Harper and Row.

Merton, Thomas. 1985. *Love and Living.* New York: Harcourt Brace Jovanovich.

Midgley, Mary. 1989. *Wisdom Information and Wonder.* London: Routledge.

Midgley, Mary. 1990. Why Smartness Is Not Enough. In *Rethinking the Curriculum,* ed. Mary Clark and Sandra Wawrytko, 39–52. New York: Greenwood Press.

Midgley, Mary. 1996a. Sustainability and Moral Pluralism. *Ethics and Environment* 1, no. 1, 41–54.

Midgley, Mary. 1996b. *Utopias, Dolphins, and Computers.* London: Routledge.

Momaday, Scott. 1993. *The Way to Rainy Mountain.* Albuquerque: University of New Mexico Press.

Montessori, Maria. 1994. *From Childhood to Adolescence.* Oxford: Clio Press.

Murray, Michael. 2004. Payback and Currencies of Energy, Carbon Dioxide, and Money for a 60kW Photovoltaic Array. Senior honors thesis, Oberlin College.

Murray, M., and J. E. Petersen. 2004. Payback in Currencies of Energy, Carbon Dioxide and Money for a 60 KW Photovoltaic Array. In *Conference Proceedings of the American Solar Energy Society.*

Newman, Frank, Lara Couturier, and Jamie Scurry. 2004. Higher Education Isn't Meeting the Public's Needs. *Chronicle of Higher Education,* October 15, B6–B8.

Odum, Howard, and Elisabeth Odum. 1990. *A Prosperous Way Down.* Boulder: University of Colorado Press.

Oppenheimer, Andrea, and Timothy Hursley. 2002. *Rural Studio: Samuel Mockbee and an Architecture of Decency.* New York: Princeton Architectural Press.

Oppenheimer, Todd. 2003. *The Flickering Mind: Saving Education from the False Promise of Technology.* New York: Random House.

Orr, David W. 1992. *Ecological Literacy.* Albany: State University of New York Press.

Orr, David W. 2002. The Architecture of Science. In *The Nature of Design,* 135–142. New York: Oxford University Press.

Orr, David W. 2004. *Earth in Mind.* 10th anniversary ed. Washington, DC: Island Press.

Pelikan, Jaroslav. 1992. *The Idea of the University.* New Haven, CT: Yale University Press.

Petersen, John. 2002. Appraising Success of the Adam Joseph Lewis Center. *Oberlin College Environmental Studies Program Newsletter* (Spring).

Pevsner, Nikolaus. [1943] 1990. *An Outline of European Architecture.* London: Penguin.

Plato. 1961. *The Collected Dialogues,* ed. Edith Hamilton and Huntington Cairns. Princeton, NJ: Princeton University Press.

Pless, Shanti, and Paul Torcellini. 2004. *Energy Performance Evaluation of an Educational Facility.* NREL/TP–550–33180. Golden, CO: National Renewable Energy Laboratory.

Press, Eyal, and Jennifer Washburn. 2000. The Kept University. *Atlantic Monthly* 285, no. 3 (March): 39–54.

Putnam, Robert. 2000. *Bowling Alone.* New York: Simon and Schuster.

Rafferty, Milton. 1980. *The Ozarks: Land and Life.* Norman: University of Oklahoma Press.

Rees, William, and Mathis Wackernagel. 1996. *Our Ecological Footprint*. Philadelphia: New Society Press.

Roberts, Paul. 2004. *The End of Oil*. Boston: Houghton Mifflin.

Rocky Mountain Institute. 2002. *The 2020 Report*. Old Snowmass, CO: Rocky Mountain Institute.

Rodes, Barbara, and Rice Odell. 1992. *A Dictionary of Environmental Quotations*. Baltimore, MD: Johns Hopkins University Press.

Rogers, Elizabeth. 2001. *Landscape Design: A Cultural and Architectural History*. New York: Harry Abrams.

Rogers, Everett. 1995. *Diffusion of Innovations*. 4th ed. New York: Free Press.

Rogers, Richard. 1997. *Cities for a Small Planet*. London: Faber and Faber.

Rogers, Richard, and Anne Power. 2000. *Cities for a Small Country*. London: Faber and Faber.

Rudofsky, Bernard. 1964. *Architecture without Architects*. Albuquerque: University of New Mexico Press.

Rudolph, Frederick. 1977. *Curriculum: A History of the American Undergraduate Course of Study since 1636*. San Francisco: Jossey-Bass.

Ruskin, John. [1880] 1989. *The Seven Lamps of Architecture*. New York: Dover.

Rybczynski, Witold. 2001. *The Look of Architecture*. New York: Oxford University Press.

Sacks, Oliver. 1993. To See and Not See. *New Yorker*, May 10, 59–73.

Sax, Linda. 2004. Research on the Assessment of Civic Engagement. Los Angeles: Comparative Institutional Research Program, University of California.

Schama, Simon. 1995. *Landscape and Memory*. New York: Knopf.

Schwartz, Barry. 1994. *The Costs of Living*. New York: W. W. Norton.

Schweitzer, Albert. 1981. *The Philosophy of Civilization*. Tallahassee: Florida State University Press.

Schwenk, Theodor. 1989. *Water: The Element of Life*. Hudson, NY: Anthroposophic Press.

Schwenk, Theodor. 1996. *Sensitive Chaos*. London: Rudolf Steiner Press.

Scofield, John. 2002. Early Performance of a Green Academic Building. *ASHRAE Transactions* 108:2.

Scott, Robert. 2003. *The Gothic Enterprise*. Berkeley: University of California Press.

Senge, Peter. 1994. *The Fifth Discipline*. New York: Doubleday/Currency.

Senge, Peter. 2000. The Academy as Learning Community. In *Leading Academic Change*, ed. Ann Lucas and associates, 275–3000. San Francisco: Jossey-Bass.

Senge, Peter, Art Kleiner, Charlotte Roberts, Richard Ross, George Roth, and Bryan Smith. 1999. *The Dance of Change*. New York: Doubleday/Currency.

Sewall, Laura. 1999. *Sight and Sensibility*. New York: Tarcher.

Sherman, Thomas. 1997. *A Place on the Glacial Till*. New York: Oxford University Press.

Shunturov, Vladislav. 2005. Socio-Technical Feedback for Improving the Environmental Performance of Buildings. Senior honor's thesis, Oberlin College.

Sinsheimer, Robert. 1978. The Presumptions of Science. *Daedalus* 107, no. 2: 23–36.

Smil, Vaclav. 2003. *Energy at the Crossroads*. Cambridge: MIT Press.

Smith, Adam. [1759] 1976. *The Theory of Moral Sentiments*. Indianapolis: Liberty Press.

Smith, Adam. [1776] 1965. *The Wealth of Nations*. New York: Modern Library.

Smith, April. 1993. *Campus Ecology*. Los Angeles: Living Planet Press.

Smuts, Jan. [1926] 1996. *Holism and Evolution*. Highland, NY: Gestalt Journal Press.

Smith, Page. 1990. *Killing the Spirit: Higher Education in America*. New York: Viking.

Solomon, Robert. 1992. Beyond Reason: The Importance of Emotion in Philosophy. In *Revisioning Philosophy*, ed. James Ogilvy, 19–48. Albany: State University of New York.

Spirn, Anne Whiston. 1998. *The Language of Landscape*. New Haven, CT: Yale University Press.

Steffen, Will, et al. 2004. *Global Change and the Earth System*. New York: Springer.

Steiner, Frederick. 2002. *Human Ecology*. Washington, DC: Island Press.

Steiner, George. 2001. *Grammars of Creation*. London: Faber and Faber.

Sunstein, Cass. 2004. *The Second Bill of Rights*. New York: Basic Books.

Sutton, Sharon. 2001. Reinventing Professional Privilege as Inclusivity. In *The Discipline of Architecture*. ed. Andrzej Piotrowski and Julia Robinson, 173–207. Minneapolis: University of Minnesota Press, 2001.

Swimme, Brian, and Thomas Berry. 1992. *The Universe Story*. San Francisco: HarperCollins.

Tainter, Joseph. 1988. *The Collapse of Complex Societies*. Cambridge: Cambridge University Press.

Thayer, Robert. 2003. *Life Place: Bioregional Thought and Practice*. Berkeley: University of California Press.

Thompson, D'Arcy. [1942] 1992. *On Growth and Form: The Complete Revised edition*. New York: Dover.

Todd, Nancy Jack. 2005. *A Safe and Sustainable World: The Promise of Ecological Design*. Washington, DC: Island Press.

Tower Engineering. 2003. A. J. Lewis Center Energy Study. July 30.

Tsui, Eugene. 1999. *Evolutionary Architecture: Nature as a Basis for Design.* New York: John Wiley.

Tuchman, Barbara. 1984. *The March of Folly.* New York: Knopf.

Tucker, Mary Evelyn. 2003. *Worldly Wonder.* Chicago: Open Court.

Turner, Paul Venable. 1995. *Campus: An American Planning Tradition.* Cambridge: MIT Press.

Uhl, Christopher. 2004. *Developing Ecological Consciousness.* New York: Rowman and Littlefield.

U.S. Department of the Interior and U.S. Geological Survey. 1998. *Status and Trends of the Nation's Biological Resources.* Washington, DC: U.S. Superintendent of Documents.

U.S. Government Printing Office. 1980. *Global 2000 Report.* Washington, DC: U.S. Government Printing Office.

Van der Ryn, Sim. 2005. *Design for Life: The Architecture of Sim Van der Ryn.* Layton, UT: Gibbs Smith.

Van der Ryn, Sim, and Stuart Cowan. 1996. *Ecological Design.* Washington, DC: Island Press.

Vitruvius. 1960. *The Ten Books of Architecture.* New York: Dover.

Vogel, Steven. 1988. *Life's Devices.* Princeton, NJ: Princeton University Press.

von Frisch, Karl. 1974. *Animal Architecture.* New York: Harcourt Brace Jovanovich.

Washburn, Jennifer. 2005. *University Inc: The Corporate Corruption of Higher Education.* New York: Basic Books.

Weil, Simone. 2002. *The Need for Roots.* London: Routledge.

Whitehead, Alfred North. 1967. *The Aims of Education.* New York: Free Press.

Whybrow, Peter. 2005. *When More Is Not Enough.* New York: W. W. Norton.

Whyte, William Foote, and Kathlees King Whyte. 1988. *Making Mondragon.* Ithaca, NY: New York State School of Industrial and Labor Relations, Cornell University.

Willis, Delta. 1995. *The Sand Dollar and the Slide Rule.* Reading, MA: Addison-Wesley.

Wills, Garry. 2002. *Mr. Jefferson's University.* Washington, DC: National Geographic.

Wilshire, Bruce. 1990. *The Moral Collapse of the University.* Albany: State University of New York.

Wilson, Alex, and Peter Yost. 2001. Buildings and the Environment: The Numbers. *Environmental Building News* 10, no. 5 (May): 1, 10–13.

Wilson, Edward O. 1984. *Biophilia*. Cambridge, MA: Harvard University Press.

Wilson, Edward O. 2002. *The Future of Life*. New York: Knopf.

Wittfogel, Karl. 1957. *Oriental Despotism*. New Haven: Yale University Press.

Wright, Frank Lloyd. 1993. An Organic Architecture. In *Frank Lloyd Wright Collected Writings*, ed. Bruce Brooks Pfeiffer, 3: 299–334. New York: Rizzoli International Publications.

Yunis, Muhammad. 1999. *Banker to the Poor*. New York: Public Affairs Press.

# Index